Companion to the Calendar

Second Edition

A Guide to the Saints, Seasons, and Holidays of the Year

Kathy Coffey
Donna M. Crilly
Mary G. Fox
Mary Ellen Hynes
Julie M. Krakora
Corinna Laughlin
Robert C. Rabe

LTP

LITURGY
TRAINING
PUBLICATIONS

Nihil Obstat
Very Reverend Daniel A. Smilanic, JCD
Vicar for Canonical Services
Archdiocese of Chicago
December 2, 2011

Imprimatur
Reverend John F. Canary, STL, DMIN
Vicar General
Archdiocese of Chicago
December 2, 2011

Additional information about Christmas Time ("The Liturgical Times") provided by Margaret Brennan.

COMPANION TO THE CALENDAR, SECOND EDITION: A GUIDE TO THE SAINTS, SEASONS, AND HOLIDAYS OF THE YEAR © 2012. Archdiocese of Chicago: Liturgy Training Publications, 3949 South Racine Avenue, Chicago IL 60609; 1-800-933-1800, fax 1-800-933-7094, e-mail orders@ltp.org. All rights reserved. See our website at www.LTP.org.

Full color cover art by Kathy Ann Sullivan. Interior and back cover line art by Lawrence Klimecki. Night sky art on front cover by Julie Lonneman. Back cover calendar art by Joseph Malham.

Front cover (Saints and observations in Ordinary Time Summer): World Environment Day (June 5); Flag Day, the United States of America (June 14); the Summer Solstice (June 21), Saint John the Baptist (June 24); Month of the Precious Blood (month of July); Canada Day (July 1); Independence Day, the United States of America (July 4); Saint Benedict (July 11); Blessed Kateri Tekakwitha (July 14); Ramadan, Islam (as beginning on July 20, 2012); Tisha'B'Av, Judaism (July 29); the Immaculate Heart of Mary (month of August); El Salvador del Mundo (August 6); Our Lady of LaVang (August 15). Back cover: Saint Francis (October 4); Saint George (April 23).

Printed in the United States of America

Library of Congress Control Number: 2011944914

16 15 14 13 12   1 2 3 4 5

ISBN 978-1-56854-260-7

COMCAL2

Contents

INTRODUCTION

Christ yesterday and today
the Beginning and the End
the Alpha
 and the Omega
All time belongs to him
 and all the ages
To him be glory and power
 through every age and for ever. Amen.

Each year, at the Easter Vigil, these words are prayed during the blessing of the paschal candle. The priest celebrant marks the candle with a cross, and between the arms of the cross he inscribes the numerals of the current year. In this rite, so full of meaning, we glimpse the meeting of "through every age and for ever," the intersection of the Paschal Mystery with the here and now of our daily lives. We recognize, once again, that the Paschal Mystery of Christ—his saving life, Death, and Resurrection—are historical events, yet, so much more. For Christian believers, they are living realities. Through the celebration of

the Eucharist, they are now. For us, time and eternity are not opposites; they are mysteriously intertwined.

There is a definite tension between the Church's calendar and the secular calendar. This becomes obvious during our penitential liturgical times of Advent and Lent. In Advent, as we quietly await the coming of Christ, we are inundated with all the trappings of the secular observance of Christmas Time, and just when we are decorating our Christmas trees, the world is putting them away! Then, in Lent, we are surrounded with bunnies and chocolate Easter eggs during our weeks of preparation for Easter. We do everything a little differently. For us, the new liturgical year begins not on January 1, but on the First Sunday of Advent; New Year's Day is celebrated as the Solemnity of Mary, the Holy Mother of God.

The calendar itself echoes this tension. It is full of the echoes of the pre-Christian world. Our month names come from ancient Rome ("July" and "August" are named for two famous Caesars, Julius and Augustus). The days of the week are mostly from Old

Images of Saints and Feasts of the Liturgical Year (L to R): Saint Benedict (July 11),
The Holy Family (Christmas Time), Saint Josephine Bakhita (February 8).

English, named for North Germanic gods and goddesses ("Wednesday," named for Wodin, "Friday," named for Freya) or for celestial bodies ("Sunday," sun's day, "Monday," moon's day, "Saturday," Saturn's day). And yet we number our years from Christ's birth; it is the point from which believers and nonbelievers alike count the years.

The tension between the liturgical calendar and the secular calendar—sometimes intersecting, sometimes not—is a good reminder for us. We are called to be in the world, yet not of the world.

The liturgical year is divided into six periods of liturgical time or "seasons." These six periods comprise the temporal cycle. The year begins with Advent, the time of waiting for the second coming of the Lord and of preparation for Christmas Time. Christmas Time follows, lasting about three weeks, until the Feast of the Baptism of the Lord. Lent begins a few weeks after Christmas Time ends and is a period of preparation for Easter Time. The Sacred Paschal Triduum is the shortest time of the year, lasting just three days, but also the most important: just as the Passion, Death, and Resurrection of Christ is the heart of our faith, so this commemoration is the heart of our liturgical year. Easter Time lasts 50 days—because we are a people of the Resurrection! The weeks between Christmas Time and Lent and between Easter Time and preceding Advent, about 33 or 34 weeks in all, are known as Ordinary Time (which means ordinal or "numbered" time).

Within the periods of time during the liturgical year, there are special observances, which are ranked according to their importance for the Church. The highest ranking observances are called solemnities: these include Easter Sunday and the Nativity of the Lord (Christmas); Our Lord Jesus Christ, King of the Universe; Immaculate Conception of the Blessed Virgin Mary; Saints Peter and Paul; and other saints. There are local solemnities as well, like the anniversary of the dedication of a church.

Next in rank are feasts, which celebrate mysteries of Christ (the Feast of the Exaltation of the Holy Cross, for example), and the Blessed Virgin Mary, as well as important saints like the Apostles

and Evangelists. Next come memorials, which are mainly of saints. Some memorials are obligatory, like Saint Thérèse of the Child Jesus (also often referred to as Saint Thérèse of Lisieux) on October 1 or Saint Scholastica on February 10. Others are optional in most places, like Saint Patrick on March 17 or Saint Nicholas on December 6.

About This Book

This book is intended to help you pray your way through the Catholic liturgical year. It includes introductions to each liturgical time and brief reflections on the saints, feasts, memorials, and commemorations of the year from the *Proper Calendar for the Dioceses of the United States of America* and the *Proper Calendar for the Dioceses of Canada*.

The *Proper Calendar* is a complete listing of all the saints that are observed in these particular countries. There are hundreds of saints, and it would be impossible to honor them all throughout the course of the liturgical year. Calendars were therefore created for each country. There are variations from diocese to diocese and parish to parish because of local patron saints (i.e., the patron saint of a diocese or the patron saint of a parish). These variations are not included in this book.

It is easy to find in this book the saints that are celebrated on the *Proper Calendars* of the United States and Canada. Throughout this book you will see noted in the largest heading the designations of solemnities, feasts, memorials, or optional memorials. An image of the American and Canadian flags have been placed in the headings to designate the proper country (these flags are also included with civic celebrations; see below).

It is important to note that biographies of saints that are not on the *Proper Calendars* of the Dioceses of the United States and Canada have also been included in this book. *Companion to the Calendar, Second Edition* reflects a new awareness of our global Church, with many new entries on sanctoral and devotional observances around the world, from Asia; North, Central, and South America; Europe; and Africa. These entries help us to see our faith through other eyes. To differentiate between the *Proper Calendars* and saints of cultural significance, the headings do not include the ranking of solemnity, feast, memorial, or optional memorial. Only the saints' name is given.

This book also includes major civic holidays of the United States, Canada, Australia, and Mexico, in addition to special sections describing the most important holy days for our Orthodox Christian, Jewish, and Muslim brothers and sisters.

About the Authors

Kathy Coffey is the author of *Hidden Women of the Gospels, Women of Mercy, God in the Moment: Making Every Day a Prayer, Mary* (Orbis), *Immersed in the Sacred: Discovering the Small s Sacraments* (Ave Maria), catechetical resources such as *Understanding the Revised Mass Texts, Leader's Edition: Second Edition* with Father Paul Turner (LTP), *Children and Christian Initiation, Baptism and Beyond* (Morehouse), online resources at www.pastoralplanning.com and many articles in Catholic periodicals. She taught for fifteen years at the University of Colorado, Denver, and Regis Jesuit University. She has won fourteen awards from the Catholic Press Association, the Foley Poetry Award from *America* magazine, the Independent Publishers Book Award and the Associated Church Press Award for Editorial Courage. Kathy also speaks at national and international gatherings. The mother of four, she lives in Denver, Colorado.

Donna M. Crilly received her bachelor's degree from Douglass College (Rutgers University) and her master of theological studies from Weston Jesuit School of Theology (now the Boston College School of Theology and Ministry). She is currently the managing editor at Paulist Press in Mahwah, New Jersey.

Mary G. Fox is the editor of *Pastoral Liturgy* and *Catechumenate: A Journal of Christian Initiation.* Her bachelor of arts degree in journalism is from Duquesne University and her master of arts degree in religious studies is from Mundelein College.

Mary Ellen Hynes is a writer, editor, retreat leader, and spiritual director. She holds a Master's in Religious Education and a Master's in Pastoral Studies from Loyola University Chicago. She is the author of *Companion to the Calendar*, published by LTP in 1993. She is a frequent contributor to *At Home with the Word*, LTP's annual resource for the Lectionary readings of the liturgical year. She lives in Oak Park, Illinois, with her husband, John. Her two grandchildren, Brendan and Lauren, are the delight of her heart.

Julie M. Krakora received her bachelor of arts in Theology from Marquette University and her master of arts in Pastoral Studies with an emphasis in Spirituality from Loyola University in Chicago. She has been a Director of Youth Ministry for junior high and high school teens, a campus minister / theology teacher in Catholic high schools, and currently is a Director of University Ministry at the University of St. Francis in Joliet, Illinois. While always seeking to work with people in the ministerial setting, her other passion is to write anything that will bring people closer in relationship with God. She is the author of *Sunday Prayer for Catholic School Teachers 2013,* as well as a contributing author to *God's Word, Your World 2013, Sourcebook for Sundays, Seasons, and Weekdays 2013,* and *Year of Grace 2013* (all from LTP).

Corinna Laughlin serves as Pastoral Assistant for Liturgy at Saint James Cathedral in Seattle. She also serves on the Liturgical Commission for the Archdiocese of Seattle. She holds a doctorate in English language and literature from the University of Washington, and a bachelor's degree in English from Mount Holyoke College. Corinna is the co-author of LTP's *Daily Prayer 2010* as well as the *Guide for Sacristans* and *Guide for Servers* from *The Liturgical Ministry Series.* She is also a contributing author to *Sourcebook for Sundays, Seasons, and Weekdays: The Almanac for Pastoral Liturgy* for 2009, 2011, and 2012.

Robert C. Rabe is a theology teacher at Mother McAuley Liberal Arts High School in Chicago. He serves the Church in a variety of capacities, including retreat facilitation, instructor in diaconal and lay formation programs, and author and editor of theological resources for both adults and youth. Holding a Master of Divinity degree from Saint John's School of Theology Seminary, Robert possesses a solid background in scriptural interpretation. Along with a passion for Sacred Scripture, Robert has spent considerable time researching and writing about the intersection between hagiography and contemporary spirituality. His publications include *Daily Prayer 2007* (LTP), *The Bible: The Living Word of God,* and the *Year of Grace 2012* (LTP), and he is contributing author to *Sourcebook for Sundays, Seasons, and Weekdays 2011* (LTP).

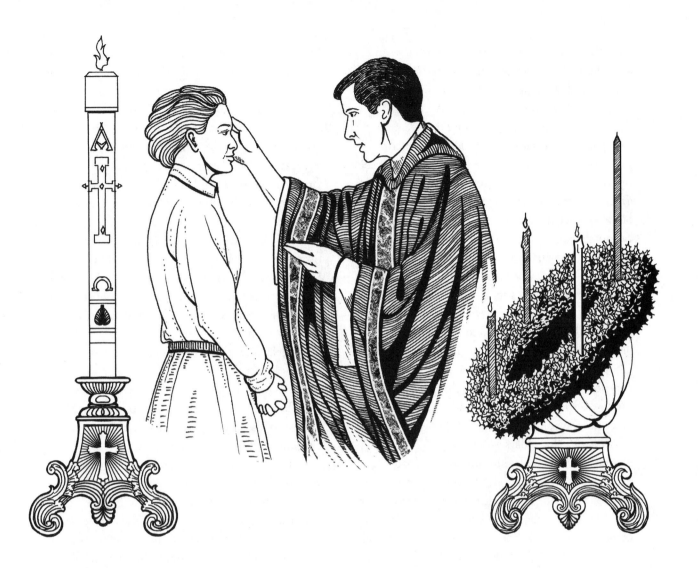

THE LITURGICAL TIMES

Sunday and the Week

Jesus lived the Jewish Law in its fullness, observing all the feasts and fasts, the processions, and the prayers of his ancestors. Each day was punctuated by prayer, and each week ended with the Sabbath observance, from sundown on Friday until sundown on Saturday. In the Book of Genesis, we hear that God created the world in six days, and on the seventh day he rested. The Jewish people understood the Sabbath as God's gift to creation. In resting on the seventh day, God made rest sacred.

The Christian liturgical observance grew out of Jewish worship. The Gospel tells us that Jesus rose "on the first day of the week," the day after the Sabbath (John 20:1). The first day—the day when God created the heavens and earth—is now the day of the new creation, when Christ's Resurrection brings life, unimagined and totally new, out of death. The earliest

Images of Symbols and Rituals of the Liturgical Year (L to R): The Paschal Candle, Distribution of Ashes, the Advent Wreath.

Christians continued to observe the Jewish Law and to keep the ancient Sabbath, but soon "the Lord's Day," as it was called, supplanted the older observance.

Sunday was, and is, the heart of Christian worship. In the year 304, the Emperor Diocletian sought to suppress Christianity by forbidding Christians to gather on Sunday. When some Christians in Abitene, in what is now Tunisia, defied his command to gather on Sunday morning to break the bread, they offered no defense except to say, "without Sunday, we cannot live" (quoted by Pope Benedict XVI in a homily for Esplanade of Marisabella, May 29, 2005).

The Sunday Eucharist is the most important prayer of our week, the "center of the whole of Christian life" (*General Instruction of the Roman Missal*, 16), but we are called to be people for whom prayer is our "daily bread" (The Lord's Prayer). Our Church's liturgy marks every single day with the celebration of the Eucharist and the praying of the Liturgy of the Hours, which (as its name suggests) sanctifies the hours of the day with prayer. The week unfolds with "ferial days"—weekdays—special commemorations of saints and mysteries of faith, and occasional solemnities, all of which open up windows on the living of the Christian life. We are nourished by the Eucharist and by the word of God; through the celebrations of the saints, we are made aware of the great "cloud of witnesses" (Hebrews 12:1) that surrounds us and urges us on. Through their heroic lives we see how we can live in Christ. In the course of the year we contemplate the mysteries of Christ from his birth through his Death, to his Resurrection and Ascension, and along the way we pause simply to be aware of the mystery of his love in solemnities like the Most Holy Body and Blood of Christ and the Most Sacred Heart of Jesus. The solemnities, feasts, and memorials of Mary span the entire year, to keep before our eyes the example of the first and best disciple of Christ.

The Sanctoral Cycle

Our liturgy exists to celebrate the Paschal Mystery of the Passion, Death, and Resurrection of Christ.

Through the liturgy, Christ's saving work is remembered and accomplished, for the sacrifice of Christ is renewed in every Mass. In a certain sense, every day, and especially every Sunday, is Easter. Saints' days, too, are celebrations of Christ and of his Paschal Mystery, for in celebrating the saints we are really celebrating the Christ whose grace strengthened them, whose word guided them, and whose power working through them made them living examples of holiness.

When a member of one's family dies, survivors often share a belief that they now rely upon the deceased to relay their prayers to God. Many call upon their deceased loved ones for inner strength and in times of need. Some ask for a deceased grandfather or mother to give them advice, or show them a sign to help guide them on life's journey. These actions usually do not shock people. Yet some appear surprised to learn that Catholics pray through saints and offer them special days and celebrations at Mass. For Catholics, praying to a saint is not all that different from praying through Grandma.

The Church distinguishes saints as men and women outstanding in holiness. In an exemplary way, they model what it looks like to imitate Christ Jesus in a particular time and place. Their life so clearly reflects the kind of living set out by the Gospel that once a person is declared a saint, the Church believes that they enjoy all the benefits of heaven.

Recalling the lives of the saints is one of the defining characteristics of our Catholic identity. Woven into the Church's calendar, which normally celebrates the events in the life of Christ Jesus (known as the temporal cycle), exists what some have described as a garland of saints' feasts and memorials. This calendar of saints is known as the sanctoral cycle.

Who are the saints? The calendar includes men and women from every century and every place, famous names and not-so-famous names. They are martyrs—people who were killed for their faith in Christ. They are priests, bishops, and popes, shepherds of the flock. They are virgins, who consecrated their lives to Christ, in a monastery or convent, or outside of it. They are laypeople, married people, mothers and fathers, leaders of families, and rulers of nations. They are holy men and women. The calendar of saints includes young people like Saint Maria Goretti (July 6), who was martyred at the age of twelve, and Saint Anthony (January 17), who is said to have lived to the ripe old age of 105! There are saints from five continents and from almost every nation on earth. There are saints who spent their lives in silent contemplation, and saints who spent their lives in crowded cities. There are saints who advocated tirelessly for justice, and saints who dedicated themselves to the sick, to the arts, to administration and leadership, to children, to the education of priests, and so much more. The saints remind us of what Jesus said to his friends—"In my Father's house, there are many dwelling places" (John 14:2). There are many ways to live the Christian life; there are many calls to holiness.

Usually, on saints' days, the color of the vestment changes from the color of the liturgical time to red or white. Red, the color of witness, is reserved for martyrs; for all other saints, white vestments are worn.

Saints' days are ranked in various ways. Solemnities are rare—the only saints honored with a solemnity on the calendar are the Queen of Saints, Mary (January 1, August 15, December 8), Joseph (March 19), Peter and Paul (June 29), and John the Baptist (June 24). The feast day of the titular saint of any church is celebrated as a solemnity in that church. And, of course, all the saints are honored on the Solemnity of All Saints (November 1).

Apostles and Evangelists are honored with feasts, including John (December 27), James (July 25), Luke (October 18), and the Archangels (September 29). Important saints have obligatory memorials, meaning they must be observed throughout the world—saints like Teresa (October 15), Jerome (September 30), Vincent de Paul (September 27), and many others. Finally, there are dozens of optional memorials, which the priest may choose to celebrate or not—saints like the martyrs Cosmas and Damian (September 26 in the United States) and Maria Goretti (July 6) fall into this category.

The Temporal Cycle
Advent

Advent begins the liturgical year for the Church. The beginnings of things usually need some advance preparation, and the liturgical year is no different. One way to approach the beginnings of the Christian life is to look at Christ himself. Advent prepares the faithful though joyful waiting and hopeful expectation for Christ's coming.

Advent begins four Sundays prior to the Solemnity of the Nativity of the Lord (Christmas), December 25. While Advent readies us for this joyful anniversary of Christ Jesus' birth, there is more. Advent contains a double purpose. In addition to the Christmas preparations, it also prepares us for the second coming of Christ at the very end of time.

The first part of Advent draws our attention to the end of time. At Mass during the Eucharistic Prayer, the congregation jubilantly sings "We proclaim your Death, O Lord, / and profess your Resurrection / until you come again." He will come, as the Nicene Creed says, "to judge the living and the dead." We sometime refer to this as the second coming. He will rule over all nations. He will judge with justice tempered with mercy. His coming is to bring about a complete integration of peace among all living things: people, animals, nature, and the whole cosmos. We do not know when this will happen. The Scriptures tell us that we do not know the day (see Luke 12:40), but we are to be on the watch (see Matthew 24:42). This waiting and watching characterize the spirituality of Advent. The readings, traditions, and rituals of this liturgical time help Catholics practice the art of joyful anticipation and holy patience.

The second part of Advent serves as a prelude to celebration of the infant birth of Christ Jesus. The focus of the prayers and Scripture during this part of Advent feel much more like Christmas Time. The Scriptures tell the story of the angel Gabriel coming to Mary, and her journey with Joseph to Bethlehem unfolds.

It is said that Advent signifies the four thousand years of waiting for the Messiah to come and fulfill all the hopes and longings of the people and to bring about the fullness of God's reign. It looks toward the justice and the redemption God has promised with hopefulness and joyful anticipation.

Part of waiting for the Lord's coming includes being ready. Sin and injustice weaken our readiness. They rob us of joy. Advent seeks to restore this joy by our acts of repentance. The Sunday readings of Advent include the stories of John the Baptist proclaiming a baptism of repentance for the forgiveness of sins (see Matthew 3:7–10; Mark 1:4; Luke 3:7–9; John 1:27), for one mightier is coming who will baptize with the Holy Spirit (Matthew 3:11; Mark 1:8; Luke 3:16). To more fully prepare for the Messiah, the people acknowledge their sins. Repenting does not need to be an avoided activity. We can easily lose sight of its larger purpose. John the Baptist encouraged repentance for the sake of receiving the Messiah who comes with the Holy Spirit.

Advent offers a time to prepare for oncoming joy. Part of that preparation involves a loving and honest acknowledgement of all that is unloving, unfaithful, and unjust in our lives. As we prepare for the Lord of all nations, we examine our own societies and admit the structures of corruption and injustices that pervade them. Advent affords us the reflection time to see our incompleteness and to ask for his forgiveness. We pray that when he comes, he may be merciful.

The Days of Advent

Gaudete Sunday

Third Sunday of Advent

The Third Sunday of Advent is also known as *Gaudete Sunday*, from the first words of the Entrance Antiphon for the Mass: *Gaudete in Domino semper*, "Rejoice in the Lord always; again I say, rejoice. / Indeed, the Lord is near" (Philippians 4:4–5). Like the Fourth Sunday of Lent (*Laetare Sunday*), it is a day for rejoicing in the midst of a penitential liturgical time. The organ returns, flowers again grace the altar, and the liturgical color may shift from violet to rose. Why do we rejoice? Because, as Saint Paul says,

"the Lord is near" (Philippians 4:5). Even as we continue to await the Lord's coming, we know that he is already with us: in his word and in his sacraments, and in the Church, which is his body. In a special way, he is with us in his beloved poor.

A new *Gaudete Sunday* custom has developed in Rome in recent years. Each year on the Third Sunday of Advent, the children of Rome bring the *Bambinello* (the figure of the Christ Child) from their home manger scenes to Saint Peter's Square for a special blessing by the Holy Father. In just a few years, this has become a well-loved tradition, so much so that some Romans call the Third Sunday of Advent *Bambinelli Sunday*!

Advent Traditions

The "O" Antiphons

December 17–23

An antiphon is a short passage or verse, usually from Scripture, which is prayed before and after the Psalms and canticles in the Liturgy of the Hours. In the last days of Advent, from December 17 through December 23, the antiphons for the Magnificat at Evening Prayer call upon Christ under the many names used by the prophets in the Old Testament, and ask him to hasten his return. Each of these antiphons begins with "O" (hence their name). The first "O" Antiphon begins, *O Sapientia* (O Wisdom). Then comes *Adonai* (Sacred Lord), *Radix Jesse* (Root of Jesse), *Clavis David* (Key of David), *Oriens* (Dawn), *Rex gentium* (King of peoples), and finally *Emmanuel* (God-is-with-us). The favorite Advent carol, *O Come, O Come Emmanuel,* is actually John M. Neale's translation of these ancient antiphons.

Medieval poets loved intricacies of language, and the first letters of the titles by which Christ is addressed in the "O" antiphons—*Sapientia, Adonai, Radix,* and so on—form a reverse acrostic, spelling the Latin words that mean "I will be there tomorrow."

Advent Wreath

The Advent wreath is a devotion that originated among the Lutherans of Eastern Germany hundreds of years ago. The wreath, made of yew, fir, or laurel branches, is often suspended from the ceiling or placed on a table. On the wreath are placed four candles, one for each of the weeks of Advent. Each Sunday, another candle is lit, until, just before the Solemnity of the Nativity of the Lord (Christmas), all four candles glow. Often, the candles echo the liturgical colors of Advent, with three violet candles, and one rose candle, lit on Gaudete Sunday, the Third Sunday of Advent (although four violet candles or four white candles may also be used). This devotion began in Germany but has now spread all over the world, and is loved by Christians of many different denominations. We have Advent wreaths at home, at school, and in the church as well.

Why is the Advent wreath so popular? Perhaps because it is such a powerful sign of what we celebrate at Christmas. The wreath of evergreen branches reminds us that even in the darkest days of the year, there is life. And the gradually increasing light of the candles speaks of the fact that at Christmas, Christ, the true light, came into the world: "the light shines in the darkness, and the darkness did not overcome it" (John 1:5).

Jesse Tree

"A shoot shall come out from the stump of Jesse" (Isaiah 11:1). The prophecy of Isaiah finds its fulfillment in Christ, sprung, like King David, from Jesse's line. In recent years, the Advent devotion of the Jesse Tree has gained in popularity. Each day during Advent, a Scripture passage is read, and an ornament is hung on the Jesse Tree. Gradually, the story of the love of God for the human family unfolds, from the creation of the world in the book of Genesis, to the exile and homecoming of the chosen people, to the journey of Joseph and Mary, and, finally, to the birth of Jesus. The Jesse Tree can be an actual tree or a bare branch from which ornaments can be hung. It can also be a poster or wall hanging. Through the Jesse Tree, we come to know the people who prepared the way for the Lord, from Adam and Eve to John the Baptist.

Christmas Time

When children think of Christmas Time, gifts, ribbons, ornamented trees, and Santa Claus come to mind. Families begin preparing weeks in advance. Retailers start months ahead. Family traditions preserve special recipes of sweets and chocolates enjoyed only during this liturgical time. Even with the massive influx of nonreligious objects infused into this time by a secular society, many communities and families retain a strong sense of its core: Christmas remembers God's gift of his son Jesus who comes as the savior of the world.

Christmas Time is one of the two majestic pillars of the Church's liturgical year. It has a set date, December (with a Vigil Mass the preceding evening), from which follows a series of celebrations. The Solemnity of the Nativity of the Lord (Christmas Day itself) celebrates the birth of our Lord Jesus Christ to Mary, his mother, and Joseph, her husband. Yet for Catholics that is only the beginning. The Nativity of the Lord (Christmas Day) carries such importance within the life of the Church that it is an entire period of liturgical time lasting nearly three weeks.

The day itself is known by a variety of names. Christmas ("Christ's Mass") is most common. Officially, the Church titles it the Solemnity of the Nativity of the Lord. When referring to the solemnity celebrating this event several words are used interchangeably: Christmas, the Nativity, or the Incarnation.

The celebration marks an event of the Lord and also expresses a part of Church doctrine. The doctrine of the Incarnation states a fundamental Christian belief that God's divine nature assumed a human nature. In other words, the unseen God became human. Both human and divine natures come together in the person of Jesus Christ. This became known as the "holy exchange," which tells us that the divine became a human being so that humans could become divine.

Parishes ususally offer various opportunities to celebrate Christmas. Following the custom of our Jewish ancestors, a special feast day can begin the evening before, as soon as the sun sets. Thus, many parishes will begin Christmas Masses on the evening of December 24. These are known as the Vigil Masses. The Mass during the Night (previously called Mass at Midnight) is a great tradition for many Catholics. The Christmas story from Luke's account of the Gospel tells how the angel of the Lord came to the shepherds in the fields during their night watch. Some celebrate Christmas Mass at dawn, and others will attend Christmas morning or day. Catholic are expected to go to only one of these options to prayerfully celebrate the Christmas mystery.

December 25 is not likely the literal day on which Jesus was born. The actual day of his birth is unknown. It was not until after Jesus died and was resurrected that his friends and followers truly realized the significance of his life. Thus, his childhood received little historical attention.

December 25 has remained through the years largely due to its symbolism; however, historical circumstances had a great deal to do with the development of Christmas. In the fourth century, the Church was faced with its first great controversy—the Arian heresy, which denied the divinity of Jesus. At the Council of Nicaea in 325, the Church condemned Arianism, proclaiming Jesus as "God from God, Light from Light, / true God from true God, / . . . consubstantial with the Father" (Nicene Creed). Jesus was not simply a holy creation of God, as the Arians said. Jesus was God Almighty, with God from the beginning, "begotten, not made" (ibid.). Even after the Council of Nicaea, Arianism continued to fester in the Church; the matter was not definitively settled until the Council of Constantinople in 381. It was in this climate of controversy that Christmas developed. The first Christmas at Rome has been dated at around 330, just a few years after the Council of Nicaea.

Christmas proclaims Jesus as the Emmanuel, God-with-us. Other historical circumstances also contributed to the development of Christmas. In 274, the Emperor Aurelian had decreed that December 25—the time of the winter solstice—be dedicated to *Natale Solis Invicti*, a pagan feast in honor of the "Unconquered Sun God." Given the frequent scriptural references to Christ as light—the true light, the light of the world—it was easy for the early Christians to "baptize" this pagan feast, and turn the celebration of the sun into a celebration of the Sun of Justice.

There was still another, more potent reason for the celebration of Christmas on December 25: for the early Christians, this was the historical date of Christ's birth. "As early as the third century Christian theologians were endeavoring to calculate the date of Christ's birth, which is not mentioned in the Gospel. The Christ-as-sun symbolism that was so deeply rooted in the Christian consciousness caused them to pay special attention to the equinoxes and solstices" (*The Liturgical Year* by Adolf Adam, p. 123). As a result, the birth of John the Baptist was placed at the summer solstice ("I must decrease," John 3:30) and the birth of Jesus six months later, at the winter solstice ("he must increase," ibid.). For people whose lives were impacted by the sun, moon, and natural seasons far more than our own, these times of the year held tremendous meaning. The early Christians could see the Incarnation of the Lord—his birth, his Death, his Resurrection—written in the cosmos.

This mystery of God becoming flesh in the life of Christ Jesus strikes the heart of Christian believers. So rich is this mystery of the Christian faith that Catholics take several weeks and multiple celebrations to ritually unfold this expression of God's love.

The Days of Christmas Time

Octave of the Nativity of the Lord

December 25–January 1

Octave comes from a Latin word meaning "eight." In music, an octave is an interval of eight notes. In the Church's calendar, an octave is a special period of celebration following a major feast, particularly the Nativity of the Lord (Christmas) and Easter. The Christmas Octave, which ends with the Solemnity of Mary, the Holy Mother of God on January 1, is a special time to reflect on the great mystery we have celebrated at Christmas: the Incarnation. The Octave of Christmas is full of variety. It includes a number of saints' days—Saint Stephen on December 26; Saint John the Evangelist on December 27; the Holy Innocents on December 28; Saint Thomas Becket on December 29; and Saint Sylvester on December 31. These Christmas saints are sometimes called the *Comites Christi*, the companions of Christ. They are old, young, and in between, martyrs, teachers, bishops, popes. What did they have in common? They were faithful disciples of Jesus, following him on the way of the cross.

During the Octave of Christmas, we observe a special feast in honor of the Holy Family of Jesus, Mary, and Joseph (see below).

Feast of the Holy Family of Jesus, Mary, and Joseph
Sunday within the Octave of the Nativity of the Lord, or, if there is no Sunday, December 30

The Feast of the Holy Family of Jesus, Mary and Joseph, which is observed on the Sunday in the Octave of Christmas (except when Nativity of the Lord [Christmas] falls on a Sunday, when it is moved to December 30), is quite a new feast, added to the calendar by Pope Leo XIII in 1893. The pope wanted to highlight the importance of the Christian family and to point to the Holy Family as a model for all families to follow. Mary and Joseph could not surround the newborn Jesus with material things: he was born in poverty, with, as we sing in the carol, "no crib for his bed" (*Away in a Manger*). Yet, what they had, they lavished on Jesus: love, tenderness, and care. Love transformed the stable, making it a source of light and hope, just as love can transform every home, even the poorest, and make it a place where children can grow as Jesus did, in wisdom, love, and grace. This feast urges us to see in the Holy Family of Jesus, Mary, and Joseph, a "shining example" for all family life (Collect, Feast of the Holy Family of Jesus, Mary, and Joseph). In their mutual love and forbearance, in their patience in times of trial, and in their total obedience to God's will for them, the Holy Family shows us how to live together in peace.

The Feast of the Holy Family is a fitting time for blessings related to the family, including blessings of married couples, children, and engaged couples. These blessings are found in the *Book of Blessings,* chapter 1.

Solemnity of the Epiphany of the Lord
January 6 (traditional date)
Sunday between January 2 and January 8 🇺🇸 🍁

The Gospel according to Matthew speaks of wise men, Magi from the East, who saw a star and came in search of the infant Christ, and then returned home. Through the years, tradition has added many other details to the story, giving the names of Caspar, Melchior, and Balthasar to the wise men, and explaining the significance of their gifts: precious gold, given to a king; frankincense, offered to God; and bitter myrrh, for one doomed to die. The Magi have so captivated the Christian imagination that in some countries, including Spain, the Solemnity of the Epiphany is referred to as *Los Tres Reyes*, the Three Kings!

But Epiphany is not just about the Magi. The word *epiphany* is Greek for "manifestation" or "showing forth," and this solemnity is about Christ revealing his glory to the nations. That is of course what happened when the Magi, foreigners from the East, followed the star: they recognized Christ as God, and worshiped him. In past centuries (and to this day in the Orthodox Church and Byzantine Catholic Church) other mysteries were remembered on this day in addition to the visit of the Magi: especially Jesus' baptism, and his first miracle at Cana, both moments in which his glory appeared for all to see. In the Office of Morning Prayer (Liturgy of the Hours) for this solemnity, an antiphon brings the three "epiphanies" together in a wonderful way: "Today the Bridegroom claims his bride, the Church, since Christ has washed her sins away in Jordan's waters; the Magi hasten with their gifts to the royal wedding; and the wedding guests rejoice, for Christ has changed water into wine, alleluia" (volume I, p. 564).

Many wonderful traditions are associated with Epiphany. It is a day for the blessing of homes: one ancient tradition calls for the letters 20 + C + M + B + XX [the numerals of the current year], to be written above the door with blessed chalk (the letters C, M, and B stand for the names of the Magi). In some countries, Epiphany is another day for gift-giving, and children will leave a shoe out the night before, in hopes that the Magi, who of course brought precious gifts for Christ, will leave a gift for them as well. Another favorite tradition throughout most of Europe is the Kings' Cake, a special cake in which a coin (or a bean) is hidden. The cake is cut and eaten, and the person who finds the hidden coin is the "king" or "queen."

Epiphany traditionally takes place on January 6, twelve days after Christmas, though in many countries where January 6 is not a public holiday, the solemnity is now observed on the Sunday after January 1.

Feast of the Baptism of the Lord

Sunday after January 6

Christmas Time always ends with a feast in honor of the baptism of the Lord. This feast is celebrated on the Sunday after Epiphany, except when Nativity of the Lord (Christmas) falls on a Sunday; then, in the United States of America, the Baptism of the Lord is transferred to a Monday.

When Jesus came to the Jordan to be baptized, John the Baptist exclaimed: "I need to be baptized by you, and yet you are coming to me?" (Matthew 3:14). We might want to ask the same question. Why does Jesus come to be baptized? He is sinless; why does he need to receive John's baptism of repentance? Jesus answers, "it is fitting for us to fulfill all righteousness" (Matthew 3:15). In other words, Jesus is baptized because this is God's plan for him—and for us. Jesus is baptized because we need Baptism. He opens the way for us, sanctifying the water, to wash away our sins. An antiphon at Evening Prayer uses vivid imagery to express what happened when Jesus was baptized: "In the Jordan river our Savior crushed the serpent's head and wrested us free from his grasp."

Jesus' baptism marks a change. After his baptism, he begins to proclaim the kingdom of God, to gather disciples, to teach, to heal and to work miracles. He begins his active ministry, leaving behind the "hidden years" of his quiet life with Mary and Joseph in Nazareth. It is the same for all Christians who follow Jesus into the waters of Baptism. Baptism is not an ending, but a beginning. As we receive forgiveness for our sins, we also receive a calling, to live as faithful disciples, and so build up the kingdom.

This feast is usually celebrated on the Sunday after January 6; however, if Epiphany is celebrated on January 7 or 8 (Sunday), in the United States, the Feast of the Baptism of the Lord is celebrated on the following Monday.

Solemnity of Mary, the Holy Mother of God

January 1

This solemnity is the most ancient liturgical observance of Mary in the Church's calendar. It honors Mary as *theotokos* or "Mother of God," the title accorded her at the Council of Ephesus in 431. Mary is not just the Mother of Jesus: she is the Mother of God, because Jesus is both God and man, divine and human. As other Marian feasts entered the calendar, January 1 acquired a different focus. The eighth day after birth was the traditional day for the circumcision and naming of a child, and so this became the Feast of the Circumcision of the Lord (and the naming of Jesus). It was only in 1969 that the Marian character of this ancient feast was restored.

Christmas Time Traditions

Christmas Tree

The Christmas tree is almost certainly the favorite of all the home traditions of Christmas. Like the Advent wreath, it began in Germany, where it is traced to the middle ages, when the performance of mystery plays was one of the ways people learned their faith. One such play was called the *Paradise Play*, telling the story of the creation and the fall. At the center of the performance was the *Paradise Tree*, covered in apples and surrounded by candles. The play, usually performed in Advent, would end with the expulsion of Adam and Eve from Paradise and with God's consoling promise that one day he would bring humanity to a new paradise, through Christ, who would die upon the tree of the Cross. When the mystery plays were suppressed, people began to place the *Paradise Tree* in their homes, and gradually the custom of the Christmas tree developed, with ornaments taking the place of the apples.

The primary symbols of the Christmas tree, like the Advent wreath, are life and light. The *Book of Blessings* (BB) includes a prayer for the lighting of a Christmas tree that recalls the origins of the tradition: "your Son, / . . . rescued us from the darkness of sin / by making the cross a tree of life and light. / May this tree, arrayed in splendor, / remind us of the life-giving cross of Christ" (BB, 1587).

Some parishes and schools set up a Giving Tree during Advent. On the tree are hung ornaments with the name of a person in need from a local nursing home, care center, senior housing facility, or family shelters. Each person asks for a gift—usually something simple but necessary like a winter coat or school supplies. Parishioners are invited to take the ornament away with them, and come back before Christmas with the wrapped item. Giving trees allow the community to reach out to those who may not otherwise receive a gift at Christmas.

Las Posadas

December 16–24

Las Posadas ("Lodgings") is one of the most popular Advent and Christmas devotions in Mexico and Central America. Part drama, part prayer, it reenacts the journey of Joseph and Mary through Bethlehem, as they seek a place to stay. Children dressed as "Joseph" and "Mary" knock at the doors of houses, accompanied by "shepherds" who carry lanterns. A traditional song is sung, alternating between those outside and those inside. At last Mary and Joseph find a welcome. *Las Posadas* is not a one-time event but a novena of prayer, repeated each evening, beginning on December 16, and offering each household the opportunity to welcome the Holy Family. *Las Posadas*

is a vivid reminder that the Holy Family still seeks a place to stay, and that when we answer "yes," Christ is born in us again.

Simbang Gabi

December 16–24

Simbang Gabi, a novena of Masses in honor of the Blessed Virgin Mary, is form of the Christmas Novena, originating in the Philippines. The Masses were traditionally offered at dawn, so that fishermen and laborers could attend before going off to work (hence the novena's other name—*Missa di Gallo* or Mass of the Rooster). Associated with *Simbang Gabi* is the *parol*, or star-shaped lantern, which recalls the star that led the Magi to the infant Christ.

Las Parrandas

December 16–26

If you didn't have a telephone, e-mail, parish bulletin, or website, how would you get people to come to Mass each evening during the days before Christmas? You might do what Father Francisco Vigil de Cañones did in 18th century Cuba: he sent children through the town of Remedios, with noisemakers and songs to bring people to the cathedral for Mass. Years went by, and the tradition survived—and grew. Today, the novena of Masses has been somewhat overshadowed by one of the biggest street parties in the world, with floats, lights, and incredible music.

The Manger Scene or Crèche

The manger scene or crèche has been part of how we celebrate Christmas for centuries. The custom is traced to Saint Francis of Assisi, who created the first manger scene in the Italian village of Greccio on Christmas Eve, 1223. He wanted people to do more than read about the Christmas story: he wanted them to see the stable at Bethlehem, and the poverty that surrounded Jesus on the night he was born. And so Francis placed the image of the Christ Child in a real manger, filled with hay, and brought in a live ox and ass to take their places in the scene. The people crowded around this vision of Bethlehem and were so moved that the manger scene became an annual tradition.

Today, the manger scene continues to be a beloved custom in our homes and churches. Some parishes and schools have a "live crib," where real people play the roles of Mary and Joseph, the shepherds, and the Magi, and a real newborn baby lies in the manger!

Lent

When people hear "Catholics" and "Lent" spoken in the same sentence, the imagination flashes images of a fish fry in the church basement, meatless Fridays with mac 'n' cheese, or Stations of the Cross. Many Catholics recall giving up something they crave such as soda pop, and those of an older generation recall making their pre-Easter obligation to confess their sins.

Lent engages the faithful in rich spiritual renewal unlike any other liturgical time. Catholics exhibit a special devotion to this liturgical time that uniquely distinguishes Roman Catholicism. While Lent entails many things, three central themes emerge. Lent prepares us for Easter and our renewal of our baptismal promises by deepening our identity with Christ through penitential practices. For the adults preparing for Baptism at Easter, Lent affords them rituals to enter into the mystery of Christ Jesus.

This period of liturgical time admits human sin and frailty more clearly than others, yet it emphasizes the strength, growth, and holiness that God offers in the midst of strife. Lent's promise of redemption reveals Catholicism's optimism. It demonstrates how the sinful are the very recipients of God's redeeming grace. Because of God's grace, freely offered as a gift, we have reason to be joyful.

Lent begins on Ash Wednesday and concludes on Holy Thursday. Traditional hymns and common thought claim that Lent lasts for forty days. However, counting the days from Ash Wednesday to Holy Thursday amounts to forty-four. How did it grow by four days?

The Council of Nicaea (325) officially recognized Lent as a period of forty days. It prepared the unbaptized for the more glorious fifty days of Easter. Saint Athanatius, a fourth-century bishop, described a forty-day fast in the vein of Moses, David, and Daniel. He makes no reference to Jesus' forty days in the desert, an image for Lent that is common today.

Originally, Lent began six Sundays prior to Easter Sunday and concluded as it does today on Holy Thursday. In 1091, Pope Urban II argued for a universal rite of ashes to precede the Lenten fast. Through the years, the distribution of ashes became customary on the Wednesday before the First Sunday of Lent. This practice remains today. Hence, four extra days snuck into Lent's calendar.

The actual dates change every year because Easter's date depends upon the lunar and solar calendars. Lent begins sometime in February or March and concludes in late March or most usually April. Check an annual Church calendar (such LTP's *Year of Grace*) for exact dates.

Lent is a time of collaborating with God to create something new and divine. Entering into this period of liturgical time with outward rituals of prayer, fasting, and almsgiving, combined with the inner work of prayer, believers will be renewed and arrive at Easter eager to welcome the new life of the Resurrection.

The Days of Lent

Ash Wednesday

Ash Wednesday is one of the most-loved days on the entire liturgical calendar. Coming together to hear the Lord's call to repentance, and to receive the blessed ashes, is part of what makes us Catholic.

The Collect for Ash Wednesday is one of the most startling prayers we hear all year. This prayer uses imagery of warfare in describing Lent: "Grant, O Lord, that we may begin with holy fasting / this campaign of Christian service, / so that, as we take up battle against spiritual evils, / we may be armed with weapons of self-restraint." This is a different kind of warfare: it is a battle that takes place within us. Our prayer, fasting, and almsgiving, our "self-restraint," are the only weapons we have in our fight against evil. But with God's grace to help us, these weapons are enough.

The use of ashes as a sign of repentance goes back thousands of years, and is referenced frequently in the Old Testament. In the early Church, penitents —baptized persons who had committed grave sins— would come to the bishop at the beginning of Lent, and be marked with ashes as a sign of their repentance. After a period of rigorous penance, they would be welcomed back to the sacraments at the Evening Mass of the Lord's Supper on Holy Thursday. As time passed, the ashes began to be given to all the faithful at the beginning of Lent. The ashes are a reminder of where we come from—ashes to ashes, dust to dust— but they are also a call to repentance. Traditionally, the ashes are made from the burning of palms from last year's observance of Palm Sunday: in that sense, they are also reminders that we are destined for glory with Christ.

Rite of Election

Usually the First Sunday of Lent

The Rite of Election takes place at the beginning of Lent, usually in the cathedral church of the diocese. The catechumens, those preparing for Baptism, gather with their sponsors, catechists, and pastors. They are presented to the bishop, who inquires about their preparation. Have they listened to the words of Christ in the Scriptures, and begun to live by his commands? Have they joined with their parish community in prayer? Have they, in short, changed their lives in response to the Gospel? If they have, then the bishop invites them to enroll their names in the *Book of the Elect*. Speaking on behalf of the entire Church, the bishop declares them to be members of the "elect," chosen by God for the Easter sacraments. After the Rite of Election, the elect enter the most intense part of their preparation to receive the Sacraments of Initiation at the Easter Vigil.

In some dioceses, the candidates for full communion—those already baptized in other Christian churches—also participate in the Rite of Election. Because they are already baptized, they do not inscribe their names in the *Book of the Elect*.

Instead, they participate in a rite called the "Call to Continuing Conversion." The bishop asks their sponsors and catechists about their readiness to be received into the Church: have they deepened their awareness and appreciation of their Baptism? Have they lived a life of service of others? Have they joined the community for prayer? Have they reflected on the tradition of the Church? If they have, then the bishop calls them to observe Lent with the Church, as they prepare for the Sacraments of Confirmation and Eucharist at Easter.

Penitential Rite

Second Sunday of Lent

On the Second Sunday of Lent, the Church provides a special rite for candidates for full communion— those already baptized in other Christian churches who are preparing to be received into the full communion of the Catholic Church at Easter. The rite resembles the three Scrutinies of the catechumens that take place on the Third, Fourth, and Fifth Sundays of Lent. After the homily, the candidates come forward, along with their sponsors. The candidates then kneel down and the entire parish community prays for them, that they may come to a deeper appreciation of their Baptism, that they may grow in faith, love, and service of others, that they may change where they need to change, and overcome their lingering doubts and hesitations. The priest then says a prayer over them, asking God to forgive their sins. He then lays hands on the head of each candidate, an ancient gesture of prayer that signifies the presence of the Holy Spirit. The candidates for full communion then take their places in the midst of the assembly. Though they do not yet partake of the Eucharist, by their Baptism they are already members of the Body of Christ.

The Scrutinies

Third, Fourth, and Fifth Sundays of Lent

For the elect, those preparing for Baptism at the Easter Vigil, Lent is a time of intense prayer, marked by special rites, including the three Scrutinies, which take place on the Third, Fourth, and Fifth Sundays of Lent. To "scrutinize" something means to look carefully at it, to see it in all its aspects. For the elect, the Scrutinies are prayers that are meant to help them examine their lives: "to uncover, then heal all that is weak, defective, or sinful . . . to bring out, then strengthen all that is upright, strong, and good" (*Rite of Christian Initiation of Adults*, 141). Through these prayers, the elect continue to grow in awareness of the reality of sin. At the same time, they are strengthened in their fight against evil, and in their desire for salvation.

Each of the Scrutinies follows the same pattern. The elect come forward before the assembly. Special intercessions are prayed for them. Then the priest prays an exorcism, asking God to free them from the power of Satan. The priest then lays hands on each of them, an ancient ritual gesture. Finally, they are dismissed from the assembly.

Laetare Sunday

Fourth Sunday of Lent

"Rejoice, Jerusalem, and all who love her. / Be joyful, all who were in mourning; / exult and be satisfied at her consoling breast" (Isaiah 66:10–11). These words of hope, spoken by the prophet Isaiah to a people in exile, form the Entrance Antiphon for the Fourth Sunday of Lent. In Latin, this antiphon begins with the word *Laetare*, "rejoice," and so this Sunday is also known as *Laetare Sunday*. Like *Gaudete Sunday* in Advent, it is a day of joy in the midst of a penitential time. Flowers may be used at the altar; the organ and other musical instruments—used only to accompany the singing of the assembly during Lent—make a brief return; rose-colored vestments may be worn.

Why do we rejoice on this day? The answer has its roots in the early Church, when catechumens preparing for Baptism at Easter received the Creed and the Our Father for the first time during the fourth week of Lent. It was another sign that they were soon to receive adoption, in Baptism: a fitting reason for the Church to rejoice! (The *Rite of Christian Initiation of Adults* has restored this ancient custom: catechumens are given the Creed during the week

following the first Scrutiny, just before Laetare Sunday, and the Lord's Prayer following the third Scrutiny, during the Fifth Week of Lent).

In 1216, Pope Innocent III gave another reason for rejoicing. We need this brief respite from our Lenten fasting, he said, so that we "may not break down . . . but may continue to bear the restrictions with a refreshed and easier heart" (Weiser, Francis X. *Handbook of Christian Feasts and Customs: The Year of the Lord in Liturgy and Folklore.* New York: Harcourt, Brace and Company, 1958. pp. 177–178).

Easter is drawing near: reason enough to rejoice!

Palm Sunday of the Passion of the Lord

Sixth Sunday of Lent

"The next day the great crowd that had come to the festival heard that Jesus was coming to Jerusalem. So they took branches of palm trees and went out to meet him, shouting, 'Hosanna! / Blessed is the one who comes in the name of the Lord—the King of Israel!'" (John 12:12–13). Each year, on Palm Sunday, these words come to life in our churches as we walk in the traditional Palm Sunday procession. We, too, carry branches, and sing Hosanna. And just as the people welcomed Jesus to Jerusalem, we welcome the Christ, the One who comes, in our midst. Our long Lenten observance is drawing to an end, and we hail the Lord with joy and recognition.

Through the centuries, Christians have celebrated the procession of palms with great fanfare. In the Middle Ages, a carved figure of Christ sitting on a donkey (called a *palmesel* or "palm-donkey") would figure in the procession, drawn on a rolling platform. In other places, choirs of boys would be stationed high on the city walls, to greet the procession with the words of the ancient Palm Sunday hymn as the procession entered the gates: "Glory and honor and praise be to you, Christ, King and Redeemer, / to whom young children cried out loving Hosannas with joy" (*The Roman Missal*).

Today, palms can be shipped across the world, so even in the far north people can carry palms grown in Mexico or in the Holy Land. But it is also appropriate to carry branches of whatever trees are beginning to bud. In Italy, branches from olive trees are often carried, and in some parts of England and Germany people carry willow branches. In Eastern Europe, people often carry branches of pussy willow or forsythia.

As soon as the procession is done, the mood of the liturgy shifts. In the Collect, we pray that we may "heed [Christ's] lesson of patient suffering," knowing that it is not by following him in his triumph, but by walking in the way of his Cross, that we can "share in his Resurrection" (*The Roman Missal*). The readings speak of the suffering of the Lord's chosen One: in the song of the suffering servant from Isaiah (50:4–7; First Reading), the Church hears the voice of Christ. The Second Reading is a hymn from the letter of Saint Paul to the Philippians, which speaks of Christ emptying himself, and suffering as one of us. These readings prepare us for the reading of Christ's Passion according to Matthew, Mark, or Luke. The lesson of patient suffering Christ gives us can be hard to hear, and it takes a lifetime to learn it.

Holy Week

Begins with Palm Sunday of the Passion of the Lord

With Palm Sunday, Holy Week begins. We celebrate the Resurrection of the Lord every day of our lives, and especially every Sunday: "It is *Easter* which returns week by week, celebrating Christ's victory over sin and death," as Blessed Pope John Paul II has written (*Dies Domini*, 1). But from very early times, there was also an annual celebration of the Resurrection of the Lord, which came to be celebrated shortly after the vernal equinox. And from this great feast flowed others: first a fast in preparation for the great day, then a week, and finally a whole period of preparation—Lent.

Holy Week is about remembering: we trace the events of Jesus' last days, from his triumphal entry into Jerusalem, to his arrest and trial, to his Crucifixion, Death, and burial, to his Resurrection. We need to be reminded of these historic events, because for us they are more than history: the Passion, Death, and Resurrection of Jesus, his Paschal Mystery, is a living

reality that shapes our lives. The mysteries we ponder are not past, but present; they are not outside us, but rather, by our Baptism, they have become part of our very being. That is why, at the beginning of the great Easter Vigil, the priest traces the number of the current year on the Paschal candle. Jesus is not then, but now: "all time belongs to him / and all the ages."

And so, we do more than remember during Holy Week. We share in the mysteries we celebrate. We sit among the disciples in the upper room on Holy Thursday. We stand at the foot of the Cross on Good Friday. We wait beside the tomb on Holy Saturday. And on Easter Sunday, we will share the joy of the holy women at the Good News of Jesus' Resurrection.

Lenten Traditions

"What are you doing for Lent this year?" It's a question we often ask, and get asked, as Lent draws near. On Ash Wednesday, in the reading from the Gospel according to Matthew, Jesus clearly lays out what it is we are to do: to undertake the time-honored practices of prayer, fasting, and almsgiving.

In Lent, our prayer is a prayer of repentance for our sins, a prayer that we may come back to God where we have strayed away from him, a prayer of conversion. But it is also prayer for others, and prayer for the world. Through devotions like the Stations of the Cross, in which we meditate on the last journey of Jesus to the mount of Calvary, we remind ourselves of what Jesus endured for us, and we confront our own sinfulness. We can gain insight to recognize those in our world today who are suffering as Jesus suffered, from violence and injustice. In the *Via Matris*, we meditate on the Seven Sorrows of Mary, from the prophecy of Simeon to the burial of Jesus, pondering the mystery of Christ through the compassion of his Mother. Another time-honored practice for Lent is to read the Gospel accounts of the Passion narratives during Lent, particularly on the Fridays of Lent. There is no better way to ponder the Passion of the Lord than through meditation on the Gospel accounts of the Passion, Death, and Resurrection of Christ.

Through our Lenten fasting and abstinence we deprive ourselves of unnecessary things to become more aware of our hunger for God. There are two fasting days in Lent: Ash Wednesday and Good Friday, and all the Fridays of Lent are days of abstinence, when we refrain from eating meat. In addition, most Catholics choose to abstain from other practices that may not be harmful in themselves, but that can absorb our time and energy: whether it's watching TV, surfing the Internet, going on Facebook, playing video games, or eating dessert. Through our fasting and abstinence, we increase our power of self-control, and learn to be aware of our deepest hunger: our hunger for God.

The third spiritual practice Jesus gives his disciples is almsgiving: we are to use the gifts God has given us in the service of the poor and the afflicted, God's beloved ones. But we are to give quietly and humbly—so quietly and humbly that our left hand does not even know what our right hand has done! Through our sacrificial giving, we can help those who are in need, but we can also grow in awareness of the root causes of poverty in our communities and in our world, and become advocates for justice.

The penitential nature of Lent marks an opportune time to celebrate the Sacrament of Reconciliation. Parishes extend available times for individual confession. Often, this includes an evening for communal reconciliation. For such evenings, a pastor brings a number of priests to the parish so that all who desire can privately confess their sins and celebrate the healing nature of this sacrament.

Some parishes are famous for a Lenten fish fry especially because meat is forbidden on Fridays. As an alternative, soup suppers have grown popular. Meatless soups remind the parish of the simple food that nourishes the poor most days of the year. Some community dinners ask for a free will donation, which usually is given to local charitable agencies.

For over 35 years Catholics have associated this liturgical time with Lenten rice bowls. Catholic Relief Services (CRS), an agency of the United States Conference of Catholic bishops, provides relief to the world's poorest populations. Each year at Lent, every Catholic parish in the United States receives free CRS materials for every family. Most famously, it includes a cardboard cutout, that folds into a simple "bowl" with a slot for coins. If one fasts from vending machines or snacks, the cash equivalent, along with spare change, accumulates in the bowl. They are called rice bowls, because at the end of Lent, CRS uses the money for the world's poor.

The Sacred Paschal Triduum

Annual rituals mark us. They give us an identity. Similar to a Thanksgiving meal or a Fourth of July cookout, rituals and meals reveal connections to others who share a common history and belief. The Sacred Paschal Triduum lies at the heart of the Catholic faith. It ties us with our Jewish ancestors. It celebrates who we are as God's people today. And it makes new believers for the future of the Church while promising us the awaited fullness of salvation to come in eternity.

For centuries, the Jewish faithful have celebrated the Passover. This meal connects them with their ancestor's flight from slavery to freedom. The meal and what followed forever changed the Jews and their understanding of God.

Christians also believe that at one moment in time, everything changed forever. That came on the night before Jesus died, when he sat down with his disciples for a Passover meal. Instead of bitter herbs and a lamb, he gave them bread and said, "This is my Body," and a cup of wine saying, "This is my Blood." Shortly after this Passover meal, Jesus was arrested, scourged, died on a Cross, and buried. Three days later his tomb was empty. God had raised him from the dead.

The New Testament refers to Jesus numerous times as the Lamb of God. He made the Passover radically new. The blood came not from an unblemished lamb, but from the innocent Son of God. The freedom won by this sacrifice is not just movement from one land to another, but from sin and death into life everlasting.

Catholics annually enter into the Triduum to celebrate the Passover of the Lord. *Triduum* comes from Latin meaning "a space of three days." It starts on Holy Thursday evening, continues through Good Friday and Holy Saturday, and concludes on Easter Sunday (three days). The rituals on Thursday, Friday, and Saturday comprise one sustained liturgy spanning three days.

The Three Days

Thursday of the Lord's Supper (At the Evening Mass) / Holy Thursday

The Triduum begins with radiant glory at the Evening Mass of the Lord's Supper on Holy Thursday. The laws of the Church permit no other parish Masses on this day. Like the Jewish Passover custom, this liturgy begins after sundown.

The Scriptures for the Lord's Supper remain the same each year. The First Reading from the Old Testament recalls how Moses led the Hebrew people out of the land of Egypt. The Lord commanded Moses and Aaron to instruct the people of Israel to sacrifice year-old male lambs, without blemish, and smear the blood on their door. When the angel of death came to their house, it would pass over if it saw the blood of the sacrifice, thus sparing their firstborn child. This passage ends by instituting this as a yearly memorial feast. It lays the foundation for the Christian feast of the Lord's Supper.

The Second Reading recounts the Apostle Paul instructing the people of Corinth to offer a sacrifice of praise. He tells them how on the night before he died, "Jesus took bread, and after he had given thanks, he broke it and said, 'This is my body that is for you. Do this in remembrance of me.'" The priest uses a variation of these words at every Mass to consecrate the bread and wine into the body and blood of Christ.

The Gospel comes from John's account of the Last Supper. Unique among the Gospel accounts, John omits references to bread and wine. Instead, he describes a meal during which Jesus takes a bowl and pitcher of water to wash the disciples' feet. The image

is clear: Eucharist is not simply a ritual meal. It must also move us from worship to service for one another.

Following the homily the priest may wash his parishioners' feet. By imitating the Gospel just proclaimed, the pastor and any associate priests demonstrate the commitment made at their Ordination to serve the community in the likeness of Christ Jesus. The Liturgy of the Eucharist continues as normal, though with these vivid Eucharistic images in the minds of those assembled.

This evening's liturgy ends differently from other Masses. There is no official ending, as this was the beginning of a three-day liturgy. Following the distribution of Holy Communion, an elaborate Eucharistic procession makes its way through the assembly. Using incense, candles, and a processional cross, the priest processes with the consecrated Eucharistic bread to a chapel or side altar. There the faithful can remain in the presence of the Lord. The procession and prayer hint at the somber tone to come on Good Friday.

Friday of the Passion of the Lord / Good Friday

Good Friday commemorates the Crucifixion, Death, and burial of Christ Jesus. Only one liturgy is permitted this day, and it continues the one begun on Holy Thursday evening. The Good Friday liturgy consists of reading the Passion of Jesus Christ, the Adoration of the Cross, and concludes with the reception of Holy Communion.

The liturgy begins in silence as the priest enters the sanctuary and prostrates himself on the floor before the altar and cross. The assembly silently kneels in this gesture of penance. After arising, the Scriptures follow in the usual way.

The First Reading comes from the prophet Isaiah. He tells of an unnamed suffering servant who will give his life for the sins of others. Like an innocent lamb led to slaughter, yet bearing the guilt of many, this servant will see the fullness of light for his sacrifice. The Second Reading offers the image of Christ Jesus as the priest offering his own life. Saint

Paul states this great high priest became the source of eternal salvation.

The highlight of the Scriptures for Good Friday is the Passion reading from John's account of the Gospel. Various details reveal how John's Passion differs in tone and content from the others. Jesus is clearly in command of the course of events. Jesus and Pilate exchange powerful dialogues. John's account of the Gospel introduces an unnamed beloved disciple, who appears at the foot of the Cross with Mary and two others.

Following the homily, the priest or deacon, along with other ministers, presents a large cross to the assembly. The priest chants, "Behold the wood of the Cross, / on which hung the salvation of the world." All respond, "Come, let us adore." So closely identified with Christ himself, the cross receives the adoration of the faithful. One by one all approach, to genuflect, kneel, caress, touch, or softly kiss it in an act of worship. This simple liturgy ends with the distribution of Holy Communion from hosts consecrated at the Holy Thursday liturgy. All depart in silence, longing for a joyful conclusion to this prayer come Saturday night.

The Easter Vigil in the Holy Night / Holy Saturday

Lent and Holy Week reach a climax at the Easter Vigil. This solemnity of all solemnities begins after sundown on Holy Saturday. Like the ancient Jewish custom, Catholics believe the sun's setting completes a day, and therefore the festivals for the next day (Easter Sunday) may begin. The Vigil starts outdoors with all gathered around a fire. A new and stately paschal candle takes its flame from the fire, and the priest blesses it as the light of Christ. All process into the empty church, illuminated only by vigil candles to hear the *Exsultet* (Easter Proclamation), an ancient text summarizing the significance of this holy night. The procession of light concludes and leads to the Liturgy of the Word.

This night calls for a more generous use of the Scriptures to emphasize God's saving work throughout history. The rite offers no fewer than seven Old Testament readings, each followed by a Responsorial Psalm. Fittingly, the creation story itself is first, followed by Abraham's sacrifice of Isaac. The vivid imagery of Moses leading the Hebrew people thought the Red Sea to freedom from their Egyptian oppressors prominently highlights the significance of this night. Passing through water to new life foreshadows the Baptisms that will take place in this celebration. Readings from Isaiah and the prophet Hosea are also offered.

The New Testament reading is always from Romans, when Paul reminds the believers of the significance of their Baptism. In that ritual they died to Christ and were given the divine promise to live with him forever in his Resurrection. After fasting from Alleluias for six weeks of Lent, musicians jubilantly lead the community in this act of praise before the Gospel account of the Lord's Resurrection from the dead.

The third major act of this night, the Baptism of the elect, follows the homily. The priest baptizes each adult and then must confirm them with the oil of chrism. Having witnessed these new believers professing their faith, the entire assembly then renew their own baptismal promises and sign themselves with the fresh baptismal waters.

Clothed in radiant white garments, like the image of the Risen Lord, the newly baptized join the assembly for the first time at the Lord's table for the Liturgy of the Eucharist. The liturgy concludes in the normal way, with the addition of a double Alleluia to the final blessing to signify the jubilant nature of this solemnity.

Easter Sunday of the Resurrection of the Lord

Easter Sunday crowns the Triduum celebrations and begins a new period of time within the liturgical year. Easter Sunday is the pattern and purpose for all other Sunday celebrations of the year. Having fasted from the Gloria and Alleluias during Lent, both return with joyous song on this day. Like all other Sundays, two readings and a Psalm precede the Gospel. The First Reading now comes from the Acts of the Apostles. Easter Sunday begins a time of reflecting upon how the followers of Jesus came to receive and understand Christ's Resurrection from the dead.

On Easter Sunday, a special Sequence is sung before the Gospel account. In beautiful poetry, it speaks of the joy of the disciples at the Good News of Christ's Resurrection.

In the United States, the priest renews the baptismal promises of the faithful and sprinkles them with the fresh waters of Baptism blessed at the Vigil. The Liturgy of the Eucharist follows as normal. Like the Vigil, Easter Sunday concludes with a dismissal to go in peace, which is followed by a double Alleluia. This punctuates the day with a final exclamation mark signifying the extraordinary works God has done for those who place their faith and trust in his saving works. *Alleluia! Alleluia!*

Sacred Paschal Triduum Traditions

The most important prayers of the Triduum are, of course, the Evening Mass of the Lord's Supper on Holy Thursday; the celebration of the Passion of the Lord on Good Friday; and the Vigil in the Holy Night of Easter. But through the centuries, the faithful have prayed during the Sacred Triduum in many other ways, and these traditions—many of them alive today—can help focus our attention on the great mysteries we celebrate during these holiest of days.

On Holy Thursday, at the conclusion of the Evening Mass of the Lord's Supper on Holy Thursday, the Blessed Sacrament is carried to an altar of repose, a special place for adoration, usually adorned with flowers. It is placed in the tabernacle, and the faithful remain in adoration through the evening hours, until midnight. In many cities around the world, the custom developed of making a pilgrimage on Holy Thursday night, to pray at the altar of repose at seven different churches.

Many devotions developed around Good Friday, which has touched the world's imagination in a special way. The best-known of these is the *Via Crucis*, the Way of the Cross, which consists of fourteen stations or moments in Jesus' last hours, from his condemnation by Pilate to his burial. The Stations of the Cross are especially associated with Good Friday but they are prayed throughout Lent. On this day in Rome, the Holy Father prays the Stations in the Colosseum, with tens of thousands of people.

In some parts of the world, there is a procession of the dead Christ on Good Friday, as a statue of the dead body of Jesus is carried in silence through the streets, accompanied by throngs of the people, who walk in procession, like mourners at a funeral. Passion plays are also a familiar element of Holy Week and of Good Friday in some countries, as the events of Christ's Passion and Death are reenacted in the streets, to bring the events of Holy Week vividly before the eyes of the faithful.

The Seven Last Words is a devotion around the seven last sayings ("words") of Jesus from the Cross, with readings from scripture, homilies, and reflections on the Passion of Christ. It is often incorporated into a *Tre Ore* or "Three Hours" service, commemorating the hours Jesus hung upon the cross, from noon until three o'clock.

A number of Holy Week devotions are associated with the Blessed Virgin Mary, including devotions to Our Lady of Sorrows, and, on Holy Saturday, the *Ora della Madre* or *Ora di Maria*, an hour-long vigil recalling the sadness, patience, and hope of the Blessed Virgin Mary, waiting at the tomb of her Son.

Various devotions have sprung up around Easter as well. A well-loved tradition has it that the risen Christ first appeared to his mother Mary. This meeting is commemorated in some countries with a celebration called the *Encuentro*, or "the encounter." Two processions, one with the image of Our Lady of Sorrows, the other with the image of the Risen Christ, meet at the doors of the Church, with music and prayer.

Easter marks the end of our long Lenten fast, and in some places the traditional blessing of food for the first meal of Easter takes place before or after the Easter Vigil. For centuries, eggs have been a traditional part of the Easter meal, since eggs were considered "meat" and were not eaten during Easter Time. A blessing for Easter food is found in chapter II of the *Book of Blessings*.

Easter Time

When Easter arrives, children proudly show off new clothes and bright dresses. Families assemble baskets with chocolates and other favorite indulgent foods. The Lenten fast has finished. Signs of new life abound, from greening lawns and flowering trees, to images of bunnies, lambs, and chicks. All this, expresses the bold and fascinating mystery of Jesus Christ, the crucified One, who has been resurrected from the dead.

Easter Time announces Christ is risen! This gives reason to sing Alleluia with full voice! Christ Jesus, having endured the suffering and death on the Cross, did not allow evil to be the last word. He defeated death. Like a morning star, Christ Jesus illuminates the darkness of fear and gives believers a path to eternal hopefulness. As Christ emerges from the tomb of death, the Church proclaims salvation for all. God's peace will reign.

The redemptive work of Christ celebrated on Easter Sunday becomes the pattern for all Sunday liturgies and in fact, for all feasts throughout the liturgical year. It is so significant an event that the Church celebrates Easter Time for fifty days. To absorb its powerful impact on the human family, the Church celebrates a week of weeks (seven times seven) plus one extra day. It symbolizes the fullness of time. The long duration ritualizes Easter as the perfect event restoring all of creation and pointing it toward eternity.

Celebrating the Newly Baptized

Easter Time rejoices with those who were baptized at the Easter Vigil. Easter Time acts as one extended celebration. Baptism initiates a new life of faith. With it comes the promised gift of salvation. Saint Paul's words to the Romans, recounted at the Easter Vigil, summarizes the connection between Baptism and Resurrection in this way: "Are you unaware that we who were baptized into Christ Jesus were baptized into his death? . . . For if we have grown into union with him through a death like his, we shall also be united with him in the resurrection. . . . If, then, we have died with Christ, we believe that we shall also live with him" (Romans 6:3ff.).

In the early Church, baptismal fonts were pools described as a tomb and a womb. As a tomb, it drowns out one's sins. Yet as a womb, the font gives birth to a life of faith in the Church and in Christ Jesus. Still today, Baptism by immersion is a living icon of Christ, rising from the tomb, radiant with new life.

With the neophytes (the newly baptized), the Church uses Easter Time to reflect upon the extraordinary events of the Vigil. This process is called *mystagogy*. The neophytes should continue deepening their faith and their understanding of how Christ Jesus is present to them in the word and sacraments of the Church. Homilies during Easter can develop a spiritual awareness of the Easter Sacraments of Baptism, Confirmation, and Eucharist. The power of Christ's unseen presence in those rituals is so rich, that it deserves the luxury of time to thoroughly unpack layers of meaning.

The Days of Easter Time

Octave of Easter

Easter Sunday through the Second Sunday of Easter

Easter Time, like Christmas Time, is too big for just one day: it overflows into an entire period of liturgical time, lasting fifty days. The first eight days, the Octave of Easter, is a time of special celebration, lasting until the Second Sunday of Easter. In the early Church, the neophytes—those who had been baptized at the Easter Vigil—wore their white garments throughout this week. In fact, the Second Sunday of Easter was called *Dominica in albis*, "Sunday in white" because of this!

Today, our liturgy marks these special days with the singing of the Gloria and the Alleluia, and with the Easter Sequence, *Victimae Paschali laudes*, "Christians, to the Paschal Victim," which recalls the meeting of Mary Magdalene with the risen Christ. "Speak, Mary, declaring / What thou sawest, wayfaring. / 'The tomb of Christ, who is living; / The glory of Jesus' resurrection; / Bright angels attesting; / The shroud and napkin resting.'" During the Masses of this week, we hear the Gospel accounts of the appearances of the risen Christ to his disciples, and we begin reading from the Acts of the Apostles, which we will hear throughout Easter Time. The Resurrection changes everything: it made fearful disciples fearless, and doubters believers. It can do the same for us.

Second Sunday of Easter / Sunday of Divine Mercy

On April 30, 2000, Blessed Pope John Paul II canonized Saint Faustina Kowalska, a Polish nun and visionary to whom Christ had appeared with red and white rays streaming from his heart, an image that has since become famous as the "Divine Mercy." Saint Faustina realized that God sees the world through the wounds of his Son, and that God's gaze is full of mercy and love. We need not fear, therefore, but only trust in Jesus.

The Divine Mercy chaplet is a special prayer using Rosary beads, but with a different sequence of prayers, emphasizing the saving Passion of Christ. One of the prayers of the chaplet summarizes the devotion, which focuses on Christ's Passion and God's mercy: "For the sake of His sorrowful Passion, have mercy on us and on the whole world."

Another prayer associated with the Divine Mercy devotion is a novena of prayer concluding on the Sunday of Divine Mercy (thus beginning on Good Friday). On each day of the novena, a different group is prayed for, encompassing, by Divine Mercy Sunday, the whole world. It is a prayer of trust in the love of Christ.

Good Shepherd Sunday

Fourth Sunday of Easter

In the Vatican Museums, there is an ancient statue of a young man, carrying a lamb on his shoulders. He holds the lamb gently and carefully, and his face is watchful, with eyes looking into the distance. This is one of the oldest existing representations of Christ, and it shows Christ as the Good Shepherd.

In the Gospel according to Matthew, the angels announce to poor shepherds the Good News of Jesus' birth, and Jesus refers frequently to shepherds and sheep in his parables and sayings. In the Gospel according to John, he helps his disciples understand his saving mission by describing himself as a shepherd. "'I am the good shepherd. The good shepherd lays down his life for the sheep. The hired hand, who is not the shepherd and does not own the sheep, sees the wolf coming and leaves the sheep and runs away—and the wolf snatches them and scatters them. The hird hand runs away because a hired hand does not care for the sheep. I am the good shepherd. I know my own and my own know me, just as the Father knows me and I know the Father. And I lay down my life for the sheep. . . .'" (John 10:11–15).

Solemnity of the Ascension of the Lord

Thursday of the Sixth Week of Easter or Seventh Sunday of Easter

The Gospel does not tell us exactly how long after his Resurrection Jesus ascended to the Father. In celebrating the Ascension forty days after Easter, the Church looks to the Acts of the Apostles 1:3. "After his suffering he presented himself alive to them by many convincing proofs, appearing to them during forty days and speaking about the kingdom of God."

With his Ascension into heaven, Jesus is no longer visible to his disciples. And yet, far from being sad, Luke tells us that they "returned to Jerusalem with great joy" (Luke 24:52). The Church, too, celebrates the Ascension with great joy; there is not a note of sadness in the liturgy today. Why? Because the Ascension is our feast, too. When Jesus ascends into heaven, he goes to make room for us there. In the memorable words of Pope Benedict XVI: "You have risen and have made a place for our transfigured flesh in the very heart of God" (*Way of the Cross*, Pauline Books and Media, pp. 134–135). Jesus is the head, and we are members of his body; where he has gone, we hope to follow. "There is an upward movement in the whole of creation," said Saint Maximus of Turin in a homily long ago, "each element raising itself to something higher . . . . In one and the same movement, our Savior's passion raises men from the depths, lifts them up from the earth, and sets them in the heights" (Office of Readings, Volume II, p. 816).

But the Ascension isn't just about looking up. It's also about looking around us. In the Entrance Antiphon for the Mass during the Day, we hear words from the Acts of the Apostles: "Men of Galilee, why gaze in wonder at the heavens? / This Jesus whom you saw ascending into heaven / will return as you saw him go, alleluia" (Acts of the Apostles 1:11). We do not need to gaze into the sky, searching for our Lord. Because even as he goes, he remains with us: " I am with you always, to the end of the age" (Matthew 28:20). We need only look around us to find signs of his abiding presence in our midst, in his Body, the Church, in the sacraments, and in his beloved poor.

The Solemnity of the Ascension of the Lord traditionally takes place on Thursday of the Sixth Week of Easter, exactly forty days after Easter. But because for most people that is a working day, many ecclesiastical provinces in the United States of America observe this day on the nearest Sunday, and it takes the place of the Seventh Sunday of Easter. The readings and prayers of the Ascension of the Lord will then replace those of the Seventh Sunday of Easter.

Solemnity of Pentecost

Last Sunday of Easter Time

Easter Time comes to its glorious conclusion with the great Solemnity of Pentecost.

Pentecost was a Jewish harvest feast, celebrated fifty days after Passover (hence the name "Pentecost," which means *fiftieth* in Greek). At Pentecost, bread made from the newly-harvested grain would be offered to God. The feast also commemorated the giving of the Law on Mount Sinai.

It was while Jews from every nation were gathered in Jerusalem to celebrate this feast that the Spirit came upon the disciples gathered in prayer, like wind and fire. They must have remembered the Exodus account of the giving of the law to Moses, when there was a sound like a trumpet blast, and fire and smoke (see Exodus 19:16–19). But the contrasts between the giving of the Law and the giving of the Spirit are even more striking than the similarities. At Sinai, Moses alone went up to receive the immutable

word of God carved on tablets of stone. On the day of Pentecost the Spirit came down to the people and rested on each of them in a play of wind and fire. The Spirit cannot be contained, or written down. The special sequence, *Veni, Sancte Spiritus*, "Come, Holy Spirit," that is prayed during Mass today addresses the Spirit with many different titles and images—the Spirit is "Father of the poor," "comforter," "sweet refreshment," "solace," and "light." The multitude of images suggests the free play of the Spirit.

In the Middle Ages, this free play of the Spirit was expressed in many creative ways in the great cathedrals. In some parts of France, wind instruments would fill the church with sound, while roses and other flowers would be dropped on the assembly. In other places, live doves would be set free to fly through the church. These customs spoke to the people about the nature of the Holy Spirit: gentle, yet impossible to contain or control.

Pentecost is sometimes called "the birthday of the Church," because it was only after they were filled with the gifts of the Spirit that the Apostles set forth on the mission Christ gave them, to preach the Good News, and to baptize all nations. The Spirit transformed them, and transforms us.

Easter Time Traditions

Lent is full of special devotions, and Easter Time has its devotions as well. One of the best-known of these is certainly the Divine Mercy. Another is the *Via Lucis* or Way of Light. Modeled on the Way of the Cross (*Via Crucis*), the *Via Lucis* is a journey with the risen Christ, from the first Easter morning to Pentecost.

The blessing of families in their homes is an old custom, particularly associated with Easter Time. In some small communities, it is still possible for the priest, deacon, and assisting clergy to visit every home in the parish during Easter Time, bringing the message of Christ's peace. Though that has become more and more difficult, the tradition of blessing the family and the home remains, and the useful resource *Catholic Household Blessings & Prayers*, published by the United States Conference of Catholic Bishops, includes an order of blessing that can be used by anyone to bless their home (p. 128). A house blessing is especially appropriate for Easter Time, when we celebrate Christ's abiding presence in our world, our Church, our hearts—and our homes.

The word *novena* is Latin for "nine," and it refers to a special time of prayer to God, to the Blessed Virgin Mary, or to a particular saint. The nine days between Ascension and Pentecost form the "first" novena. When Jesus ascended, he told his disciples, "I am sending upon you what my Father promised; so stay here in the city until you have been clothed with power from on high" (Luke 24:49). And the disciples remained in Jerusalem, in prayer, until the coming of the Spirit at Pentecost sent them forth to preach the Good News to the whole world. These nine days continue to be a special time of grace, and the novena is observed with prayer to the Holy Spirit in the home, and in many parishes.

The gifts of the Spirit are wisdom, understanding, counsel, fortitude, knowledge, piety, and fear of the Lord. The Pentecost novena is the perfect time to pray for a fuller outpouring of these gifts upon ourselves, upon the Church, and upon our communities and our world.

World Day of Prayer for Vocations

Fourth Sunday of Easter

The Fourth Sunday of Easter is also known as *Good Shepherd Sunday* (see page 19), because the readings and prayers speak of Jesus as the Good Shepherd. Since 1964, this day has also been designated the World Day of Prayer for Vocations. Pope Paul VI instituted this day of prayer to Christ, the great shepherd of souls, that Christ might inspire many young men and women to dedicate their lives to service in the Church.

Our need today is greater than ever. We need priests to build up the Body of Christ by celebrating the sacraments, especially the Eucharist. We need dedicated, religious men and women to pray, to teach, and to serve in the name of Christ. Today, let us pray in obedience to Christ, who told his disciples to "ask the Lord of the harvest to send out laborers into his harvest" (Matthew 9:38) . . . .

World Communication Day

Sunday before the Solemnity of Pentecost

On the Sunday before Pentecost, the Church observes the World Day for Communications. This observance was established in response to *Inter mirifica*, the Decree on Social Communications of the Second Vatican Council. The Council Fathers wrote: "Among the wonderful technological discoveries which men of talent, especially in the present era, have made with God's help, the Church welcomes and promotes with special interest those which have a most direct relation to men's minds and which have uncovered new avenues of communicating most readily news, views and teachings of every sort. The most important of these inventions are those media which, such as the press, movies, radio, television and the like, can, of their very nature, reach and influence, not only individuals, but the very masses and the whole of human society, and thus can rightly be called the media of social communication. The Church recognizes that these media, if properly utilized, can be of great service to mankind, since they greatly contribute to men's entertainment and instruction as well as to the spread and support of the Kingdom of God" (*Inter Mirifica*, 1–2). Since the Council, the Internet has opened up many new avenues of communication, and true to the Council's teaching, the Church has striven to keep up. Blessed Pope John Paul II became the first pope to send an e-mail; Pope Benedict XVI is the first to send a text message and to have his own Facebook page! We are all called to share the Gospel with the world in whatever way we can.

Ordinary Time

Ordinary Time: even the name of this period of liturgical time gives this time period an air of unimportance. The word *ordinary* usually equates to boring, unfulfilling, or stagnant. Yet, life is not meant to be lived always at fever pitch. The Latin derivative *ordinarius* means "following the usual course." The word *ordinary* also comes from the word *ordinal* meaning "counted." This period of 33 or 34 weeks is counted time outside of the other liturgical times.

As taught by Jesus, the usual course was one of teaching, ministering, and then going off—alone—to pray. Jesus called his disciples, and calls us, to do that same. While the "usual course" that Jesus followed is rather different than our usual course of life, we are called to pause and reflect upon the love taught for both others, and individually, in this down time.

The Collect for the Third Sunday in Ordinary Time shares the depth of this counted time:

> Almighty ever-living God,
> direct our actions according to your
> good pleasure,
> that in the name of your beloved Son
> we may abound in good works.
> Through our Lord Jesus Christ, your Son,
> who lives and reigns with you in the unity
> of the Holy Spirit,
> one God, for ever and ever.

We need this "ordinary time" in life. In fact, we need to protect the "ordinary time" so we can claim ourselves, our identity, our roots, and our strength. This is the gift Ordinary Time offers.

In every other liturgical time—Advent, Christmas Time, Lent, Triduum, and Easter Time—there is great intensity of life, reflection, prayer, and a big celebration focusing on a very specific aspect of the life of Jesus. Yet scripture is not complete without a full understanding of Jesus' own identity, his own call, his own proclamation to understand his message. Thus, Ordinary Time gives the Church a space to breathe and each of us time to gain a deeper understanding into the heart of Jesus.

Ordinary Time officially begins following Evening Prayer on the Feast of the Baptism of the Lord; thus, there is no First Sunday in Ordinary Time. This liturgical time continues until the Tuesday before Ash Wednesday. The length of this segment of Ordinary Time varies depending upon the date of Easter. In some years, this can seem too quick of a time between Christmas and Lent. Thus, as with a typical growing child, if one doesn't pay attention, the milestones of life are missed. During Ordinary Time we are called to be aware of both Jesus' milestones and also be conscious of our own spiritual growth.

The Scripture readings during the first segment of Ordinary Time teach us of Jesus' early life, his little-known childhood, and his public ministry. The focus is on how we can model our lives and faith from Jesus' own actions and growth. The symbolic color of Ordinary Time is green, symbolizing new life, growth, rebirth, and rootedness. The Church is always alive and growing.

Lent arrives and calls us to strengthen our inner souls, but it is a long and intense time followed by fifty days of great celebration. After Lent, the Sacred Paschal Triduum, and Easter Time, we enter the longest period of Ordinary Time to continue to learn about Jesus and his many teachings that define our identity. This time in Scripture we hear of Christ's vision for the Kingdom of God, how we are to get there, and give full honor to Jesus as Christ, King of the Universe. This latter solemnity falls on the last Sunday or Thirty-fourth Sunday in Ordinary Time.

We are ordinary people following an extraordinary God calling us to better ourselves in the call to holiness each day, each week, each time we receive the Eucharist. The liturgical appropriateness of Ordinary Time fits the spiritual nuances of life. One cannot live on the mountaintop forever nor disappear into the valleys for too long. The climb in between might be quiet, but it is just as important as all the other moments. The Church knows this and understands the time needed to craft our souls into that deep longing for the big moments, for without valuing ordinary time, all other time would lose its full importance.

The Days of Ordinary Time

Carnival

Sunday before Ash Wednesday

Our Lenten laws of fasting and abstinence today are very mild compared to those of previous centuries. We have only two obligatory fasting days

(Ash Wednesday and Good Friday), though we are encouraged to fast on other days as well; and only eight days of abstinence from meat (though, again, we are encouraged to abstain more if we are able). But imagine giving up not only meat, but butter, cheese, milk, and eggs, and not just on Fridays, but on every day of Lent! It's no wonder that the tradition of Carnival developed, a kind of "last fling" before the beginning of Lent. It had a practical function —to eat up all the foods that would be forbidden during Lent, rather than let them go to waste—but it rapidly became an excuse for an enormous party, with parades, processions, races, and feasting. The very word *Carnival* refers to Lent—it comes from the Latin *carnem levare*, which means "the taking away of meat." Carnival spread across Europe to the New World, and today the most famous of all carnival celebrations is Mardi Gras in New Orleans (*Mardi Gras* is French for "Fat Tuesday," and refers to the Tuesday before Ash Wednesday). "Rose Monday," or *Rosenmontag*, is a similar celebration in Germany, Austria, and Switzerland, and takes place on the Monday before Ash Wednesday.

The excesses of Carnival led Pope Benedict XIV, in 1748, to institute a devotional practice called "Forty Hours of Carnival," a time of prayer and reparation for the excesses of the festive days.

Rose Monday

Monday before Ash Wednesday

Rosenmontag, Rose Monday, is a public celebration that takes place in many parts of Germany on the Monday before Ash Wednesday. It is part of the larger folk tradition we call Carnival. Children get the day off from school, and parents get the day off from work. People dress up in costumes, and cities put on elaborate parades with music and highly-decorated floats. All kinds of good things to eat and drink are shared in abundance. *Rosenmontag*, like *Mardi Gras*, is a time of laughter and feasting before the sobriety and abstinence of Lent begins.

Shrove Tuesday

Tuesday before Ash Wednesday

Shrove Tuesday is the name given to the Tuesday before Ash Wednesday. The word "shrove" comes from the English word "shrive," meaning to "absolve." It was customary to go to confession before the beginning of Lent, and this day marked the last opportunity to be "shriven."

Shrove Tuesday has many other names as well, but most of them refer not to prayer but to food: *Mardi Gras* (Fat Tuesday), Pancake Tuesday, and even Butter Week. Because meat and butter were typically off-limits during Lent, people would eat their fill of them on this last day before the fast.

Solemnity of the Most Holy Trinity

Sunday after the Solemnity of Pentecost

The Solemnity of the Most Holy Trinity, observed on the Sunday after the Solemnity of Pentecost, dates to the seventh century; it has been on the Church's universal calendar for nearly 700 years. "The mystery of the Most Holy Trinity is the central mystery of Christian faith and life," the Catechism tells us. "It is the mystery of God in himself. It is therefore the source of all the other mysteries of faith, the light that enlightens them" (*Catechism of the Catholic Church*, 234). As Christians, we believe in one God, in three Persons: Father, Son, and Holy Spirit.

Through the centuries, saints and artists have helped us to understand the Holy Trinity through images and comparisons. Saint Patrick is said to have explained the Trinity to the people of Ireland by showing them a shamrock, with its three leaves on one stem. Saint Ignatius Loyola compared the Trinity to a chord played on an instrument: three distinct notes forming one sound. The early iconographers of the Church in the East depicted the Trinity with imagery from the Old Testament story of Abraham's angelic visitors. A familiar symbol of the Trinity is a triangle with rays radiating from it, and in the middle of the triangle an open eye, representing the all-seeing Providence of God.

On the Solemnity of the Most Holy Trinity, the liturgy provides additional images to help us ponder this great mystery of our faith. The Trinity is relationship: "The Father is Love, the Son is grace, the Holy Spirit is their bond of fellowship; O blessed Trinity." The Trinity is God's truth: "The Father utters the Truth, the Son is the Truth he utters, and the Holy Spirit is Truth; O blessed Trinity" (Antiphons for the Office of Readings, Volume III, p. 581).

Solemnity of the Most Holy Body and Blood of Christ (*Corpus Christi*)

Second Thursday after Pentecost (traditional date)

Second Sunday after the Solemnity of Pentecost 🇺🇸 🍁

This Eucharistic day, observed with such solemnity throughout the world, began in a quiet Belgian convent in the thirteenth century, with the vision of a holy nun, Saint Juliana. In her vision, she saw the moon, full and bright. It was glorious, except that one part of its disk was in shadow. The meaning of the vision was then revealed to her: the moon represented the liturgical year; the shadow, a missing feast in honor of the Blessed Sacrament. Juliana spoke to her confessor about what she had seen. Amazingly, within thirty-five years, Pope Urban IV had established the Feast of *Corpus Christi*, the Body of Christ, in the Church's universal calendar. Hundreds of years later, in 1849, Pope Pius IX added the Feast of the Precious Blood celebrated on July 1. Following the Second Vatican Council, the two liturgies became one solemnity in honor of the Most Holy Body and Blood of Christ.

Of course, we already had a feast honoring the Eucharist: the Evening Mass of the Lord's Supper on Holy Thursday, which even includes a procession with the Blessed Sacrament. But the purpose and the mood of the two processions are strikingly different. On Holy Thursday, we walk with Jesus to the Mount of Olives, to keep watch with him on the night of his betrayal. The sacrament is carried in the ciborium, covered with the humeral veil: and Christ's glory, too, is veiled as he undergoes his passion. On *Corpus Christi*, we walk in the afterglow of Easter Time, in company with the risen Lord. This time, the Blessed Sacrament is exposed in a monstrance: the Lord's glory is not hidden, but visible to all.

Corpus Christi is one of the most Catholic of days, an expression of our faith in the real presence of Christ in the Blessed Sacrament. And yet, this celebration is also outward looking, carrying the liturgy out of the church and into the streets. We come together in all our diversity and we celebrate our unity. As Pope Benedict XVI has said, "The Eucharist is a public devotion that has nothing esoteric or exclusive about it. . . . we did not choose to meet one another, we came and find ourselves next to one another, brought together by faith and called to become one body, sharing the one Bread which is Christ. We are united over and above our differences of nationality, profession, social class, political ideas: we open ourselves to one another to become one in him" (Homily for Thursday, May 22, 2008).

Solemnity of the Most Sacred Heart of Jesus

Friday after the Solemnity of the Most Holy Body and Blood of Christ (*Corpus Christi*)

One of the most beloved aspects of our Catholic tradition is our devotion to the Sacred Heart of Jesus. In honoring the Sacred Heart, we are honoring the compassion and love of Christ: his human heart, moved with pity for his flock, his divine heart, pierced for the sins of his people. From the heart of Christ, pierced by the soldier's lance, blood and water poured out, "the wellspring of the Church's Sacraments" (Preface for the Sacred Heart).

While saints and mystics, notably the thirteenth century Benedictine, Saint Gertrude, have long found the heart of Christ a rich subject matter for meditation, it was not until the seventeenth century, in France, that devotion to the Sacred Heart of Jesus began to take the form we know today. It was a time when the heresy of Jansenism was rampant. People were convinced that human sinfulness was too great to be forgiven; that salvation would only be granted to a few. In this climate of fear, the revelations of the Sacred Heart to Saint Margaret Mary

Alocoque, a Visitandine nun in the French town of Paray-le-Monial, France, must have come as a complete and wonderful surprise. The devotion spread, and the feast of the Sacred Heart of Jesus was added to the universal calendar in 1856.

There are many devotions associated with the Sacred Heart of Jesus, especially the Litany of the Sacred Heart, and the devotion of the nine First Fridays, in which people attend Mass on the First Friday of each month, celebrating the Sacraments of Reconciliation and Eucharist, in keeping with the words of Christ to Saint Margaret Mary, when he promised grace, peace, and consolation to those who would honor him in this way.

On the Solemnity of the Most Sacred Heart of Jesus, we give thanks to God for the infinite love of Christ, represented by the image of his heart on fire with love. Through our prayer, we also seek to make reparation for the ways that love has been rejected by human beings. This is why in the familiar image, Christ's heart is pierced, and surrounded with thorns. In the words of the great Litany of the Sacred Heart of Jesus: "Heart of Jesus, pierced with a lance, have mercy on us. / Heart of Jesus, source of all consolation, have mercy on us."

Memorial of the Immaculate Heart of the Blessed Virgin Mary

Saturday after the Solemnity of the Most Sacred Heart of Jesus

On the day after the Solemnity of the Most Sacred Heart of Jesus, we celebrate a memorial in honor of Mary's Immaculate Heart. It was Saint John Eudes, a priest and a contemporary of Saint Margaret Mary, who helped make devotion to Mary's Immaculate Heart part of the life of the universal Church. When Mary brings the baby Jesus to the Temple, the aged Simeon tells her that her heart will be pierced by a sword (Luke 2:35). And Mary, quietly listening and pondering the life of her Son, "treasured all these words and pondered them in her heart" (Luke 2:19). Mary's heart is the treasury of the Lord's deeds and words; and it is the place of her anguish, in witnessing the sufferings of her Son. Blessed Pope John Paul II

raised this commemoration, a liturgical sister to yesterday's Solemnity of the Most Sacred Heart, from an optional to an obligatory memorial.

Just as the Nine First Fridays are associated with the Sacred Heart of Jesus, so the Five First Saturdays are associated with the Immaculate Heart of Mary. Through celebrating the Sacraments of Reconciliation and Eucharist, and taking fifteen minutes on the First Saturday of each month to ponder the mysteries of the Rosary, the devotion is focused on reparation to the Immaculate Heart of Mary.

Solemnity of Our Lord Jesus Christ, King of the Universe

Thirty-fourth or Last Sunday in Ordinary Time

"Where is the child who has been born king of the Jews?" (Matthew 2:2) the Magi ask Herod, filling him with fear. And on the day of his Crucifixion, another fearful leader, Pontius Pilate, asks Jesus, "Are you the King of the Jews?" (John 18:33).

Both Herod and Pilate thought they knew what a king was: a king of the Jews would threaten their position and authority, seize control by force. But Jesus is not that kind of king. He tells Pilate, "'My kingdom is not from this world. If my kingdom were from this world, my followers would be fighting to keep me from being handed over to the Jews. But as it is, my kingdom is not from here'" (John 18:36).

On the Solemnity of Our Lord Jesus Christ, King of the Universe, we honor the unique kingship of Christ. His kingdom is not here: his kingdom is with his Father, and yet it is being mysteriously built in our very midst. His is "an eternal and universal kingdom, / a kingdom of truth and life, / a kingdom of holiness and grace, / a kingdom of justice, love and peace" (Preface of Christ, King of the Universe).

This solemnity honoring Christ as king developed at a time of crisis, as communism and totalitarian regimes were denying the presence of God in the world. Pope Pius XI added this day to the Church's calendar in 1925, who hoped that it would help to bring about "the signal benefits of true liberty, of calm order, of harmony, and of peace" (quoted in *The Liturgical Year* by Adolf Adam, p. 177). He placed the solemnity in October; it was moved to its present position in the reform of the calendar following the Second Vatican Council. Now, it is celebrated on the Last or Thirty-fourth Sunday in Ordinary Time.

Memorials of the Blessed Virgin Mary on Saturday

Saturdays in Ordinary Time without an obligatory memorial

Just as Fridays are associated with the Passion of Christ, so Saturdays have been associated with the Blessed Virgin Mary. This dates to at least the ninth century. Some say that Saturday became associated with Mary because of Holy Saturday, the day on which Christ rested in the tomb, and Mary alone waited in hope for the Resurrection. Another explanation points out that Saturday is the day on which God rested, having completed all his work; and that this day is appropriately dedicated to Mary, in whom the Word of God came to "rest." Whatever the explanation, Saturdays continue to be days especially devoted to Mary, and on the Saturdays of Ordinary Time, the Church offers an optional Memorial of the Blessed Virgin Mary. Most often, when we celebrate Mary, we celebrate some particular aspect of

her life: her Immaculate Conception (December 8), her Nativity (September 8), and her Assumption (August 15). On Saturdays, our devotions don't necessarily have a particular focus. Instead, we recognize Mary's living presence in the Church, as advocate and model of discipleship. We ask her intercession, "now and at the hour of our death" (Hail Mary).

World Youth Day

Thirtieth Sunday in Ordinary Time

World Youth Day was established by Blessed Pope John Paul II in 1985. It grew out of his experiences as a pastor in Poland, when he recognized the need of young people to come together to learn and pray together and celebrate their shared faith.

Each year, World Youth Day is celebrated in the local diocese. Every two to three years, an international gathering is held that draws as many as a million young people from all over the globe. They come together for worship, learning, and service, to pray with the Holy Father and to experience the global Church of which they are a part. World Youth Days have been held all over the world, from Rome, to Denver, to Manila, to Australia.

He helped Americans realize that racism existed everywhere, not just in the South.

In 1964, King received the Nobel Peace Prize, a great international honor. Because of King and other civil rights leaders, important new laws were passed that protected the civil rights of all Americans. In 1968, when he was 39 years old, Martin Luther King was shot and killed by an assassin.

Martin Luther King, Jr. helped millions of Americans turn against racism and against violence. In 1983 a national holiday was declared in his honor. It falls on the third Monday in January. That day is on or soon after January 15, which is the day he was born. On Martin Luther King Day we take for our own these words of the prophet Amos: "Let justice roll down like waters / and righteousness like an everflowing stream" (Amos 5:24).

Catholic Schools Week

Begins the Last Sunday in January

This week we participate in a nationwide celebration of Catholic education. It's a chance to share the good news about Catholic education with our community and to celebrate the high academic standards grounded in strong moral values that Catholic schools provide, as well as the great contributions Catholic school graduates have made to our communities and our nation. According to recent data, more than 2 million young people are enrolled in over 7,000 Catholic Schools in the United States of America. Catholic Schools across the country will be hosting open houses and activities for students, administrators, faculty and staff, the community, and families. It's a good week to pray for all the children in our Catholic Schools, as well as their teachers and families.

Lunar New Year

Second New Moon after the Winter Solstice
January or February

The word *month* comes from the word *moon*. The "months" of most ancient calendars were the 29 1/2-day periods from one new moon to the next. That's how the Jewish and Muslim calendars work.

The ancient calendars of the peoples of east Asia are organized like that, too.

Nowadays, most Asian countries keep the Western calendar, in which New Year's Day is January 1. However, the Vietnamese and the Chinese people love their old New Year's festival, which begins on the second new moon after the winter solstice (December 21)—sometime between January 21 and February 19 on the Western calendar. The Lunar New Year is celebrated in China and southeast Asia as the beginning of spring.

Chinese, Korean, and Vietnamese communities around the world celebrate the Lunar New Year (also called Chinese New Year, or Tet in Vietnamese) as a heritage festival. In North America you can join the celebration in New York, San Francisco, Vancouver, Los Angeles, and other big cities that have East Asian populations.

In Chinese communities, a huge dragon—the symbol of prosperity and good luck—slithers through street parades held at night. It's made of bamboo covered in paper, silk, and velvet, and it can be up to 125 feet long. A crew of dancers supports it from underneath. Firecrackers are set off, and gongs clang to chase troubles away. The streets are packed with acrobats, lion dancers, floats, clowns, and stilt walkers.

Red is the good luck color, the color of life. People hang red scrolls bearing wishes for a healthy and prosperous new year. Spring flowers are everywhere. Piles of oranges and sweet pastries are set up as signs of abundance.

The celebration lasts for two weeks, from the new moon until the full moon. In Baltimore, it includes a fashion show of traditional Chinese gowns. In San Francisco, the city with the largest North American Chinese community, more than 50,000 people celebrate outdoors. Drama, opera, and athletic demonstrations are staged. The Golden Dragon Parade is held at sunset of the last day. Its dragon glitters with lights.

Gung Hay Fat Choy! Happy New Year!

1

SOLEMNITY OF Mary, the Holy Mother of God

Please see page 8 for more information.

THE Octave Day of the Nativity of the Lord

Please see page 6 for more information..

World Day of Prayer for Peace

Since 1967, January 1 has been observed not only as the Solemnity of Mary, the Holy Mother of God, but also as the World Day of Prayer for Peace. On Christmas night, the angels announced to the shepherds the Good News of "Glory to God in the highest heaven, / and on earth peace among those whom he favors!" (Luke 2:14). On this Octave Day of the Nativity of the Lord, and the first day of the New Year, we pray for peace in our world and for the intercession of the Blessed Virgin Mary for all who suffer from war and violence.

New Year's Day

On New Year's Eve, some people "pray in" the new year. Church bells peal out the old and ring in the new. With noisemakers and fireworks, people make a racket to try to scare away their troubles. The next morning, many people attend church services. It is the Roman Catholic Solemnity of the Mary, the Holy Mother of God, the Lutheran and Episcopalian Feast of the Holy Name of Jesus, and the Byzantine Feast of the Circumcision of Jesus. In Greece, January 1 is also Saint Basil's Day. A bread, *vasilopita*, is baked with a coin in it; whoever gets the coin is crowned queen or king for the new year. (The name Basil means "royalty.")

In some countries January 1 is the official day to exchange Christmas gifts. Everywhere, feasting is customary. In Japan, where pink and red are colors of good fortune, a pink fish called red snapper is served. Strawberries are eaten as a taste of spring.

In many European countries, a dinner of roast pork is supposed to bring a bountiful year. Swedes drink a toast to the new year with glögg—hot spiced wine. In the southern and southwestern United States, black-eyed peas are cooked in a traditional New Year's dish called "hoppin' John."

On this day people visit friends to settle any misunderstandings from the previous year. People also call on the folks they want to spend time with during the next year. In some families, parents bless their children. Many people pay a visit to their godparents.

Hospitality is the rule of the day. At the new year many people make a special effort to be loving and outgoing. Perhaps extra good will on this day is a Christmas hope that this spirit will last all year long.

Saint Basil's Day (Greece)

New Year's Day in Greece also celebrates people named Basil. It's a day for gambling and eating a special cake called *vasilopita*, which contains a coin. Whoever receives the piece of cake with the coin should have good luck in the year ahead. The herb basil, also connected to this day, is believed to have healing powers. Many households tie a sprig of basil around a wooden cross and hang it over water, so that the power of the cross can protect the family against demons. Any vessel containing water is replaced with fresh water. A famous quote from the Liturgy of Saint Basil is: "The bread that you use is the bread of the hungry; the garment hanging in your wardrobe is the garment of him who is naked; the shoes you do not wear are the shoes of the one who is barefoot; the acts of charity that you do not perform are so many injustices that you commit."

2

MEMORIAL OF
Saints Basil the Great and Gregory Nazianzen, BISHOPS AND DOCTORS OF THE CHURCH

Saints Basil the Great (329–379) and Gregory Nazianzen (329–390) became close friends as boys in Cappadocia. They both were sent for advanced studies in Athens, where the future emperor, Julian the Apostate, was among their classmates. As emperor, Julian would return to paganism and start a severe persecution of Christians.

Basil was from a wealthy family of saints and martyrs in Cappadocia, which is in modern-day Turkey. His grandmother, father, and several siblings—his sister, Macrina, and brothers Peter of Sebaste and Gregory of Nyssa—are all venerated as saints. Gregory, too, came from an illustrious family. His father, also named Gregory, was bishop of Nazianzus in southwest Cappadocia.

After returning from Athens, Basil dedicated himself to God and studied monasticism, traveling to its sites of origin in Egypt, Palestine, and Mesopotamia. He founded a monastic community on the family estate and wrote two rules, *The Longer Rules* and *The Shorter Rules*. They are the basis of monasticism in the Eastern Church and are referred to in *The Rule of Saint Benedict*.

Basil and Gregory were both consecrated as bishops, and together they fought against the Arian heresy, which denied the full divinity of Christ. Their writings also aided the Church's understanding of the Holy Spirit and the Trinity. With Basil's brothers, Gregory of Nyssa and Peter of Sebaste, they are among the Cappadocian Fathers. Gregory is known as "the Theologian" by the Eastern Churches. Basil is known as the "Father of Eastern Monasticism."

He influenced the liturgy of both Eastern and Western Churches: Eucharistic Prayer IV in *The Roman Missal* is based on the Anaphora of Saint Basil, which dates back to the fourth century and is still used on some occasions in the Eastern Catholic and Orthodox Churches.

3

OPTIONAL MEMORIAL OF THE
Most Holy Name of Jesus

Names are important. They tell us something of who we are, and where we come from, and they speak of our parents' hopes and dreams for us. The name of *Jesus* is especially important. It means "God saves." Jesus' name is not chosen for him by his family but given him by God before he is born: "She will bear a son, and you are to name him Jesus, for he will save his people from their sins" (Matthew 1:21). In Jesus' name is not only his identity, but his mission. Jesus' name is powerful: "I will do whatever you ask in my name" he tells his disciples (John 14:13). In the letter to the Philippians, Saint Paul sings a hymn to the power of Jesus' name: "Therefore God also highly exalted him / and gave him the name / that is above every name, / so that at the name of Jesus / every knee should bend, / in heaven and on earth and under the earth, / and every tongue should confess / that Jesus Christ is Lord, / to the glory of God the Father" (Philippians 2:9–11).

In Jewish tradition, a boy was named and circumcised eight days after birth. That is why the Church celebrates this memorial so close to January 1, the octave day of Jesus' birth.

4

MEMORIAL OF **Saint Elizabeth Ann Seton,** RELIGIOUS 🇺🇸

Born in New York City in 1774, Saint Elizabeth Ann Seton, the daughter of a prominent New York doctor, was raised Episcopalian. At the age of nineteen, she married William Magee Seton, a wealthy trader, with whom she had five children. Unfortunately, in 1802 the business went bankrupt as a result of the Napoleonic blockade and the loss of several ships at sea. Subsequently, William contracted what was probably tuberculosis, and on the recommendation of his doctors, he moved to Italy for the climate, accompanied by Elizabeth and their eldest daughter, Anna Maria. On arrival at the port of Livorno, they were kept in quarantine, where William died before they were released. Elizabeth and Anna Maria were aided by one of William's wealthy business associates, Antonio Filicchi, who took them into his home. For the first time, Elizabeth met cultured and educated people who were Catholic, very different from the poor Irish immigrants who had already begun arriving in New York. When she returned to New York two years later in 1805, she was received into the Catholic Church, and as a result, friends and family cut her off. She was destitute, with no one to turn to for help. To support her children, Elizabeth first attempted to start a hospital, which failed. She then accepted the invitation of the Sulpicians to start a school, Saint Joseph's Academy, in Emmitsburg, Maryland. This was the first free Catholic school in the United States of America, and it was staffed by the newly founded Sisters of Charity, the first community of religious women founded in the new nation. Elizabeth Ann Seton endured many losses during her lifetime, starting with the deaths of her mother and her husband, and estrangement from family and friends after her conversion to Catholicism. She agonized over her children and watched three of her daughters die young. Elizabeth herself died of tuberculosis in 1821, when she was only forty-six years old. In 1975, she became the first native-born citizen of the United States to be canonized. She is the patron saint of Catholic schools.

5

MEMORIAL OF **Saint John Neumann,** BISHOP 🇺🇸

Saint John Neumann (pronounced "Noi-mahn," not "New-man" / 1811–1860) emigrated to the United States of America from Bohemia in what is now the Czech Republic. He began studies in Prague in hope of being ordained to the priesthood, but at the time, Bohemia had a high number of priests, and the bishop was not accepting new candidates. John decided to emigrate to the United States, and in 1836 he was ordained in New York City. His first assignment was to work with German immigrants near Niagara Falls and establish missions. In 1840, he entered the Redemptorists, and in 1848 was appointed provincial superior. In 1852, John was consecrated fourth bishop of Philadelphia. He organized the first diocesan school system and doubled the number of Catholic schools. A gifted linguist, he was fluent in Italian as well as German and was able to minister to Italian immigrants and founded the first national parishes for them. Neumann expanded the Church in his diocese and drew the attention of the "Know Nothings," a virulently anti-Catholic political party that wanted to deprive foreigners and Catholics of civil rights and burned down convents and schools. John Neumann wrote many newspaper and magazine articles and published two catechisms. (He should not be confused with Blessed John Henry Newman, the English priest and writer who was beatified in 2010.) John Neumann, bishop of Philadelphia, was canonized by Pope Paul VI in 1977. His memorial is celebrated both in the United States, on January 5, the day he died, and on March 5 in the Czech Republic.

6

SOLEMNITY OF
the Epiphany of the Lord

January 6 is the traditional date for the celebration of the Epiphany of the Lord. However, in the United States of America and Canada, Epiphany is celebrated on the Sunday between January 2 and January 8. Please see page 7 and below under "The Twelfth Day of Christmas" for more information.

OPTIONAL MEMORIAL OF Saint André Bessette, RELIGIOUS

Saint André Bessette (1845–1937), known as Frère André, was born to an impoverished working-class French-Canadian family. His father worked at various trades, trying to make enough to support his family. Eventually he found work as a lumberjack but was tragically killed by a falling tree, leaving behind a widow and ten children. Three years later, André was orphaned at the age of twelve when his mother died of tuberculosis. He was taken in by his aunt and uncle. He tried his hand at several trades, but his poor health and lack of education made it difficult for him to hold a job, so he emigrated to the United States and spent time working in a textile mill in New England. André was always exceptionally pious, and he eventually returned to Canada and entered the Congregation of the Holy Cross in Montreal. He was made doorkeeper at Notre Dame College in Côte-des-Neiges, Quebec. He held this position for forty years and developed a great following once his reputation for wisdom and holiness spread. In 1904 he began building a small chapel on Mount Royal, which later developed into Saint Joseph's Oratory. Thousands of miraculous healings were attributed to him during his lifetime, but he always gave credit to Saint Joseph, to whom he had a great devotion. When he died in 1937, aged ninety-one, a million people paid their respects. André Bessette was canonized by Pope Benedict XVI on October 17, 2010.

The Twelfth Day of Christmas

The English count twelve days of Christmas from December 26, making today the twelfth day. Today is also the traditional date for Epiphany. The word *epiphany* means "manifestation"—in a star, in water or wine, in humanity. The wise ones who brought gifts to Jesus followed a star to Bethlehem, where they found him with his parents, and rejoiced exceedingly.

El día de los Reyes Magos
(Three Kings)

Today Spanish-speaking countries celebrate the arrival of the three kings in Bethlehem. Beforehand, Mexican children write letters to the wise men (or their favorite one), asking for gifts. These are attached to a helium balloon and flown up to the sky. Puerto Rican children put a shoe box filled with grass under their beds for the kings' camels to eat—their "wish list" is placed on top. Finally, the figures of the kings are added to the family crèche. The evening of January 6, friends and family share a meal called the *Merienda de Reyes* and *Rosca de Reyes*, doughnut-shaped pastries that contain a hidden plastic baby Jesus. Parades with live camels, music, lights, puppets, candies, pastries, and children wearing crowns are also part of the holiday.

7

MEMORIAL OF
Saint André Bessette, RELIGIOUS

Please see above for biography. Today is obligatory in Canada.

OPTIONAL MEMORIAL OF
Saint Raymond of Penyafort,
PRIEST 🇺🇸

Saint Raymond of Penyafort (c. 1175–1275) was born near Barcelona, Catalonia into a prominent family. He received his education in Barcelona and at the University of Bologna, Italy, earning doctorates in both civil and canon law. While teaching canon law at Bologna, he heard the preaching of Blessed Reginald, the prior of the Dominicans there, and joined the order in 1222. By 1238, he was made General of the Dominicans, and during his term, he revised the order's constitutions. In 1230, Pope Gregory IX asked him to come to Rome to lend his legal expertise to the organization of the canon law. At that time, there was no systematic codification of canon law, which was scattered among multiple sources. Raymond aided in organizing canon law into a collection known as the *Gregorian Decretals*, which replaced the *Decretals of Gratian* and was considered the standard collection of Church law until the promulgation of the first *Code of Canon Law* in 1917. When he returned to Spain, his focus shifted to the conversion of Jews and Muslims to Christianity, and he encouraged the Dominicans to study and teach Arabic and Hebrew. Legend has it that it was he who prompted Saint Thomas Aquinas to write the *Summa contra Gentiles*, a work thought to have been composed as a response to the teachings of Islam and Judaism for use by Dominican missionaries. In an unfortunate footnote to history, Raymond was among those who established the Inquisition in Catalonia. Saint Raymond is the patron saint of canon lawyers.

8

OPTIONAL MEMORIAL OF
Saint Raymond of Penyafort,
PRIEST

Please see above for biography.

9

The Black Nazarene (Philippines)

The Black Nazarene is a life-size statue of Christ carrying his Cross, carved in Mexico by an unknown artist and brought to the Philippines by Catholic missionaries in 1606. According to legend, the image was blackened when a fire broke out on the galleon that brought it to the Philippines. Every year on January 9, the Feast of the Black Nazarene, the image is carried in procession, and not just any procession! Devotees turn out by the millions, making the procession barefoot in honor of the Black Nazarene. Many believe the image possesses miraculous properties, and some say that miraculous healings have occurred for those who are able to touch the image. The procession expresses the profound devotion of the people of the Philippines to Christ in his Passion. With love and faith, they follow Christ, who carried his Cross on the road to Calvary, knowing he can help all of us to carry our own burdens—our troubles, our fears, our illnesses, our anxiety for those we love.

12

MEMORIAL OF
Saint Marguerite Bourgeoys, VIRGIN 🍁

The first Canadian woman to be canonized, Saint Marguerite Bourgeoys, was born in France on April 17, 1620. When she was nineteen, her mother died, and Marguerite took on the responsibility of caring for her brothers and sisters. A year later, during a procession in honor of Our Lady of the Rosary, she felt inspired to consecrate herself to the service of God. She tried joining the Carmelites and the Poor Clares, but both communities refused her entrance. Once Marguerite learned about the French settlement at Ville Marie in Canada—later known as Montreal—she realized that her vocation was to missionary work. The founder and governor of the settlement, Paul Chomody de Maisonneuve, persuaded her to dedicate herself to the education of French and Indian children. She started a school but soon realized she would need help and returned to France to recruit other young women. These became the founders of the Congregation de Notre-Dame. Originally, Marguerite intended her community uncloistered and take simple vows, an innovation at the time that enabled the sisters to pursue an active apostolate rather than remain in a cloister. Soon French Canadian and Native American women joined the group. The Congregation of Notre Dame received approval from the Vatican in 1698, and by the late 19th century, the sisters had spread through Canada and into the United States. Marguerite Bourgeoys is considered the co-foundress of Montreal, where she died on January 12, 1700 after offering her life for the cure of a younger sister. She was canonized by Blessed Pope John Paul II in 1982.

13

OPTIONAL MEMORIAL OF
Saint Hilary, BISHOP AND DOCTOR OF THE CHURCH

Saint Hilary (c. 315–367) was born to pagan parents in Poitiers, France. He was from an upper-class family and received a better education than most of his contemporaries, even studying Greek, which was rare at the time. At first, he embraced the philosophy of Neo-Platonism, but after studying the Old and New Testaments, he decided to become a Christian, along with his wife and daughter. At this early time in the history of the Church, married men could be ordained, and in 353, the people of Poitiers elected him bishop. Hilary found himself in the midst of the Arian heresy, which taught that the Son was not fully divine, and he fought for the correct understanding and expression of the divinity of Christ. He was known as the "hammer against Arianism" and the "Athanasius of the West," after the bishop of Alexandria who fought the heresy in the East. In an attempt to halt the persecution of Orthodox Christians by Arians, Hilary wrote to the emperor Constantius II. Constantius exiled him to Phrygia in modern-day Turkey, where he spent four years, managing to run his diocese from a distance. While in exile, Hilary composed *De synodis* and *De fide Orientalium*, his most important contributions to theology. The Christian world was so divided by Arianism that Hilary was exiled twice. His great contribution was the successful expression in the Latin language of theology about the nature of Christ, or Christology, that had been developed by Greek theologians.

Saint Kentigern, Bishop (Scotland)

Commonly known as Saint Mungo, Saint Kentigern (c. 518–603) was the "apostle" of the Kingdom of Strathclyde in what is now Scotland, and the patron saint and founder of the city of Glasgow. His mother, Thenaw, was the daughter of a king who ruled in an area of present-day Scotland, probably the Kingdom of Gododdin. A manuscript in the British library relates that she was seduced by Owain mab Urien and became pregnant. As a result, her father had her thrown from a hill, Traprain Law, but she survived and was put in a small boat that drifted to Culcross in Fife where Kentigern was born sometime in the late sixth century.

Kentigern was raised by Saint Serf, who was ministering to the Picts, a people that lived in early medieval Scotland. He gave Kentigern the nickname by which he is known, Mungo. When Kentigern, or Mungo, was twenty-five, he joined Serf in missionary activities, directing his attention to the people living in what is now Glasgow. He built a cathedral on the River Clyde on the site where the present cathedral stands.

Because of persecution by an anti-Christian king, Mungo fled to Wales, where he stayed with Saint David. While there, he founded the cathedral at Llanelwy and installed Saint Asaph as bishop. He made a pilgrimage to Rome and returned to Scotland when the new king asked him to return. Mungo eventually settled in Glasgow, where a community formed around him, attracted by his holiness. Saint Mungo died on January 13 in either 602 or 614. The cathedral in Glasgow was built on the site of his burial, and even after the Reformation, his remains were left in the crypt. They are said to be there still. A miraculous spring called Saint Mungo's Well flows from the eastern side of the cathedral apse. Saint Mungo is the patron saint of Glasgow, of Scotland, and is invoked against bullies.

15

The Black Christ of Esquipulas (Guatemala)

The Black Christ of Esquipulas is a crucifix venerated in the Basilica of Esquipulas in Guatemala, Central America. The image dates from the late 16th century. Tradition offers two explanations for the dark color of the image. One is that the smoke of countless candles illuminating the shrine darkened the crucifix over time. Another tradition says that the native peoples venerating the image wanted a representation of Christ with dark skin, like their own, and that Jesus performed a miracle for them. For more than 400 years, the crucifix has been devoutly venerated in the town of Esquipulas, but devotion to the image reaches far beyond Guatemala. Each year on this day, millions of pilgrims from throughout Latin America and abroad flock to the shrine to pray before the image. On this day, we can all pause before the image of Christ crucified, and give thanks to the Lord who became one of us, taking on our humanity so that we could be one with him in glory.

16

World Day of Refugees and Migrants

Refugees are people who have fled their homes and crossed an international border to escape persecution or conflict. Migrants are those who travel to another nation in order to find work. Pope Pius X instituted this World Day of Refugees and Migrants in 1914 to bring greater awareness to the challenges they face.

17

MEMORIAL OF
Saint Anthony, ABBOT

Early in his life, Saint Anthony of Egypt (251–356) discovered the grace of solitude. Solitude provides the vehicle through which one battles demons and removes worldly distractions that distance the heart from the will of God. Saint Anthony journeyed to the desert, and for nearly thirty years he lived a life of solitary prayer and self-discipline—a life of utter dependence on God. After his time in the desert, he emerged as a man of balance, ready to share all he learned regarding the human thirst for God. Realizing that the spiritual life takes root within a community of believers, he founded a group of monks. While serving as abbot, a spiritual father, to the monks, Saint Anthony mentored them in the ways of contemplative prayer and helped them overcome illusory thinking. His dynamic personality continued to attract others. As a result, he counseled a steady stream of pilgrims and laid the foundation for many monasteries.

A biography of Anthony (*Life of Antony*) written by Saint Athanasius of Alexandria popularized the monastic ideal of withdrawing from society to dedicate oneself to God. As a result, many followed Anthony's example and went out to the desert to live lives of asceticism. Saint Anthony is invoked against skin diseases.

18–25

Week of Prayer for Christian Unity

Each year, Christians from many denominations observe a special week of prayer for Christian Unity. Coming together in a variety of ways, through joint prayer and meetings, we remember how much we share, and we look honestly at the issues that still keep us apart. It is a time to reflect on Christ's prayer the night before he died: "The glory that you have given me I have given them, so that they may be one, as we are one, I in them and you in me, that they may become completely one, so that the world may know that you have sent me and have loved them even as you have loved me" (John 17:22–23).

The week of prayer was begun in 1908 by an American Episcopalian priest, Paul Wattson, and since that time it has spread worldwide. Each year, a joint commission of leaders from the full spectrum of the Christian family gathers to prepare prayer resources for this week of prayer and reflection. For Catholics, the unity of all Christian believers is more than just one more dream; it is central to the Church's mission.

20

OPTIONAL MEMORIAL OF Saint Fabian, POPE AND MARTYR

Saint Fabian (+ 250) was pope from 236–250. In his *Church History*, Eusebius says that Saint Fabian was chosen to be pope when a dove alit on his head. In spite of the fact that he was still a layman, he was named pope by acclamation as was customary in the early Church. Tradition says he instituted the four minor orders—porter, exorcist, lector, acolyte—stages through which candidates to the priesthood passed. Fabian improved the Church's organization, dividing Rome into seven districts, each headed by a deacon assisted by subdeacons whose task it was to record the deeds of the martyrs. A fairly reliable tradition says that Fabian sent missionary bishops to Gaul, among whom were Saint Denis of Paris. Martyred under Emperor Decius, he is buried in the catacomb of Callixtus in Rome.

OPTIONAL MEMORIAL OF
Saint Sebastian, Martyr

Saint Sebastian was martyred under Diocletian in about 288. Tradition says he was a Roman soldier who was appointed captain of the Praetorian Guard before Diocletian knew he was Christian. Although little is known of his life, he appears in many paintings, represented as tied to a post and shot through with arrows, the first method by which Diocletian attempted to have him killed. His body was recovered by Saint Irene, but when she went to prepare him for burial, she found he was alive and nursed him back to health. Later, Diocletian had him clubbed to death. Saint Sebastian was invoked during the Middle Ages as a protector against the bubonic plague, and he is counted among the Fourteen Holy Helpers (a group of saints honored together because they are believed to intercede against disease). He is also the patron saint of soldiers and of athletes.

21

MEMORIAL OF Saint Agnes, VIRGIN AND MARTYR

Saint Agnes (c. 292–305) is one of the women whose name is mentioned in Eucharistic Prayer I. She is thought to have been a member of Roman nobility, and was martyred at the age of twelve under Diocletian on January 21, 304, for refusing to marry a prefect's son. She is the patron saint of Christian virtue and is often represented with a martyr's palm and a lamb (a translation of her name in Latin). This gave rise to the tradition of blessing lambs at the Roman Basilica of Saint Agnes on this day. The wool from these lambs is then used to weave the pallium worn by archbishops and others of metropolitan rank.

Our Lady of Altagracia
(Dominican Republic)

Today the Dominican Republic observes a holiday in honor of their patroness, Our Lady of "Altagracia," or "High Grace." This is a painting dating from the 16th century, showing the Virgin smiling tenderly down at the Christ Child, who lies naked in the manger. In the background, we see Saint Joseph in a red cap and cloak, while the star of Bethlehem beams overhead. Mary wears a blue mantle covered in stars. Tradition tells us that a rich merchant, on his way to do business in Santo Domingo, was asked by his daughter to bring her a portrait of Our Lady of Altagracia. The father sought high and low for the image, but no one had ever heard of Our Lady of Altagracia. On his way home, he stopped at an inn and was explaining his dilemma, when a mysterious man pulled a rolled canvas out of his bag and offered it to him. Ever since, the image has been venerated by the people of the Dominican Republic. Blessed Pope John Paul II visited the shrine on January 25, 1979 and personally crowned the image with a precious tiara, his own gift to the Virgin, whom he called "first evangelizer of the Americas."

22

DAY OF PRAYER FOR THE
Legal Protection of Unborn Children 🇺🇸

On January 22, 1973, the United States Supreme Court handed down a decision known as *Roe versus Wade*, which made abortion legal throughout the United States, and struck down many states' laws restricting abortion. Since that decision, more than 50 million abortions have been performed in the United States. In all the dioceses of the United States, today is observed as a day of penance for violations to the dignity of the human person committed through acts of abortion, and for the full restoration of the legal guarantee to the right to life. We pray not only for the innocent children who are not able to be born, but for all mothers and fathers who are considering abortion and those who have had abortions. On this day, hundreds of thousands will participate in pro-life marches across the nation. The largest of these takes place in Washington, D.C., where some 400,000 gather on the Mall and march up Capitol Hill to witness to the Gospel of life. If January 22 falls on a Sunday, this observance is moved to Monday, January 23.

Optional Memorial of Saint Vincent, Deacon and Martyr 🍁

Saint Vincent was from Saragossa in third-century Spain. He is also known as Vincent the Deacon and served under Saint Valerius, bishop of Saragossa. He was martyred in 304 in the persecution of the emperor Diocletian. Just before he was killed on a gridiron or grill, he was offered his freedom if he would throw a copy of the Scriptures on the fire that was prepared for him, but he refused. After witnessing Vincent's faith and heroism, his executioner converted to Christianity.

Blessed Marianne Cope 🇺🇸

Blessed Marianne Cope (1838–1918) was born in West Germany, but a year after her birth the Cope family emigrated to the United States of America to seek work and educational opportunities. From a young age, she felt the call to enter religious life which led to her decision to enter the Sisters of Saint Francis in Syracuse, New York. She had a deep affection for the suffering and sick. Blessed Marianne was instrumental in the establishment of two of the first hospitals in the central New York area—hospitals that were open to all people regardless of ethnicity, religion, or race. While serving as superior general of her religious community, she accepted an invitation to care for the sick, especially those afflicted with

leprosy, in Hawaii. Blessed Marianne joined the mission to Hawaii where she helped establish homes for leprosy patients and cared for Saint Damien De Veuster of Moloka'i who contracted leprosy because of his ministry to the sick. Following the death of Saint Damien, Blessed Marianne continued his compassionate ministry of care for leprosy patients. Blessed Marianne lived the Franciscan call to serve the "crucified," the most vulnerable, in society.

At the time of this printing, the bishops of the United States have approved the inclusion of an optional memorial for Blessed Marianne. Normally, a saint's feast day is their death date, their *dies natales,* or birthday into heaven. However, Blessed Marianne died on August 9. This is the same date as the obligatory memorial for Saint Teresa Benedicta of the Cross (Edith Stein). Because of this, the American bishops have suggested this date, January 23, Blessed Marianne's birthday. Approval of the inclusion of this optional memorial is pending from the Holy See.

23

Optional Memorial of Saint Vincent, Deacon and Martyr 🇺🇸

Please see biography on January 22.

24

Memorial of Saint Francis de Sales, Bishop and Doctor of the Church

Saint Francis de Sales (1567–1622), bishop of Geneva, contributed immensely to the development of spirituality through the publication of his book

An Introduction to the Devout Life. Living during a time when most manuals on spirituality were written primarily for clerics and members of religious orders, Saint Francis' book provided a practical path to holiness for people from all states of life. He challenged the prevailing belief that only a select few could attain sanctity. Along with his accomplishments in the area of an "everyday" or "lay" spirituality, he cofounded with Saint Jane Frances de Chantal the Order of the Visitation of Holy Mary—a religious community of nuns that move beyond traditional enclosure to a blend of prayer and service to the poor. Together, Saints Francis and Jane, with their close friends Saints Vincent de Paul and Louise de Marillac, transformed the face of the Church in France. Saint Francis has been named a Doctor of the Church.

25

FEAST OF THE Conversion of Saint Paul the Apostle

Saul of Tarsus (c. 4–c. 64) had a history of persecuting Christians. He was present at the martyrdom of Saint Stephen and held the cloaks of those who stoned him. While on the road to Damascus, where Saul was headed to suppress the Christian community, he was blinded by a bright light and heard the voice of Christ saying, "Saul, Saul, why do you persecute me?" (Acts of the Apostles 9:4). He took the name Paul and became the "Apostle to the Gentiles," traveling the known world with the message of the Gospel. Saint Paul's conversion is a witness to the mercy of God and the possibility of conversion.

26

MEMORIAL OF Saints Timothy and Titus, BISHOPS

Saints Timothy and Titus, first century bishops and martyrs, are celebrated together because of their joint association with Saint Paul. Timothy is first mentioned in Acts of the Apostles 16:1–2, when Paul visits Lystra, in what is now Turkey. Timothy's mother was Jewish, Paul circumcised him so he would be accepted by the Jewish Christians. Timothy accompanied Paul on some of his journeys, and he is the one addressed in the Letters to Timothy in the New Testament. Tradition says that Paul made him bishop of Ephesus in 65. He was martyred by stoning in either the year 65 or 80 for preaching against the worship of idols.

Saint Titus was also a disciple and companion of Saint Paul. He was probably a Gentile, and Paul refused to have him circumcised because the Gospel freed Gentiles from the Law of Moses. Although he is not mentioned in the Acts of the Apostles, he is mentioned several times in Paul's letters and was probably commissioned to preach to the Gentiles. According to Paul, Titus was with Paul and Timothy at Ephesus and was sent to Macedonia to collect alms for the Christians in Jerusalem. He also spent time in Macedonia, Crete, and Dalmatia in modern-day Croatia. Tradition says that he was a bishop in Crete and died in the year 107.

Australia Day

This day of national celebration takes place during high Australian summer. A tall ships regatta adorns Sydney Harbor. Perth is famous for its fireworks. On Swanston Street in Melbourne, a "Peoples March" celebrates cultural diversity. Many towns stage concerts, flag raisings, and music festivals. Thousands of people are sworn in as new citizens. Australia Day Honours are awarded to people who have demonstrated courage and dedicated service, and

Australia Day Ambassadors offer inspiring reflections at communities around the country.

Since Australia Day takes place on the anniversary of the arrival of the British Fleet in Sydney Harbor, its date is controversial. Many indigenous people refer to this day as Invasion Day, and ask that the date of the celebration be changed.

27

OPTIONAL MEMORIAL OF
Saint Angela Merici, VIRGIN

Saint Angela Merici (c. 1470–1540) believed that young girls needed a Christian education, and so she started a school in her home. Eventually she realized that she was called to start a community of women dedicated to teaching girls, and she founded the Ursulines in 1535. She died only five years later. The Ursulines were the first order of women entirely devoted to education, and they played an important role in the development of Catholic education in the United States of America, where they founded a school in New Orleans in 1727.

28

MEMORIAL OF Saint Thomas Aquinas, PRIEST AND DOCTOR OF THE CHURCH

Saint Thomas Aquinas (1225–1274), called the "Angelic Doctor" for his writings, was born near Naples. Against his family's wishes, he joined the newly established Dominicans and went to study under Albert the Great in Paris. Thomas's theological writings, especially the *Summa Theologia*, remain preeminent texts to this day. For all his brilliance, Thomas was also a man of deep prayer who realized that the mysteries of God cannot fully be expressed by words. He contributed the liturgical texts for the Solemnity of the Most Holy Body and Blood of Christ, including the *Tantum Ergo*, which is still sung at Benediction of the Blessed Sacrament.

31

MEMORIAL OF
Saint John Bosco, PRIEST

God gifted Saint John Bosco (1815–1888) with the ability to read and interpret the signs of the times. Living during rapid industrialization and growing anti-clericalism, he became very concerned about the emotional and spiritual livelihood of people, especially the plight of the young. He worked to provide positive and affirming environments, including orphanages and oratories, where the young could learn and recognize their infinite potential. In the spirit of his favorite hero, Saint Francis de Sales, he founded the Salesians, a religious congregation devoted to works of charity, with an emphasis on empowering young people to become strong pillars of faith in a culture of instability. His work among young men living in the slums proved to be a worthy endeavor. Whether he was presiding at Mass or playing games with children or carrying the sick to hospitals, it was obvious he lived until his "last breath . . . day and night, morning and evening" for the neglected and abandoned (as quoted in *Butler's Lives of the Saints* [New Full Edition—January], p. 229).

FEBRUARY

Month of February

The second month of the year takes its name from the Latin word for *purification*.

The ancient Roman calendar had ten months, March through December. (*December* means "tenth month.") There was no January and no February. These months were left off the calendar. Strange as it seems, people didn't feel the need to keep track of the days during winter.

For the Romans, this late winter period before March became a "season" of purification and renewal, almost like Lent. When the Romans began using a 12-month calendar, the old names for the months continued to be used. The month before March was named for the time of purification.

Images of Saints in February (clockwise from left): Saint Paul Miki (February 6), Saint Scholastica (February 10), Saint Blaise (February 3).

Month of the Passion of Our Lord

For Catholics, the month of February is especially dedicated to the Passion of Our Lord, probably because Lent usually begins in this month. Through the centuries, many devotions have developed to help us focus on the Passion of Christ. Whether we pray the Stations of the Cross, or walk in the procession of the Nazarene, or pray before the crucified Christ, or reflect on the Passion narratives in the Gospel, our reflection on the Passion of Our Lord should lead us from sorrow to wonder: sorrow for our sins, wonder at the unbounded love of Christ for us.

National Day of Prayer for the African American Family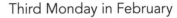

First Sunday of February

On the first Sunday of February, which is Black History Month, the United States Conference of Catholic Bishops invite us to observe a National Day of Prayer for the African American Family. This observance was instituted by Father James Goode, OFM, in 1989, as an opportunity to give thanks for our families, and to entrust every family to the loving care of Jesus. In a prayer composed for this day of prayer, Father Goode wrote:

> May we be proud of our history and never forget those who paid a great price for our liberation. . . .
>
> Bless our parents, guardians and grandparents, relatives and friends . . . .
>
> Give a healing anointing to those less fortunate, especially the motherless, the fatherless, the broken, the sick, and the lonely. . . .

World Marriage Day

Second Sunday of February

The second Sunday of February is World Marriage Day. The idea began in Baton Rouge, Louisiana in 1981. By 1982, 43 states had officially made this World Marriage Day. In 1993, Blessed Pope John Paul II imparted his Apostolic Blessing to World Marriage Day. The celebration continues to grow. This is a day to pray for all married couples: that husbands and wives may have the wisdom and courage to help one another become all God wants them to be; that they will receive the gifts of patience, imagination, and understanding, especially in their relationship with their children. We pray that married couples may find their friendship and love grows deeper with time. We also pray for all widows and widowers, that God may comfort them; and for those who suffer the pain of troubled marriages, that God will guide them into a future full of hope.

Presidents Day

Third Monday in February

Today is a celebration of the lives and works of President George Washington and President Abraham Lincoln. Years ago, many states observed the birthday of Abraham Lincoln on February 12 and that of George Washington on February 22. In 1971 the two observances were combined and moved to the third Monday of the month. That made it possible for many Americans to enjoy a three-day weekend.

Lunar New Year

Please see page 29 for more information.

1

Saint Brigid, Virgin (Ireland)

Saint Brigid of Kildare (c. 451–c. 524) is, along with Saint Patrick, a patron saint of Ireland. Many legends grew surrounding her life, but she was probably the daughter of a slave in the court of her father, King Dubhthach of Leinster. Tradition says that she made monastic vows and founded twin monasteries at Kildare (*Cill-Dara* or "the church of the oak"), one for men and one for women, and as was not uncommon at the time, was abbess over both. Brigid is remembered for her great joy.

2

FEAST OF THE
Presentation of the Lord

Forty days after Christmas, we celebrate the Feast of the Presentation of the Lord, which recalls the event described in the Gospel according to Luke: "When the time came for their purification according to the law of Moses, they brought him up to the Lord (as it is written in the law of the Lord, 'Every firstborn male shall be designated as holy to the Lord')" (Luke 2:22). Joseph and Mary bring Jesus to the Temple, and while they are there, they meet two extraordinary people. First they meet Simeon, who, taking Jesus in his arms, recognizes him as the long-awaited Messiah. Not only that, Simeon knows that this Messiah has come not only to the Jewish people, but to all. He is "a light for revelation to the Gentiles" (Luke 2:32). There is a note of sorrow in this joyful encounter: Simeon prophesies over the child, telling Mary that Jesus will encounter great opposition, while her own heart is pierced by a sword. They also meet Anna, a widow, 84 years old, who prays and fasts in the Temple night and day, and who also recognizes who Jesus is, and begins to proclaim him: "At that moment she came, and began to praise God and to speak about the child to all who were looking for the redemption of Jerusalem" (Luke 2:38).

Jesus is the light to the nations, and from the moment of his birth, people are drawn to his light. That is why on this Feast of the Presentation of the Lord, we carry lit candles, and the priest blesses the candles to be used in the celebration of the liturgy during the coming year. Because of this, today's Mass is often called Candlemass.

World Day for Consecrated Life

On the Feast of the Presentation of the Lord, we also observe the World Day for Consecrated Life. The Gospel today tells the story of Mary and Joseph taking Jesus to the temple "to present him to the Lord" (Luke 2:22). Simeon and Anna recognize in this little child the Savior whom they have awaited with eager expectation. It's the perfect feast to take some time to give thanks to God for the gift of consecrated life—for all the men and women who have dedicated their lives to the Lord and to service in his Church. Men and women religious throughout the world renew their commitment to the consecrated life this day. It's also a time to encourage young men and women to consider whether God might be calling them to this mode of life. "What would become of the world if there were no religious?" Saint Teresa of Avila once asked. "This is a question which brings us to give unceasing thanks to the Lord, who by this singular gift of the Spirit continues to enliven and sustain the Church in its demanding journey through this world" (Pope John Paul II, Message for the First World Day for Consecrated Life, 1997).

Groundhog Day 🇺🇸 🍁

The Celtic people divided the year differently than we do now. For them, February 1 was the first day of spring. The first days of May, August, and November marked the beginnings of the other natural seasons. That way of dividing the year makes a lot of sense in northern Europe, where the change in the length of days is dramatic.

Saint Brigid's feast day and the Presentation of the Lord (Candlemas Day) are associated with folklore about the arrival of spring, or at least the arrival of lengthening days. German farmers say that on Candlemas the badger interrupts its winter nap to check the weather. If the day is sunny, the badger sees its shadow and gets scared, and then goes back to hibernate for six more weeks. The bright, cold days of winter aren't over yet. But if the day is cloudy, the badger cannot see its shadow. That means that hibernation is over, and the cloudy, warmer weather of spring is about to arrive. Good news for the farmers!

German farmers who immigrated to Pennsylvania did not find badgers. They decided that groundhogs would provide the spring forecast, instead. So on Candlemas Day we wonder if the groundhog will see its shadow or if spring is coming soon.

3

OPTIONAL MEMORIAL OF
Saint Blaise, BISHOP
AND MARTYR

Saint Blaise was a physician, bishop of Sebaste (Turkey), and martyr who was born sometime in the third century and died around the year 316. The earliest written reference to him doesn't appear until the fifth or sixth century, where he is reputed to have healed a boy who was choking on a fish bone. For this reason, his intercession is invoked for illnesses of the throat, and it is customary for throats to be blessed on his memorial, using crossed candles. The instruments of his martyrdom were steel combs that would normally have been used to comb wool, and for this reason he is the patron saint of the wool trade. He was very popular in the 11th and 12th centuries, and is one of the Fourteen Holy Helpers whose story is retold in the Golden Legend. The Fourteen Holy Helpers are a group of saints who are invoked against diseases.

OPTIONAL MEMORIAL OF
Saint Ansgar, BISHOP

Saint Ansgar (c. 801–865), the "apostle of the north," was an orphan who was raised at the Benedictine abbey of Corbie in France. The source for most of his life is the *Life of Ansgar*, written by his disciple, Rimbert, who succeeded him as archbishop and is also a saint. Ansgar became a monk at Corbie and was sent as a missionary to Jutland in what is now Denmark. Later, at the request of King Björn, he went to Sweden to preach the Gospel. In 831, Ansgar was appointed archbishop of Hamburg, a diocese that had a special responsibility to evangelize the northern countries in Scandinavia. Although he lived during the period of political upheaval that followed the death of Charlemagne and the accession of his sons and subsequent division of his empire, Ansgar managed to establish Christianity and build churches and monasteries. He died in Bremen in 865 and is the patron saint of Denmark.

Our Lady of Suyapa (Honduras)

Today, in Honduras, the Blessed Virgin Mary is venerated under the title of Our Lady of Suyapa. Devotion centers on a tiny 18th-century statue, less than two and a half inches high. Legend has it that a laborer was hard at work clearing the corn fields, and was overtaken by nightfall as he journeyed home. He went to sleep on the ground and was awakened by a pain in his side. He found he was sleeping on a tiny statue of the Blessed Virgin Mary! He took the statue home with him and placed it on the family altar, where it was venerated for many years. In 1768, the little statue was credited with its first miracle and was placed in its own chapel. In the 1950s, a large basilica was built next to the chapel. Diminutive as the image is, Our Lady of Suyapa dominates the basilica and is venerated as the patron saint of all Honduras. Our Lady of Suyapa, pray for us, and for the people of Honduras.

4

Saint John de Britto, Martyr (India)

Saint John de Britto (1647–1693) was born in Lisbon, Portugal, the son of an aristocratic Portuguese family. He entered the Jesuits in 1662, and after completing his studies at the University of Coimbra, he was sent in 1673 to the missions of Madura in southern India (Tamil Nadu). He returned to Europe in 1687 but returned to India with twenty-four new missionaries in 1690. In the Madura mission, John attempted to establish an Indian Catholic Church free of European cultural domination, similar to the work of Matteo Ricci in China. He assumed native dress and customs such as strict vegetarianism and learned the local languages. Because of his success and his preaching, he was condemned to death by the Setupati of Marava on January 28, 1693 and was executed on February 4. He was canonized by Pope Pius XII in 1947.

Te Deum as they went. At Nagasaki, they were crucified. When Christian missionaries returned to Japan in the nineteenth century, they found that a secret Christian community had survived by transmitting the beliefs and prayers from generation to generation.

5

MEMORIAL OF Saint Agatha, VIRGIN AND MARTYR

Saint Agatha was born in Sicily, probably around the year 231 and is one of the women mentioned by name in Eucharistic Prayer I. According to legend, she was the daughter of a prominent family and was very beautiful. The Roman senator Quintianus wished to marry her, but when Agatha spurned him, he had her put in a brothel. In spite of this, Agatha held to her Christian faith. Quintianus then had her tortured by having her breasts cut off. She eventually died in prison in 253. Saint Agatha is the patron saint of the city of her martyrdom, Catania, and is invoked against fire, earthquakes, and eruptions of Mount Etna. In recent years, because her breasts were cut off as part of her torture, she is considered the patron saint of breast cancer patients.

6

MEMORIAL OF Saint Paul Miki and Companions, MARTYRS

Saint Paul Miki (c. 1562–1597), a Jesuit priest, was one of the twenty-six martyrs of Japan. The local governor felt threatened by the growing influence of the Jesuits and had members of the Christian community arrested and thrown in jail. They were forced to walk six hundred miles from Kyoto to Nagasaki as a deterrent to other Christians, but they sang the

8

OPTIONAL MEMORIAL OF Saint Jerome Emiliani

Saint Jerome Emiliani (1481–1537), was born in Venice. As an adult, he joined the army and was later appointed magistrate of Castelnuovo. All the while, he devoted himself to studying theology and performing charitable works. After he was ordained to the priesthood in 1518, he most often could be found among the poor and sick. The plague and famine of 1528 resulted in a spike in the number of orphans, and Jerome obtained a house where they could be taken care of. By 1532, Jerome had founded a number of hospitals, orphanages, and homes for former prostitutes. He had attracted followers to help him in his work and started a religious community at Somasca, whose main work would be the care of orphans, the poor, and the sick; they would become known as the Somaschi. He became ill while tending to the sick and died at Somasca in 1537. Members of his order still work among the poor today in Europe and the United States, as well as Honduras, El Salvador, India, Sri Lanka, the Philippines, and Australia. Saint Jerome is the patron saint of orphans and abandoned children.

OPTIONAL MEMORIAL OF Saint Josephine Bakhita, VIRGIN

Saint Josephine Bakhita (c. 1868–1947), was born in the Darfur region of Sudan. She recalled her early childhood as happy, but between the ages of seven and nine, she was kidnapped by Arab slave traders.

Because of the trauma, she forgot her own name, and was called *Bahkita*, which means "lucky" in Arabic. She suffered beatings at the hands of cruel owners, and was branded as a slave by having salt poured into wounds cut by one of her mistresses. In 1883, Bahkita was bought by the Italian Vice Counsul, Callisto Legnani, at Khartoum. For the first time since her capture, she was treated kindly, and when Legnani was recalled to Italy, she begged to be taken along. Once in Italy, she was given as a gift to the Michieli family, where she served as nanny and returned to Sudan for a time. When the Michieli family decided to sell their Italian estate and remain there, Josephine was sent to live with the Canossian Sisters until all was settled, but when the Signora Michieli came retrieve her, Bahkita refused to leave. Italian law did not recognize slavery, and she was free for the first time to set her own course. She decided to remain with the sisters, was baptized in 1890 with the name Josephine, and entered the novitiate of the Canossian Sisters in 1893. She was assigned as portress or doorkeeper of the convent and became well-known and loved in the local area for her holiness. Josephine Bahkita died in 1947 and was canonized by Pope John Paul II in 2000. She is the patron saint of Sudan.

10

MEMORIAL OF
Saint Scholastica, VIRGIN

Saint Scholastica (+ 547) is thought to have been the twin sister of Saint Benedict and was "dedicated to the Lord from infancy" (see 1 Samuel 1:24). Her story is told in Book II of the *Dialogues of Saint Gregory the Great*. Once a year Scholastica would visit Benedict at a guest house on the grounds of his abbey in order to spend time together in worship and holy conversation. At the end of one such visit, Benedict rose to leave, but Scholastica, having a premonition of her own death, begged him to stay.

When he insisted that he had to return to his cell for the night, she bowed her head and wept in prayer. A wild storm arose, making it impossible for Benedict to leave. When Benedict realized he could not return to the abbey, he complained to his sister, "God forgive you, what have you done?" She answered him, "I desired you to stay, and you would not hear me; I have desired it of our good Lord, and he has granted my petition. Therefore if you can now depart, in God's name return to your monastery, and leave me here alone" (*Dialogues*, Book II). Gregory comments that God heard Scholastica's prayer rather than her brother's because, since "God is love," it is natural that she who loved more, did more.

The next morning, the two returned to their respective monasteries, and three days later, Benedict, as he prayed in his cell, saw his sister's soul ascend to heaven in the form of a dove. Saint Scholastica is the patron saint of female Benedictine monastics. Because of Benedict's vision of her death, she is depicted in art accompanied by a dove. Saint Gregory's narrative is also found in the Office of Readings for this memorial.

11

OPTIONAL MEMORIAL OF
Our Lady of Lourdes

It was on this day in 1858 that the 14-year-old Bernadette Soubirous, a peasant girl in Lourdes, saw a "lady" in a grotto near the river Gave, at the foot of the Pyrenees Mountains in France. Over the next several months, Bernadette encountered the "lady" many times. During one of these apparitions, the Lady directed Bernadette to drink from the fountain. But there was no fountain there — only the river. At the lady's command, Bernadette began to dig in the ground near the grotto, and a spring of water began to flow. Immediately, numerous miraculous healings took place, of those who bathed in or drank the water of the spring. Only later did the

Lady reveal to Bernadette who she was: "I am the Immaculate Conception."

Today, Lourdes is one of the most popular pilgrimage places in the world. Every year, hundreds of thousands of people make the pilgrimage to the little town, to drink of the water, and to feel close to the Virgin and to her Son, Jesus Christ, healer of body and soul.

World Day of the Sick

Since 1992, the World Day of the Sick has been celebrated each year on the optional Memorial of Our Lady of Lourdes. Blessed John Paul II had already been diagnosed with Parkinson's Disease when he instituted this world day of prayer. Today we pray for all who are sick and suffering, that they may see in their suffering a share in the Cross of Christ. We pray also for caregivers, for nurses and doctors, that they may be unfailingly gentle and compassionate. We pray, too, for researchers and scientists who seek to eradicate disease. And we pray for the poor of our world, who do not have access to adequate health care.

14

MEMORIAL OF
Saints Cyril, MONK, and Methodius, BISHOP

Saints Cyril (827–869) and Methodius (815–884) were brothers born in Thessalonika (Greece), in the ninth century and are known as the "apostles to the Slavs." Cyril was a scholar and linguist, and Methodius was a monk. In 862, Prince Rastislav of Moravia asked the Byzantine Emperor Michael III and the Patriarch of Constantinople, Photius, to send missionaries to his people. It is likely that Ratislav turned to Constantinople for help rather than fall under the influence of the Franks. At the time, there was no written form of Old Slavonic, so Cyril and

Methodius developed the Glagolitic alphabet, from which their disciples developed the Cyrillic alphabet, still used today in Slavic languages such as Russian and Ukrainian, as well as by the Russian-influenced languages Moldovan, Mongolian, and Tatar, among others. As part of their work, they translated some of the Scriptures into Old Slavonic and devised a liturgy in that language. Shortly before his death, Cyril became a monk; Methodius continued the mission alone and later was made an archbishop. The Eastern Orthodox churches venerate them as saints with the title "equal-to-apostles," and they are celebrated with national holidays in Bulgaria and Macedonia. In 1980, Blessed Pope John Paul II declared them co-patron saints of Europe, an honor they share with Saint Benedict of Nursia. Their joint commemoration is celebrated on the anniversary of Cyril's death. Saints Cyril and Methodius are the patron saints of ecumenism, of unity among the Eastern and Western Churches, of Europe, as well as countries such as Bulgaria, the Czech Republic, and Moravia.

Saint Valentine's Day

An ancient, mysterious legend explains this day's origins. Two Saint Valentines, both third-century martyrs—one a bishop, the other a priest—sent letters of encouragement to people dreading persecution. Hence, we send valentines decorated with flowers, hearts, and the color red, which symbolizes the blood of martyrdom. Initially, the celebration was not meant to be exclusive; now it has taken on romantic overtones. However, to retrieve the original sense, Peter Mazar suggests handmade cards for people who might not otherwise receive them: residents of retirement centers or hospitals and members of the armed forces. While the day provides revenue for card shops, jewelers and florists, it's intended to celebrate the Christian values of thoughtfulness and tender care. And it enlivens a long winter!

17

OPTIONAL MEMORIAL OF
the Seven Holy Founders of the Servite Order

In 1233, seven young men from Florence—Alexis Falconieri, Bartholomew degli Amidei, Benedict dell'Antella, Buonfiglio Mondaldi, Gherardino Sostegni, Hugh dei Lippi-Uguccioni, John Buonagiunta Monetti—together had a vision of the Virgin Mary, telling them to change their lives and devote themselves to prayer. Acting on the vision, they withdrew from the city and moved near the Franciscans in La Camarzia. In 1240, seeking greater seclusion, they moved to Monte Senario, and the Virgin Mary appeared to them again. She gave them a black habit and told them to found an order that would follow the *Rule of Saint Augustine*. This was the Order of Servites. In 1249, the new order received official approval from Rome. It grew rapidly, expanding to four provinces by 1256. Today, in addition to the men's community, there are religious women, some cloistered, others tertiaries, religious who are involved in active ministries, founded by Saint Juliana Falconieri, the niece of one of the seven founders. The Servites are one of the original five mendicant orders (religious who rely on charity), along with the Franciscans, Dominicans, Augustinians, and Carmelites, in principle relying directly on charity for their support and owning nothing. The Servites can be found in Europe and the United States, preaching missions, spreading their signature devotion to Mary, especially as she witnessed the sufferings of her son during the Passion, Our Lady of Sorrows. In their tradition of scholarship, they also teach in colleges and founded the Marianum, a college in Rome devoted to the study of Mariology, the theological study of Mary.

21

OPTIONAL MEMORIAL OF
Saint Peter Damian, BISHOP AND DOCTOR OF THE CHURCH

Saint Peter Damian (1007–1072), was born in Ravenna, Italy. He was orphaned at a young age, but when his intellectual gifts manifested themselves, his brother, Damian, made sure he received an education. Peter was so grateful that he added his brother's name to his own. He excelled at his studies and by the age of twenty five, he was already a famous teacher. However, around the year 1035, he entered the hermitage of Fonte Avellana near Gubbio, which was part of the Camaldolese branch of the Benedictines. Peter dedicated himself to a life of penance and the study of Scripture and the Fathers of the Church. He gained a reputation among the hermits as both a gifted scholar and spiritual father and became prior in 1043. Although he lived in the monastery, Peter paid close attention to what was happening in the Church and spoke out against corruption. He was present at the Lateran synod of 1047, at which decrees were passed against simony. (Named for Simon Magus in Acts of the Apostles 8:18–24, simony is the practice of paying for sacraments and for positions in the hierarchy.) When the abbot of Monte Cassino was elected Pope Stephen IX, he was determined to make Peter a cardinal. Peter, desiring to remain a hermit, resisted, but eventually he accepted the position of cardinal, heading the diocese of Ostia. During his years as a bishop, the Church suffered from schisms, with more than one person calling himself pope, and Peter sometimes found himself negotiating or persuading the antipope to step down. After a life spent traveling in the service of the Church as papal legate, he fell ill with fever and died in 1072. Peter's work as legate and his writings were so influential that he was made a Doctor of the Church in 1828. In art he is depicted with a knotted rope (an instrument of self-mortification) or as a pilgrim carrying a papal Bull for his many journeys on behalf of the Holy See.

22

FEAST OF THE Chair of Saint Peter THE APOSTLE

On February 22, we observe the unique Feast of the Chair of Saint Peter. Saint Peter's chair is an ancient wooden chair that has been venerated at Saint Peter's Basilica for well over a thousand years. This relic is enclosed in a magnificent bronze sculpture by Bernini, which shows a chair surmounted by a stained-glass window of the Holy Spirit, and surrounded by a glory of sunbursts, clouds, angels, and enormous figures of the Doctors of the Church. Why is this chair so important? Because in our Catholic tradition, chairs are one of our primary symbols of teaching authority. Every bishop has a chair, a "cathedra," the symbol of his authority, so important to the life of the local Church that a special church is built to house it—the cathedral. The Chair of Peter is, then, a symbol of the teaching authority of the Bishop of Rome, the pope, who is the successor of Saint Peter. This is a day to pray for our Holy Father and to give thanks for the gift of our Catholic faith.

23

MEMORIAL OF Saint Polycarp, BISHOP AND MARTYR

Saint Polycarp (c. 69–c. 155) was the bishop of Smyrna in the second century. With Clement of Rome and Ignatius of Antioch, he is an apostolic father, one who was converted by the Apostles. Saint Irenaeus was taught by him as a young man and records that Polycarp had been a disciple of John the Apostle; Tertullian wrote this as well. The letter sent by the Christians of Smyrna after his death is a genuine, eyewitness account of an early martyrdom. For refusing to burn incense to the Roman Emperor, Polycarp, in spite of his great age—he may have been eighty-six at the time—was condemned to death. He was sentenced to be burned at the stake, but "the fire, making the appearance of a vault, like the sail of a vessel filled by the wind, made a wall round about the body of the martyr; and it was there in the midst, not like flesh burning, but like [a loaf in the oven or like] gold and silver refined in a furnace" (*Martydom of Polycarp* 15:2). He was subsequently killed by beheading. Polycarp is one of the earliest Christians whose writings we still have.

Venerable Samuel Charles Mazzuchelli 🏴

Venerable Samuel Charles Mazzuchelli (1806–1864), born in Milan, Italy, joined the Dominicans at the age of 17. He was sent to the American frontier where he served as a missionary priest to the Northwest Territory, from the Great Lakes to the Mississippi. He ministered to immigrant settlers, miners, farmers, traders, political leaders, and native tribes. He had a deep love for Native Americans, so he established schools that taught in their own language, and also published a Winnebago prayer book and liturgical almanac in Chippewa. Venerable Samuel also fought governmental injustices against Native Americans. Along with founding 30 parishes, he began a religious community of women, the Dominican Sisters of Sinsinawa, to continue his mission of teaching and preaching. Mazzuchelli died on this date in 1864. His cause for beatification is still pending.

MARCH

Month of March

March is the month of the vernal equinox, when day-time grows equal to nighttime, and spring begins in the Northern Hemisphere. The lengthening days warm the air and help create the March winds. A few days in March are as cold as deep winter, a few are as warm as springtime, and many of the days are stormy. No wonder March is named after Mars, the Roman god of war. The struggle against winter is a strong sign of Lent. Summer and winter seem to battle through this month.

Month of Saint Joseph

The month of March is dedicated to Saint Joseph, spouse of the Blessed Virgin Mary and the foster-father of the Lord. Saint Joseph was the favorite saint of Saint Teresa of Avila, and of many popes, including Pope Saint Pius X and Blessed John XXIII, who wrote: "O glorious Joseph! Who concealed your incomparable and regal dignity of custodian of Jesus and of the Virgin Mary under the humble appearance of a craftsman and provided for them with your work, protect with loving power your sons, especially

Images of Saints in March (L to R): Saint Patrick (March 16), Saint Joseph,
Spouse of the Blessed Virgin Mary (March 19). Saint Katharine Drexel (March 3).

entrusted to you. You know their anxieties and sufferings, because you yourself experienced them at the side of Jesus and of His Mother. Do not allow them, oppressed by so many worries, to forget the purpose for which they were created by God" (Prayer for Workers). Joseph is the patron saint of fathers, of workers, and of the universal Church. Saint Joseph, pray for us!

Daylight Savings Time

Second Sunday in March / First Sunday in November

Daylight Savings Time (DST for short) is used in the spring, summer, and fall months in many countries. During those months, simply advancing the clock one hour gains an extra hour of sunlight each day. The sun seems to rise an hour later, when most people are still sleeping, and to linger in the sky for an extra hour before twilight. Most of the United States of America uses DST. However, some states and territories with very warm climates choose to remain on Standard Time all year long.

Mexico, most of Canada, European Union countries, and many countries in the Southern Hemisphere also use DST. Some people think that using DST saves energy, but not everyone agrees on this. The motto "spring forward, fall back" helps simplify resetting the clocks each year.

World Day of Prayer

First Friday in March

Prayers will resound today from the first sunrise to the last sunset as groups of women from many Christian expressions of faith and from more than 170 countries intercede for the needs of the world. Each year the women of a different nation prepare for this day by writing a prayer service for all to use. They also express their concerns, believing that, as their motto states, "Informed prayer leads to prayerful action." The concerns they voice become the yardsticks for selecting grants that are donated to projects in many lands. Those who share in this experience increase their understanding of other cultures, increase their faith, and develop their

gifts. The ecumenical organization Church Women United represents women of the United States of America in this annual work of peace and justice.

Commonwealth Day

Second Monday in March

On this day, a number of English-speaking lands celebrates their partnership. Many, but not all, of these countries were once part of the British Empire. Together they form a sort of club of nations called the Commonwealth. Nearly the largest club on earth, the Commonwealth includes 30 percent of the world's population—almost two billion people! Commonwealth nations work together for peace, prosperity, and democracy.

Commonwealth Day honors this partnership with a series of activities, some of which continue all year. Many of these projects are designed for schoolchildren. Every fourth year a series of international sporting events called the Commonwealth Games is held. Commonwealth Day begins with an interfaith service, usually held in England's Westminster Abbey.

1

Saint David (Wales / England)

Saint David (c. 500–589) is the patron saint of Wales. There is not much reliable historical information available about him; the earliest mention of him isn't until the tenth century, in the *Annales Cambriae*, well after his death. Traditionally, he was born at Henvynyw in Cardiganshire and had a prominent role in two synods around the year 569. He was probably bishop of Menevia, a Roman port, later called Saint David's. Saint David is said to have told the Welsh to wear leeks in their hats during a battle against the Saxons, to distinguish themselves from their enemy; since then the leek has been a symbol of Wales. He was canonized in 1120 by Pope Callistus II. In art, Saint David is depicted standing on a hill with a dove on his shoulder.

3

OPTIONAL MEMORIAL OF Saint Katharine Drexel, VIRGIN 🇺🇸

Saint Katherine Drexel (1858–1955), born in Philadelphia, was the second American-born saint to be canonized. She was from the prominent Philadelphia family that founded Drexel University. Katherine's parents were devoutly religious and raised their daughters to be aware of the needs of the poor. While caring for her stepmother who was dying of cancer, she felt she might be called to religious life. In 1887, Katherine and her sisters had a private audience with Pope Leo XIII. She pleaded with the pope for a missionary priest to be sent to the Native Americans, but he asked her to be a missionary instead. This confused her, because she thought she was called to be a contemplative religious. After her father died in 1885, Katherine and her sisters traveled to several Indian reservations and witnessed firsthand the poverty endured there. She began building and supporting schools on the reservations. In 1889, on the advice of her spiritual director, Katherine founded the Sisters of the Blessed Sacrament in Bensalem, Pennsylvania, to work with African American and Native Americans peoples. She was joined by thirteen companions, and they began building elementary and high schools throughout the United States. In 1917, Katherine founded Xavier University to train teachers. Katherine was forced to cut back on her travels after suffering a heart attack in 1935, but she lived for another twenty years, praying for the missions she had founded. Katherine was an early advocate of racial tolerance and was known for her great love of Eucharist, her courage in the face of social injustice, and her selfless service. Saint Katherine was canonized on October 1, 2000, by Blessed Pope John Paul II. She is the patron saint of philanthropists and of racial justice.

4

OPTIONAL MEMORIAL OF Saint Casimir

Saint Casimir (1458–1484) was a prince of Poland and of the Grand Duchy of Lithuania. Born in the royal palace in Kraków, he was heir-apparent to the throne. When the king went to Lithuania, Casimir was left in charge of Poland from 1481 to 1483, and it is said that he ruled with great justice and prudence. Casimir was known for his piety and devotion. Weakened by fasting, he developed a lung disease that was probably tuberculosis and died. Saint Casimir is buried in the cathedral of Vilnius, in Lithuania.

4–12

Miraculous Novena of Grace
Also November 25–December 3

The Novena of Grace is observed from March 4–12, concluding on the day of the canonization of Saint Francis Xavier. It originated in Naples in 1633 with the Jesuit Father Marcello Mastrilli, who was miraculously cured of a serious injury after seeing a vision of Saint Francis Xavier. The devotion has spread far and wide and now is a popular Lenten practice. In some places, a novena of Masses is celebrated as a "preached retreat."

7

MEMORIAL OF Saints Perpetua and Felicity, MARTYRS

Saints Perpetua and Felicity are Christian martyrs who died on March 7, 203. Perpetua was a noblewoman of Carthage in North Africa and Felicity her slave. The account of their imprisonment is thought to have been written by Perpetua herself, one of the first writings by a woman in Church history. The sufferings of the two women were compounded by the fact that Perpetua was a new mother, separated from her unweaned baby, and Felicity was in the last month of pregnancy, anxious about her unborn child. Two deacons bribed the guard and were able to get into the jail, bringing Perpetua's baby with them, and she was able to keep him with her and nurse him. In spite of attempts by her father to persuade her to deny her Christian faith, Perpetua kept her resolve. For refusing to sacrifice to the gods, Perpetua, Felicity, and four companions were condemned to be thrown to the beasts in the games. Because of a law forbidding the execution of pregnant women, Felicity feared that she would be separated from the others, but she gave birth two days before their day of execution. Eventually, a basilica was built in Carthage over the site of their grave; an ancient inscription with their names can still be seen. Saints Felicity and Perpetua are patron saints of mothers, pregnant women, and the city of Carthage.

8

OPTIONAL MEMORIAL OF Saint John of God, RELIGIOUS

Saint John of God (1495–1550) was a Portuguese friar who became a leading religious figure. After a period in the army in Spain, he began to distribute religious books, using the new Gutenberg printing press. At one point, John had an intense religious experience that resulted in temporary insanity. He was thrown into a madhouse, and while there, he realized how badly treated the sick and poor were. Once he recovered, he spent the rest of his life caring for them. In Granada he gathered a circle of disciples around him who felt the same call and founded the Brothers Hospitallers of Saint John of God.

9

OPTIONAL MEMORIAL OF Saint Frances of Rome, RELIGIOUS

Saint Frances (1384–1440) was born in Rome to wealthy parents. Although she wanted to enter a monastery, her parents married her off to Lorenzo Ponziano, commander of the papal troops in Rome. It was a happy marriage that lasted 40 years. Her husband was often away at war, and Frances spent her time praying, visiting the poor and caring for the sick. Eventually, her example inspired other wealthy women to do the same. Frances founded a lay congregation of Benedictine Oblates now known as Oblates of Saint Frances of Rome.

10

Saint John Ogilvie, Priest and Martyr (Scotland)

Saint John Ogilvie (1580–1615) was born to a wealthy Calvinist family in Scotland. His father was a laird, a member of the Scottish gentry. John was educated in Europe in Catholic schools, studying with the Benedictines in Germany and later with the Jesuits in what is now the Czech Republic. In spite of the religious upheavals of the time, he decided to become a Roman Catholic and was received into the

Church in Belgium in 1596, at age seventeen. In 1608, he entered the Jesuits and was ordained in Paris in 1610. John was assigned to serve in Rouen in Normandy (France), but he begged to be sent to Scotland to help the Catholics that remained in and around Glasgow. The Reformation had taken its toll in Scotland, and in 1560, Catholic preaching or catechizing became illegal. John hoped that he would find some Catholic nobles remaining in Glasgow, but he found none and returned to Paris. In 1613, he returned to Scotland disguised as a horse trader and using the name John Watson. He preached and celebrated Mass in secret in the homes of the remaining Catholics. In 1614 he was betrayed and arrested. He was tortured in an attempt to force him to reveal the names of other Catholics, but he did not give in. On March 10, 1615, he was hanged, drawn, and quartered, the punishment for the crime of high treason for refusing to accept the king's authority over the church. On the gallows he said, "If there be here any hidden Roman Catholics, let them pray for me, but the prayers of heretics I will not have." He threw his Rosary beads into the crowd, and legend has it that one of his enemies caught them and subsequently became a Catholic. John Ogilvie was canonized in 1976, the only post-Reformation saint from Scotland.

17

OPTIONAL MEMORIAL OF
Saint Patrick, BISHOP

Saint Patrick (fifth century) was a Roman, born in Britain. At the age of 16, he was kidnapped by Irish raiders and enslaved in Ireland, where he worked as a shepherd. The isolation of his work turned him to prayer. After six years, Patrick managed to escape and returned to Britain. Eventually, he entered the priesthood and returned to Ireland as bishop, doing much missionary work in the north and west. Two of his works survive: his Confessions and a letter. There are many legends about Patrick, including the one in which he banished the snakes from Ireland, but this is probably a metaphor for his triumph over the paganism of the druids.

18

OPTIONAL MEMORIAL OF Saint Cyril of Jerusalem, BISHOP AND DOCTOR OF THE CHURCH

Saint Cyril of Jerusalem (c.315–386), bishop of Jerusalem and Doctor of the Church, is venerated as one of the great theologians of the early Church. Like his contemporaries, he was embroiled in the Arian controversy and was exiled three times for teaching that the Son is fully divine. Cyril is best known for 23 lectures to catechumens, encompassing introductory teachings through post-baptismal mystagogy. From them we learn much about catechetical methods and liturgical practices in the early Church, as well as the development of teaching on the Eucharist: "Since then He Himself declared and said of the Bread, This is My Body, who shall dare to doubt any longer? And since He has Himself affirmed and said, This is My Blood, who shall ever hesitate, saying, that it is not His blood?" (*Catechetical Lecture* 22:1). He was much loved by the people of Jerusalem during his lifetime for his charitable works and generosity—he even sold gifts from the emperor to raise money for the poor. Cyril is one of the Greek fathers of the church and is venerated by Catholics, Anglicans, and the Orthodox alike. He was named a Doctor of the Church by Pope Leo XIII in 1883.

19

SOLEMNITY OF Saint Joseph, Spouse of the Blessed Virgin Mary

Saint Joseph (first century)was the foster father of Jesus, the man entrusted with his care and upbringing. We know that Joseph was a "righteous man" who protected Mary from disgrace after she was found to be pregnant with Jesus upon her return from visiting her cousin Elizabeth (Matthew 1:19). Like the earlier Joseph in Genesis, he received instruction and reassurance from God through dreams. The Gospel gives little information about him, save that he was an artisan who lived in Nazareth, was a descendant of David, and went to Bethlehem for a census, causing Jesus to be born there in fulfillment of the prophecies. When warned in a dream that Jesus was in danger because of the evil intentions of King Herod, Joseph took Jesus and Mary to live in exile in Egypt until he learned that Herod had died (see Matthew 2:12–15). As a result, Jesus was spared the fate of the Holy Innocents. After the account of Jesus's being lost and found in the Temple during a pilgrimage, Joseph is not mentioned again. We can infer that he had died before Jesus began his ministry; he was certainly not alive at the time of the Crucifixion, because he would have been the one to claim Jesus' body, not Joseph of Arimathea. Catholic tradition describes him as dying in the arms of Jesus and Mary, and so he is invoked as the patron saint of a happy death. Because he was a man who worked with his hands, he is the patron saint of workers and especially carpenters. Devotion to Saint Joseph developed rather late, and was especially popularized by Saint Bernardine of Siena during the fifteenth century. In addition to his March celebration, he is also honored on May 1, the optional Memorial of Saint Joseph the worker. He is represented in art holding a carpenter's square or tools, the infant Jesus, or a staff with lilies. Saint Joseph is patron saint of the Universal Church, of fathers, immigrants, and workers, and is venerated as a special patron saint of Vietnam and the Philippines. In Canada, the proper title for this solemnity is Saint Joseph, Husband of the Blessed Virgin Mary, Principal Patron of Canada.

20/21

Vernal Equinox

On two days of the year, one at the beginning of spring and one at the beginning of fall, day and night are each exactly 12 hours long. That's what the word *equinox* means (equal days and equal nights). The word *vernal* means "spring." Today marks the first day of spring in the Northern Hemisphere. From now until the autumnal equinox, days will be longer than nights. The most important date of the Christian liturgical year, the date of Easter, is determined by the vernal equinox. For most Roman Catholic and Protestant Christians, Easter Sunday is the first Sunday after the first full moon after the equinox. That can fall any time between March 22 and April 25. The vernal equinox occurs during Lent. In fact, the word *Lent* is related to the word *lengthen* because during Lent the days lengthen and the nights get shorter. The word *Lent* also is an old word for *springtime*.

23

OPTIONAL MEMORIAL OF Saint Turibius of Mogrovejo, BISHOP

Saint Turibius of Mogrovejo (1538–1606) was born into the Spanish nobility and dedicated his life to bringing Christianity to the native peoples of Peru as the missionary archbishop of Lima. He traveled the whole of his enormous diocese, usually on foot, evangelizing and baptizing as he went. Among those he baptized and confirmed were Saint Rose of Lima and Saint Martin de Porres. Saint Turibius also founded the first seminary in the Western hemisphere and built roads, schools, chapels, hospitals, and convents. He is remembered for his defense of the native peoples against the injustices of the Spanish government.

25

SOLEMNITY OF
the Annunciation of the Lord

Exactly nine months before Christmas, we celebrate the Solemnity of the Annunciation of the Lord, when the angel brought to Mary the amazing news that she would be the Mother of God's Son. On this day, as in Christmas Time, we contemplate the wonder of the Incarnation: in Jesus, God took on our flesh, becoming like us in all things but sin.

This solemnity almost always falls during Lent, and this seems appropriate because it was the Incarnation that made the Passion possible. In becoming one of us, Christ became capable of suffering as we suffer; he made himself vulnerable as we are vulnerable. "Beyond our grasp, he chose to come within our grasp," wrote Saint Leo the Great. "Existing before time began, he began to exist at a moment in time. Lord of the universe, he hid his infinite glory and took the nature of a servant. Incapable of suffering as God, he did not refuse to be a man, capable of suffering. Immortal, he chose to be subject to the laws of death" (Office of Readings, Volume II, p. 1746).

The Annunciation is a Solemnity of the Lord, but it is also a day to give thanks to and for Mary. The Gospel account of the Annunciation in Luke reveals a great wonder: God sought the free consent of a young girl to carry out his plan for us. God asked for help! No wonder so many artists throughout the ages have chosen to depict this moment of decision that changed the world for ever.

APRIL

Month of April

The word *April* means "to open." This is the time of year that leaf and flower buds open. In most northern countries, this is a month of transformation. The day is now longer than the night. Even if the nights are still chilly, the daytime sun is strong and growing stronger. The earth itself seems to take part in the Passover of the Lord.

Month of the Holy Eucharist

During the month of April, we give special honor to the Holy Eucharist. The Eucharist, the Second Vatican Council taught us, is "the source and summit of the christian life" (*Lumen Gentium*, 11). What does that mean? It means that our participation in the Eucharist is the source from which we draw our strength to live as Jesus taught and to serve

Images of Saints in April (L to R): Saint Catherine of Siena (April 29), Saint George (April 23), Blessed Marie-Anne Blondin, Virgin (April 18).

in his name. It is also the summit, the high point of our communal life.

We use the word *Eucharist* to describe our celebration of the Mass. We use the same word when we speak of the Sacrament of Christ's Body and Blood. In this month of the Holy Eucharist, let us participate more fully and actively in the Church's liturgy, our celebration of the Eucharist. And let us take time, too, for quiet adoration in the presence of the Blessed Sacrament, and become more aware of the wondrous way Christ comes to us in the Eucharist.

National Arbor Day

Last Friday in April

J. Sterling Morton, founder of Arbor Day, believed that the people of each generation take the earth as trustees. He was especially convinced of the blessings trees provide, including food, fuel, wildlife habitat, pure air, climate control, soil retention, clean drinking water, beauty, and shade. His conviction lives on in the Arbor Day Foundation, a not-for-profit organization whose mission is to inspire people to plant, nurture, and celebrate trees. In addition to National Arbor Day, individual states have a state Arbor Day determined by the time best for tree planting in that locale. Many ways to celebrate this day are suggested at www.arborday.org, where a guide to identifying trees and many other resources for stewardship of our magnificent leafed heritage can be found.

1

April Fools' Day

The first of April probably became All Fools' Day in 1564. That was the year the French began to use the new Gregorian calendar. A few centuries before that, Christians had moved the start of the year from January 1 to March 25, Annunciation Day. Everyone celebrated the New Year for eight days. On April 1, the festival ended with parties where gifts were exchanged. In 1564, the first of January once again became the first day of the year, but

some people loved the old custom. They didn't give up their New Year's parties on April 1. They were called "April fools." Nowadays in France an April fool is called a *poisson d'avril*, an "April fish." Young fish that appear in streams around this time of year are more easily caught than older, cagier fish. French shops sell chocolates shaped like fish for the occasion. People try to pin paper fish on each other's backs as a joke. In some places in England, an April fool is called a "noddy." In Scotland on this day, don't let anyone send you out searching for hen's teeth or pigeon milk, or you'll be called a "gowk"—a cuckoo!

2

OPTIONAL MEMORIAL OF Saint Francis of Paola, HERMIT

Although Saint Francis of Paola (1416–1507) was attracted to the Franciscan friars, he longed for a more contemplative life grounded in solitude and asceticism. Building upon the Franciscan tradition, he founded the hermits of Brother Francis of Assisi, which eventually became known as the Minim Friars, meaning "the least" of all God's servants. The community had a strong devotion to the five wounds of Christ and the Virgin Mary. Due to his reputation for holiness and the miraculous, King Louis XI of France requested Saint Francis's spiritual guidance as he was preparing for death. Saint Francis spent the last 25 years of his life advising kings and restoring peace between France and its neighboring countries. Many miracles connected to the sea have been attributed to him; therefore, he is the patron saint of navigators and naval officers.

4

OPTIONAL MEMORIAL OF
Saint Isidore, BISHOP AND DOCTOR OF THE CHURCH

What do an archbishop of Seville, avid writer, systematic and liturgical theologian, evangelizer to the skeptic, minister to the poor, and establisher of schools have in common? They encapsulate the life and work of Saint Isidore of Seville (c. 565–636). He is credited with organizing the Church of Spain through various councils and synods. His theology of the Trinity and Incarnation were the basis for a Creed that was approved at the Fourth Council of Toledo (633 AD). Along with these two noteworthy accomplishments, he also revised the Mozarabic Rite—the accepted liturgy of Spain—and opened cathedral schools for the training of priests. Saint Isidore was named a Doctor of the Church due to his extensive writing, including doctrinal summaries, etymological studies, and rules for religious communities.

Saint Benedict the Black, the African, or the Moor

Also called "The Moor," Saint Benedict the Black was born in 1526 to slaves who were brought to Sicily and later converted to Christianity. He was freed from slavery as a reward to his parents for their service. Benedict was uneducated and illiterate and worked at a series of menial jobs, but he gave his meager wages to the poor and sick. When he was twenty-one, he was publicly insulted for his race. The superior of a local group of Franciscans hermits noted his dignity and patience in the face of this indignity, and they invited Benedict to join their community. Eventually, he became their leader. In 1564, Pope Pius IV ordered the hermits to attach themselves to an established community, and Benedict moved to Palermo to join the Friary of Saint Mary. Initially he served as cook, but his holiness was soon recognized. In spite of the fact that he was an illiterate lay brother, he was elected guardian (the title Franciscans give to their superiors) and later he was given charge of training new members as the novice master. Benedict was able to reform the friary by instituting strict observance of the *Rule of Saint Francis*. He had a reputation for his intuitive understanding of theology and the Scriptures—in spite of his lack of education—and was known as a wise spiritual counselor and healer of the sick. He died in 1589 at the age of 65, and was canonized in 1807. Benedict is a patron saint of African Americans.

5

OPTIONAL MEMORIAL OF
Saint Vincent Ferrer, PRIEST

Saint Vincent Ferrer was born around 1350, the son of an English immigrant to Spain. He entered the Order of Preachers (Dominicans) at the age of 18, and was eventually sent to study theology, earning a doctorate at Lleida. Vincent traveled widely, preaching the Gospel as he went. The saints are human and prone to mistakes as anyone, and, unfortunately, Vincent is an example: he is said to have been responsible for the forced conversion of many Spanish Jews to Catholicism. He was also a supporter of the Avignon pope, Benedict XIII, during the Great Schism, a period during which three men each claimed to be the "true" pope. Eventually, after Benedict did nothing to end the schism, Vincent withdrew his support. Vincent Ferrer died on April 5, 1419 in Brittany (France) and is buried in Vannes Cathedral. He was an eloquent speaker, and he lived a life of great asceticism and imposed severe penances on himself such as sleeping on the floor, and fasting continuously. Vincent firmly believed that the end times were near and that he had been sent to prepare humanity. Known as the "Angel of the Apocalypse," he is the patron saint of construction workers because of his work to "build" the Church.

7

MEMORIAL OF Saint John Baptist de la Salle, PRIEST

Most people have never heard of Saint John Baptist de la Salle (1651–1719) and yet have been profoundly shaped by his educational methodology. He established standard educational practices that we take for granted; for example, teaching a group of individuals simultaneously rather than private tutoring, instructing in the vernacular instead of Latin, and giving reports of student progress. Moved by pity for poor children in France, Saint John gave away his wealth to establish a religious institute called the Institute of the Brothers of the Christian Schools. The purpose of the institute was to teach the poor so they could realize their innate dignity as children of God and rise above their impoverished circumstances. The brothers developed "charity schools" based on the philosophy that ". . . not only is God so good as to have created us, but God desires all of us to come to the knowledge of the truth" (quoted on the website of the Christian Brothers University). Today, Saint John Baptist de la Salle's brothers serve in all parts of the world as teachers, social workers, counselors, and retreat facilitators. They are not to be confused with the Congregation of Christian Brothers or Irish Christian Brothers, who were founded in Cork by Blessed Edmund Rice in 1808.

11

MEMORIAL OF Saint Stanislaus, BISHOP AND MARTYR

Noted for his compassionate concern for the poor and wise counsel, Saint Stanislaus (c. 1030–1079) was appointed bishop of Krakow. His consecration as bishop was met with great joy on the part of the people. While serving as bishop he spoke out against King Boleslaus, an unjust and cruel man who incited fear in the people of Poland. Saint Stanislaus, outraged by the oppressive behavior of the monarch, declared that an unjust king has no place in the Church. In response, the king defamed his reputation, eventually ordering guards to kill him, but they refused. The king took matters into his own hands by stabbing him with a sword. Saint Stanislaus, the martyr, is the patron saint of Poland and the city of Krakow.

13

OPTIONAL MEMORIAL OF Saint Martin I, POPE AND MARTYR

Saint Martin I was a Roman of noble birth, and had a reputation for intelligence, learning, and charity. He fought against the Monothelite heresy, which claimed that Jesus had two natures—human and divine—but only one will. At that time, the government was deeply involved in theological controversies. If the Church was torn by doctrinal conflicts, the emperors felt it threatened public order. They sought peace at all costs, even sacrificing orthodoxy. Martin was tried by Emperor Constans II in Constantinople, and was imprisoned and exiled. He died from mistreatment at the hands of fellow Christians in 655.

17

Optional Memorial of Blessed Kateri Tekakwitha 🍁

Blessed Kateri Tekakwitha (c. 1656–1680), daughter of a Mohawk warrior and Catholic Algonquin woman, was born in a Mohawk fortress near Auriesville, New York. Her parents and brother died in a small-pox epidemic, and she was left with scars and weakened eyesight. Kateri's mother had made an impression on her, and she was baptized on Easter Sunday in 1676. Her conversion to Christianity caused her relatives to mistreat her, and so Kateri fled to a community of Native American Christians at Kahnawake (or Caughnawaga), Quebec. Kateri died at 24. She is called "Lily of the Mohawks," beatified by John Paul II in 1980, the first Native American to be so honored.

Venerable Maria Kaupas 🇺🇸

Born in Lithuania, Venerable Maria Kaupas (1880–1940) came to the United States to serve as a house-keeper for her brother, Reverend Anthony Kaupas. During her stay, she felt called to an apostolic form of religious life (religious who live actively in the world). She intended to enter an existing religious community of sisters. However, the American Lithuanian clergy urged her to found a new congregation of women to provide a Catholic education to the young that preserved Lithuanian culture. The new congregation, the Sisters of Saint Casimir, began in Pennsylvania, but eventually built their Motherhouse in Chicago due to a large concentration of Lithuanian immigrants and the central location of the city. Along with staffing parochial schools throughout the United States, Maria had many sisters trained to be nurses and hospital administrators to meet a growing healthcare need. Kaupas died on this date in 1940. Her cause for beatification is still pending.

18

Optional Memorial of Blessed Marie-Anne Blondin, Virgin

Born in 1809, Esther Blondin was a French Canadian who learned from the Sisters of Notre Dame to read and write—at age 22. Although she wanted to join their community, her health prohibited it. As a teacher in a parochial school, she realized that high rates of illiteracy were due to a Church ruling that allowed girls to be taught only by women and boys only by men. She founded an order of religious sisters to offset illiteracy and instruct boys and girls together, a new idea for the time.

Her order was called the Congregation of the Sisters of Saint Anne, and she took the name Marie-Anne. However, she faced stiff opposition from their chaplain, who prevented her from taking any administrative position. She spent 32 years doing the laundry, convinced that "there is more happiness in forgiving than in revenge."

Venerable Cornelia Connelly 🇺🇸

Venerable Cornelia Connelly (1809–1879), born in Philadelphia, converted to the Catholic faith while she was married to an Episcopalian priest. The tragic death of two children led to a lifelong devotion to Our Lady of Sorrows. After her husband converted to Catholicism, he renounced the marriage to become a Catholic priest. Rising from the depths of despair, Venerable Cornelia founded the Society of the Holy Child Jesus, a group of religious sisters, to educate mill girls and poor children. She established day and night schools as well as taught Sunday classes about the core tenets of the Catholic faith. Today, the Society of the Holy Child Jesus is active in fourteen countries, remaining devoted to the teaching of young women. She died on April 18. Connelly's cause for beatification is still pending.

21

OPTIONAL MEMORIAL OF
Saint Anselm, BISHOP AND
DOCTOR OF THE CHURCH

Saint Anselm was born around the year 1033 in Aosta, then part of the Kingdom of Burgundy, today part of Piedmont in the Italian Alps. Hearing of the reputation of his countryman, Lanfranc, who was prior of the Benedictine abbey of Bec in Normandy, Anselm entered the monastery there at the age of twenty-seven. When Lanfranc was named abbot of Caen, Anselm succeeded him as prior of Bec, and fifteen years later in 1079, he became abbot. In 1070, Anselm's mentor Lanfranc was made archbishop of Canterbury in England, and when he died in 1109, William II of England seized the lands and revenues of the archdiocese and left the office of archbishop empty (at this time, bishops were appointed by kings). Finally in 1093, public pressure forced William to appoint Anselm archbishop of Canterbury. Anselm's term as archbishop was not easy. He was forced into exile twice because of his support of the Gregorian Reform, which tried to do away with lay investiture, the power of secular authority to appoint bishops. Anselm is a Doctor of the Church and is called the Father of Scholasticism for his works of theology, especially the *Proslogion*, an argument for the existence of God based on reason and his treatise, *Why God Became Man*, on the saving action of the Incarnation. He is also celebrated in the Anglican and Lutheran Church.

22

Earth Day 🇺🇸

Perhaps the most important thing the astronauts on the first trip to the moon did was bring back photos of Earth. Until that time, most people probably thought of their planet as a larger version of a globe, with every country a different color edged by visible borders.

In the historic 1969 photos we earthlings saw a very different picture. The earth was mostly a vast blue ocean misted with clouds. No borders between nations could be seen on the land masses. Citizens of Earth were reminded that we all share the same home.

Just at the time the photographs appeared in magazines, scientists found out that almost every creature in Lake Erie had been killed by pollution. This discovery made many people aware of the dangers we humans cause ourselves and the creatures who share our planet, by the ways we treat our air, farmland, and water. The first Earth Day was held in 1970, and people came together all over the United States to show their concern.

Since then new laws and a new organization, the Environmental Protection Agency, have been created in the United States. Lake Erie has been cleaned. Some dangerous pesticides have been banned from use for growing fruits and vegetables. Air pollution from lead, a serious problem not long ago, has all but disappeared. That's the good news.

But we've found new reasons for concern, too. Around the world, millions of square miles of tropical rain forest are being burned. Pollution from factories and automobiles is killing northern forests. Pollution also may be causing holes to open up in the protective ozone layer of the earth's atmosphere.

The problem is global. Air pollution created in the United States doesn't stop at the borders. It drifts into Canada. It travels to Europe. Eventually it circles the world. We need to act as united citizens of the planet to protect the environment. In 1992, 178 world leaders met in the city of Rio de Janeiro in Brazil to discuss environmental concerns. This meeting was called the Earth Summit. This was the largest gathering of leaders ever held. It reflected growing hope that people everywhere might begin to work together.

During Easter Time, we Christians celebrate a reverence for all life. In the First Reading of the Easter Vigil, we hear how God created the earth and called it good. Today we pray that our children's children will still be able to describe it that way.

23

OPTIONAL MEMORIAL OF
Saint George, MARTYR

Saint George (c. + 303) was a soldier from Syria who was in the Guard of Emperor Diocletian. Although historians feel that he did, in fact, exist, the details of his life have been obscured by the many legends that grew up around him. *The Golden Legend*, a thirteenth-century collection of saints' stories, relates the account of George slaying a dragon. He is honored by Catholics, Anglicans, Lutherans, the Orthodox, and even adherents of Islam. Saint George is shown in art as a soldier on a white horse slaying a dragon, while carrying a white shield with a red cross. This red cross on a white background is known as Saint George's Cross and is on the flags of several countries, including England and Greece.

OPTIONAL MEMORIAL OF Saint Adalbert, BISHOP AND MARTYR

Saint Adalbert (c. 959–997) came from a wealthy Czech family. He became bishop of Prague before the age of thirty, but resigned because paganism persisted among the Christians there. Adalbert went to Rome and became a Benedictine monk, but in 993, after only four years, the pope sent him back to Prague to resume his role as bishop. He founded the first monastery in the Czech region, but during an uprising, all of his brothers were murdered, and Adalbert had to flee Prague. Adalbert then went to evangelize in Hungary and Poland, where he was welcomed by the rulers. He then went to Prussia where, following the custom of Christian missionaries, he chopped down the sacred oak trees to show the people that the trees were not supernatural. For this he was executed in April, 997. He is honored by both the Catholic and Orthodox Churches and is a patron saint of Bohemia, Poland, and Prussia.

24

OPTIONAL MEMORIAL OF
Saint Fidelis of Sigmaringen,
PRIEST AND MARTYR

Saint Fidelis of Sigmaringen (1578–1622) was a German Capuchin. He studied at the University of Freiburg, and after finishing he taught philosophy, but in spite of his learning, he was known for his penitential practices, prayerfulness, and humility. In 1612, at the age of thirty-five, he joined the Capuchins and took the name Fidelis, which means "faithful." Fidelis was known for his charity and prayer, and when he became superior of a Capuchin friary, many in the local area returned to Catholicism as result of his influence. At the behest of the Habsburgs, who ruled parts of Europe at the time, Fidelis went to the north of France to preach to the people who had left the Church. Although he was protected by Austrian soldiers, he was captured by Calvinists, who murdered him when he refused to renounce his faith.

25

FEAST OF Saint Mark,
EVANGELIST

Saint Mark (first century) is the traditional author of the Gospel account that bears his name. Although he has been identified with John Mark and Mark, the cousin of Barnabas, the earliest tradition sees him as a distinct individual, one of the seventy disciples sent by Jesus to preach before the Crucifixion. According to Hippolytus, a writer of the second to third century, he had such difficulty with Jesus' teaching on the Eucharist that he left but was later brought back by Saint Peter. Subsequently, he traveled with Peter and worked as his interpreter, wrote the Gospel based on Peter's preaching, and became bishop of Alexandria in Egypt. The Coptic Church claims him as their first bishop and parts of their liturgy are attributed to him. Their tradition says that he was martyred at Alexandria in 68 AD.

Anzac Day (Australia / New Zealand)

The word *Anzac* stands for Australian and New Zealand Army Corps. On this day, Australians and New Zealanders express their hopes for enduring peace as they remember those who died in war. Anzac troops in World War I experienced massive losses, especially at Gallipoli (in modern-day Turkey). Since then many more lives have been lost in wars, regional conflicts, and peacekeeping missions.

Wreath-laying services and parades happen everywhere today, but the main events take place at the Australian War Memorial in Canberra. Charles Bean, Australian war correspondent who was wounded himself, founded the Memorial. He specified that war must not be glorified there, nor victory boasted about, because "those who have fought in wars are generally strongest in their desire to prevent war."

26

OPTIONAL MEMORIAL OF Our Lady of Good Counsel 🍁

Today in Canada the Blessed Virgin Mary is honored under the title Our Lady of Good Counsel. In this well-loved image, Mary embraces the child Jesus, who has his arm around her neck. She seems to be leaning down to hear what the Child Jesus has to say—to listen to his words of "good counsel." The original image is found in Genazzano, near Rome, but the devotion has spread all over the world. Many schools, colleges, and parishes are dedicated to Our Lady under this title, and Pope Pius XII was devoted to Our Lady of Good Counsel. Our Lady of Good Counsel, pray for us, and for the people of Canada.

28

OPTIONAL MEMORIAL OF Saint Peter Chanel, PRIEST AND MARTYR

Saint Peter Chanel (1803–1841) was born in France and ordained in 1827, when he was twenty-four years old. After reading letters of missionaries, the desire to evangelize grew, and in 1831 he entered the newly founded Society of Mary (Marists). After the new order was approved by Pope Gregory XVI, they were asked to send missionaries to the South Pacific region. Chanel left France in 1836, the superior of a group of Marists. They traveled to the Canary Islands and Tahiti, and Peter ended up at Futuna. The local king was threatened by the missionaries, and when his son requested Baptism, he arranged for Peter's murder. Peter Chanel is the patron saint of Oceania, the area in the South West Pacific that encompasses Australia, New Zealand, and the islands of Polynesia, Melanesia, and Micronesia.

OPTIONAL MEMORIAL OF Saint Louis Grignion de Montfort, PRIEST

Saint Louis Grignion de Montfort (1673–1716) was born in Britanny. He developed his devotion to the Blessed Virgin Mary when young, and eventually, a benefactor paid his way through the famous seminary of Saint-Sulpice in Paris. After his ordination in 1700, he discerned the need for an order of priests dedicated to Mary. Eventually, this group became the Company of Mary and an order of women, the Daughters of Wisdom. Saint Louis Marie is thought of as a founder of the area of theology known as Mariology, and is famous for his books, *True Devotion of Mary*, the *Secret of Mary*, and the *Secret of the Rosary*. His preaching on the mercy of God served as a powerful antidote to Jansenism, a Calvinist-influenced movement that was prevalent at the time. Louis Marie de Montfort wore himself out with preaching and died in 1716, only sixteen years after his ordination.

29

MEMORIAL OF Saint Catherine of Siena, VIRGIN AND DOCTOR OF THE CHURCH

Saint Catherine of Siena (1347–1380) was a Dominican tertiary (lay member) and mystic, the twenty-fourth of twenty-five children. In spite of family opposition, she dedicated herself to Christ at a very young age and at the age of sixteen, she withdrew from her family to lead a life of intense prayer. When she emerged, she began to dedicate herself to care of the sick and poor. Her joyful spirit attracted a number of followers. After a series of mystical experiences, Catherine felt compelled to write letters to those in secular and Church authority, which she dictated to her friend, the Dominican Raymond of Capua. Her influence became so great that papal legates consulted her. At this time, the popes had moved their residence from Rome to Avignon, France. Catherine begged Gregory XI to return to Rome, which he did in 1377. Saint Catherine died in 1380 at the age of thirty-three, leaving behind her writings, the *Dialogue on Divine Providence*, letters, and prayers. She is represented in art holding a lily and wearing the habit of a Dominican tertiary, and is the patron saint of Europe and Italy. In 1970, Pope Paul VI made her a Doctor of the Church, one of the first women, along with Teresa of Avila, to be so honored.

30

OPTIONAL MEMORIAL OF Saint Pius V, POPE

Saint Pius V (1504–1572) was pope immediately following the Council of Trent (1545–1563). He was a reformer who saw the laxness that had overtaken the Church, and he fought to overcome it by paring down the papal court and enforcing the decrees of Trent. He is best remembered for promulgating the 1570 edition of *The Roman Missal*, which was used until the liturgical reforms of the Second Vatican Council, and for reforming the Liturgy of the Hours. He was a Dominican friar, and after he was elected to the papacy, he continued to wear his white habit. Since then, it has been customary for the pope to wear a white cassock.

OPTIONAL MEMORIAL OF Blessed Marie of the Incarnation, RELIGIOUS 🍁

Blessed Marie of the Incarnation (1599–1672), was born in Tours, France. She married and bore a son, and when her husband died, she devoted herself to religion and entered the Ursulines in 1620, after arranging for the care of her son. Around 1638, Marie experienced visions in which she was instructed to go to Canada and found a convent, and in 1639, she set off with two other nuns, landing at Quebec in August and settling in the section of the city that is today called Lower Town. She studied with the Jesuits to learn the languages of the Native Americans, becoming so proficient that she wrote dictionaries in Algonquin and Iroquois, as well as a catechism in Iroquois. She spent the last thirty-three years of her life teaching and catechizing. Marie of the Incarnation died in Quebec in 1672 and was beatified by Pope John Paul II in 1980. Her numerous letters are an indispensable resource for Canadian colonial history.

MAY

Month of May

The fifth month is named after the goddess Maia. She is the oldest of the Pleiades (PLEE-ih-dees), the seven sisters. According to legend, the Pleiades were placed in the sky to shine as a beautiful cluster of tiny stars. The word *mai* is also a northern European word that means fresh green growth. In England, hawthorn blossoms are called "may." Originally, maypoles were small trees that had the lower branches chopped off. They were hung with ribbons and gifts and given to newlyweds as a wish for a life filled with blessings. In some places they were set up in the centers of towns to celebrate Easter or May Day or Midsummer Day, June 24. Many central European towns continue to keep this custom.

Images of Saints in May (L to R): Saint Matthias (May 14), Our Lady of Fatima (May 13), Saint Rita of Cascia (May 22).

Month of Our Lady

May is Mary's Month. Gerard Manley Hopkins wondered about this in a lovely poem called "The May Magnificat." "May is Mary's month, and I / Muse at that and wonder why . . . . the Lady Month, May, / Why fasten that upon her, / With a feasting in her honor?" he asked. Hopkins speculates that it is the springtime explosion of new life, in birds and flowers, that make May the right month for Mary. "This ecstasy all through mothering earth / Tells Mary her mirth till Christ's birth."

Whatever the reason, May is a special time of prayer to the Blessed Virgin Mary. This is also Easter Time, so we join with Mary in rejoicing in Christ's Resurrection from the dead. We can honor Mary in this month by praying the Rosary or another Marian devotion and by participating in Mass on the Feast of the Visitation, which concludes the month on May 31. It's also a good time for quiet reflection on the seven joys of Mary, the traditional counterpart to her seven sorrows. The joys of Mary are the the Annunciation, the birth of Jesus, the adoration of the Magi, the Resurrection, the Ascension of Jesus into heaven, the descent of the Holy Spirit at Pentecost, and Mary's coronation as Queen of Heaven.

National Day of Prayer
First Thursday of May

As the First Continental Congress worked to put together a new nation, residents of the 13 colonies were asked to spend a day in prayer for God's guidance. Amidst the turmoil of the Civil War, President Abraham Lincoln asked all citizens of the country to spend a day in fasting and prayer to restore unity. Congress established an annual national day of prayer in 1952 and in 1988 specified that the first Thursday of every May would be the official date for this observance. This day serves as a reminder of the multiplicity of faiths and the great diversity of religious expression in the United States of America. It can be an opportunity to thank God for the many blessings we enjoy as citizens of this country and to ask that all the peoples of the earth be gifted with the freedoms so familiar to us.

The National Day of Prayer is an opportunity for us to give thanks for the freedom of religion we enjoy, and to remember our founding fathers and mothers, who always sought the wisdom of God when faced with critical decisions. Today, let us come humbly come before God, to seeking his guidance for our leaders, and to ask him to pour out his grace upon us as a people. In God, we trust.

Mother's Day
Second Sunday in May

In the Middle Ages, many people had to travel far from home to earn a living. They became servants where work was available or they learned a trade from someone who was willing to teach them. These people were given a special holiday every year. It came on the Fourth Sunday of Lent, on *Laetare* ("Rejoice") *Sunday*. In the liturgy on this day, the city of Jerusalem is called our mother. We rejoice because when Easter arrives, we will be reunited with mother Jerusalem. And so, *Laetare Sunday* came to be called Mothering Sunday. On this day people would go home to see their mothers. Many family reunions were held. People were even excused from the Lenten fast on that day.

The Mother's Day we have in May was started in the early twentieth century by an American woman named Anna Jarvis. After her mother died, she suggested that a memorial service be held in church to honor all mothers. The first such service was held in a Philadelphia church in 1908. Those who attended were asked to wear white carnations in memory of their mothers. People were so taken with the observance of such a day that in 1914 Congress proclaimed the second Sunday in May as Mother's Day. Other countries adopted the idea. In England, the old custom of Mothering Sunday in Lent was restored. Mother's Day is observed in many other countries, but not always on the same day.

A mother provides life and nourishment. On this day we remember all who are examples of a mother's love. This holiday has been adopted by other countries including Canada. The dates for Mother's Day vary in other countries.

Victoria Day

Monday before or on May 25

This Canadian national holiday is a remembrance of the birthday of the queen who ruled the longest of any British monarch. Queen Victoria's reign lasted 60 years. Her subjects in Canada and other countries became so used to celebrating her birthday that they continued the custom even after she died. They began to use this day to tell about the deeds of British heroes. Victoria's actual date of birth is May 24, 1819. In 1952, the celebration was moved to the Monday on or before that date. In Canada, the birthday of Queen Elizabeth II is also observed on Victoria Day, although her actual birth date is April 21.

Memorial Day

Last Monday in May

In 1868, a national day was held to remember the dead of the Civil War and to pray for reconciliation. The idea had come from Southern women who visited battlefields in late spring to decorate the graves. Some people still call Memorial Day by its original name, "Decoration Day." Memorial Day now honors all United States citizens who died in war. Every city and town has its war dead. Often they are remembered with a parade to a cemetery or to a war memorial. With bouquets strewn over the waters, coastal cities honor those who died at sea. Gettysburg, Pennsylvania, is the site of a Civil War battle where many thousands died. Today school children in that town will decorate the tombs of soldiers who could not be identified after their deaths. A service will be held at the Vietnam War Memorial in Washington, D.C. In recent years Congress has proclaimed this as a day when the nation should strive for peace. As we honor those who have died, we look forward to the day when we will be willing to settle our disagreements without war. As Christians, we also pray today for all the innocent victims of war. Across the world, millions of people are homeless because their countries are ravaged by fighting. Those people are called refugees. Many of them are orphaned children. Some are hungry. All are suffering.

A day of sorrow and mourning is hard to keep. We probably would rather celebrate the beginning of summer. But Memorial Day can bring with it much needed sorrow and forgiveness and peacemaking.

1

OPTIONAL MEMORIAL OF
Saint Joseph THE WORKER

The optional Memorial of Saint Joseph the Worker is a relatively new addition to the calendar. It was introduced by Pope Pius XII in 1955, as an alternative to secular May Day celebrations of the worker, which originated in Communist countries and which did more to promote Communist propaganda than to promote the worker. Pope Pius XII urged workers to look to Saint Joseph the carpenter and to see the dignity inherent in human labor, which could become a source of holiness. The prayers for today from *The Roman Missal* call Joseph our "wise and faithful servant" who is our patron as we "complete the works [God] set us to do."

Please see page 56 for a biography of Saint Joseph.

May Day

In Southampton, England, a choir of schoolboys will greet the sun on May Day morning by "singing in the May." In other parts of Britain, people in small villages used to rise before dawn to "bring in the May." Going out to the countryside, they gathered hawthorn blossoms and other flowers. As the sun rose, they decked doors and windows with the blooms. People of every social class, even kings and queens, joined together in this joyful work. In northern France, people gather fragrant lilies of the valley today. In Belgium, parades and street fairs are held. In Austria and Switzerland, this is a time to pray for good crops. In centuries past, just about every European village built its own maypole in the town square. Dancing around the maypole is a May Day tradition still observed in some towns in the United States of America. Dancers hold streamers that hang from the top of a wreath on the pole. As they circle around the pole they weave the ribbons into patterns under, over, and around the maypole. When they change directions, the streamers untangle again and blow free in a great jumble. Ancient Celts and Romans held spring festivals on the first of May. The custom of crowning a May queen was borrowed from the Roman festival of Flora, the goddess of spring. To counteract those leftover pagan ways, the Church began to celebrate May as the month of Mary, the mother of God. One reason we honor Mary in Easter Time is that she is an image of the Church. We remember how, after Jesus ascended into heaven, Mary gathered with the disciples in the Upper Room to await the coming of the Holy Spirit. This month, in many parishes, she is crowned *Regina Caeli*, the Queen of Heaven. In many countries May Day is Labor Day, a day to honor workers.

2

MEMORIAL OF
Saint Athanasius, BISHOP
AND DOCTOR OF THE CHURCH

Saint Athanasius (295–373), bishop of Alexandria and Doctor of the Church, contributed immensely to the development of doctrine and spirituality. He defended the teaching of the First Council of Nicaea (325 AD) that Jesus was both fully human and fully divine. The Arians, who taught that Jesus was not divine, unleashed a series of attacks upon Athanasius, resulting in exile not just once, but five times in his life, amounting to 17 years out of the 45 he was bishop. During one of these exiles, he wrote the influential biography of the renowned hermit and monk Saint Anthony of Egypt. This spiritual classic, entitled *Life of Antony*, has been and continues to be read by people longing to remove worldly distractions that keep them from mystical union with God. He is also noted for two other works: *On the Incarnation* and *Discourses against the Arians*. Many titles have been

bestowed upon him, including defender of faith, champion of orthodoxy, mystical theologian, and spiritual master. Athanasius is venerated by the Eastern Orthodox as well as Western Christians, and is especially revered by the Coptic (Egyptian) Orthodox.

3

FEAST OF Saints Philip and James, APOSTLES

Saint Philip (first century) was a native of Bethsaida, and was among John the Baptist's followers who saw John point out Jesus as the Lamb of God. He is most prominent in the Gospel according to John. It was Philip who asked Jesus to "show us the Father, and we will be satisfied," to which Jesus replied, "Whoever has seen me has seen the Father" (John 14:8–9). Legends of Philip have him preaching in Greece, Phrygia, and Syria along with Bartholomew. Philip enraged the proconsul by converting his wife to Christianity and was crucified upside-down in 54 AD. A gnostic gospel found at Nag Hammadi is attributed to him, but there is no evidence it was actually written by him. Philip is shown in art with two loaves or a basket filled with bread, because of his role in the story of the feeding of the five thousand (see John 6:5–7).

The Saint James (first century) who is celebrated today is "James the Less," described in the Gospel as the "brother of the Lord," which at that time could also mean "cousin," and in Acts of the Apostles 15 as the leader of the Church at Jerusalem. He is usually thought to be the same person as James the son of Alpheus and James the Just. He was called to be a disciple along with his brother, Jude. James appears in the lists of the Apostles, but he becomes most prominent after the Ascension, when he was made the first bishop of Jerusalem. He, along with Peter and John, authorized Paul's mission to the Gentiles. The Church historian, Eusebius, records that James was martyred by being stoned and then thrown from the highest point of the Temple in Jerusalem.

Saints Philip and James are celebrated on the same day in honor of the anniversary of the dedication of the church dedicated to them in Rome (now called the Church of the Twelve Apostles).

Santacruzan (Philippines)

Santacruzan ("Holy Cross") is a popular religious festival in the Philippines celebrating the discovery of the true Cross by Saint Helena, mother of the Emperor Constantine, an event traditionally commemorated on May 3. With its floats adorned with flowers, Santacruzan is one of the most colorful festivals in the Philippines. Young women are chosen to represent the various characters in the parade, including great women of faith as well as representations of the cardinal virtues and of the Blessed Virgin Mary under several of her different titles. The high point of the parade is the appearance of the *Reyna Elena*, or Saint Helena, accompanied by a small boy, the *Prinsipe Constantino*, representing her son Constantine. The great procession is accompanied by crowds of the faithful carrying lit candles, reciting the Rosary, or singing songs of praise.

Our Lady of Tsuwano (Japan)

Between 1868 and 1870, the rulers of Japan were determined to destroy Christianity in the islands by scattering Christians and forcing believers to recant their faith. In Tsuwano, 153 Christians were imprisoned and tortured. Unable to endure the tortures that were inflicted on them, many renounced their faith, but thirty-six died for Christ. Maria Seido, the Chapel of Our Lady, was built in 1948 to commemorate the sacrifice of these martyrs. Every year on this day, a procession starting from Tsuwano winds toward Maria Seido along the tree-lined Jujika-no-Michi (Road of the Cross).

Mary, Queen of Poland

According to legend, the dark-hued image was painted by Saint Luke the Evangelist on wood from a table built by Jesus and Joseph in their work as carpenters. The precise origins of the image are unknown, but it likely dates to the seventh century and was first venerated in Poland in 1382 at Jasna Gora Monastery. In 1655, the Swedes invaded Poland. For forty days, Swedish troops surrounded the monastery, while the monks prayed to the Virgin. The siege failed, and in gratitude, the Polish monarch, Jan Kazimierz, dedicated his throne and his country to "the Virgin Mary, Queen of Poland." The two slashes on Mary's right cheek were added to commemorate an attack made on the painting, which it miraculously survived.

Devotion to the Black Madonna has continued to grow over the centuries; this image of Mary was a favorite of Blessed Pope John Paul II.

4

OPTIONAL MEMORIAL OF
Blessed Marie-Léonie Paradis, VIRGIN 🍁

Elodie (Marie-Léonie) Paradis was born in 1840 in the village of L'Acadie in the province of Quebec, Canada. Her parents were poor, but they wanted their daughter to have a good education, so they sent her to a boarding school run by the Sisters of Notre Dame. Elodie was so inspired by religious life that she asked to join the Sisters of the Holy Cross in 1854 and took the name Marie-Léonie. In spite of her youth and poor health, she was accepted by the founder, Basile Moreau, at the age of fourteen. At first her parents were against it, but they later accepted it, and she made her vows in 1857. After working in Canada as a teacher, she was sent to New York and later transferred to the Province of Notre Dame,

Indiana. When the Holy Cross sisters dropped their ministry of serving priests by managing their households, Sister Léonie felt that the work to which she was called was no longer possible there. In 1880, under the direction of Father Camille Lefebvre, Blessed Marie-Léonie founded a new religious order, the Institute of the Little Sisters of the Holy Family, dedicated to assisting priests and seminarians by serving as housekeepers, and in 1896, the new order gained official recognition. In spite of poor health, which she suffered throughout her life, Blessed Marie-Léonie spent her life in service to her sisters and the people of God, finishing the *Rule* for her order just a few hours before she passed away on May 3, 1912 at the age of seventy-one in Nebraska. Since her death, her order has spread throughout Canada, the United States, Rome, Honduras, and Guatamala. She was beatified by Pope John Paul II on September 11, 1984.

Beatified Martyrs of England and Wales

On this day, the Church honors the men and women of England and Wales who gave their lives for their Catholic faith (1535–1680). The holy people remembered today include eighty-five blesseds, beatified by Blessed Pope John Paul II in 1987, along with forty saints, martyrs of England and Wales canonized by Pope Paul VI in 1970. These holy men and women—priests and religious, lay men and women, married and unmarried, old and young—gave their lives between 1535 and 1679, a period of great political and religious turmoil in England. At times it was considered an act of treason to participate in Mass, to acknowledge the authority of the pope, or even to possess a Rosary or other pious articles. The saints and blesseds are from every rank of life. Saint Margaret Clitherow (1556–1586) was a young wife and mother who was arrested for harboring priests. Saint Robert Southwell (1561–1595) was a Jesuit priest and a gifted poet who ministered secretly to Catholic families. Saint Philip Howard (1557–1595) was the Earl

of Arundel and died in the Tower after refusing to relinquish his faith. Martyrs of England and Wales, pray for us.

5

Saint Asaph, Bishop (Wales)

Saint Asaph is a familiar name for Catholics of Wales. Asaph was said to be the grandson of a king (there was more than one in sixth-century Wales!). As a young boy, Asaph entered a monastery at Llanelwy established by Saint Kentigern. Saint Kentigern used to pray standing in the ice-cold waters of a nearby stream. One day he was so cold he asked young Asaph to fetch some coals to warm him. Not having anything to carry the coals in, the young boy brought them back in his apron. Saint Kentigern marveled that neither the boy nor his clothes were burned, and he interpreted this wonder as a sign of the boy's sanctity. Asaph later became the second bishop of the diocese, which is now named in his honor.

In art Saint Asaph is usually shown as a bishop, with miter and pastoral staff, holding a book—but sometimes he appears as a young monk holding a live coal!

Cinco de Mayo (Mexico)

On May 5, 1862, greatly outnumbered Mexican soldiers repelled invading French troops in the Mexican state of Puebla, leading to the eventual withdrawal of French forces from Mexican soil. The event became known as Cinco de Mayo ("fifth of May" in English). People sometimes confuse this day with Mexican Independence Day, which takes place on September 16, celebrating liberation from Spanish rule. Cinco de Mayo is honored in Puebla and some other Mexican cities, but in the United States of America it is celebrated much more universally, especially in cities with a large Mexican population, and towns near the United States-Mexico border. The number of such American fiestas grows larger each year. They feature flamenco and salsa dancing, mariachi musicians, traditional Mexican foods, and parades.

6

OPTIONAL MEMORIAL OF
Blessed François de Laval, BISHOP

Blessed François de Laval (1623–1708), was the first Roman Catholic bishop of Canada. He was born in France, a member of the noble Montmorency family, who are believed to go back to pagan Gaul. In spite of its rank, the family was not wealthy, and when his older brothers were killed in battle, François inherited the responsibility for his family and interrupted his studies for the priesthood in order to arrange for their financial security. In 1658, he was appointed vicar apostolic for New France, as French Canada was then known. In spite of difficulties caused by politics—both ecclesiastical and secular—Bishop Laval traveled extensively, confirming hundreds, founding parishes, and instituting a seminary. Seeing the damage caused to Native Americans by alcohol, he worked to stop traders from paying them for furs with liquor. As a result of his work, at the time of his retirement the number of parishes had increased from 5 to 35, the number of priests from 24 to 102, and the number of religious women from 32 to 97. He was known for his holiness, his spirit of poverty, and his generosity to the poor. Bishop Laval died in 1708, exhausted from his work, and was immediately acclaimed by the people as a saint. He was beatified by Blessed Pope John Paul II in 1980.

8

OPTIONAL MEMORIAL OF
Blessed Catherine of Saint Augustine, VIRGIN

Blessed Catherine of Saint Augustine (1632–1668) was born near Cherbourg, France. Her family was very devout, and she learned to care for the sick from her grandmother, who used to take invalids into her home. In 1644, Catherine entered the Augustinian Hospitaller Sisters, an order dedicated to caring for the sick. In spite of her family's opposition—her father even went to court to stop her—she volunteered for the mission in Quebec and arrived there in 1648. Upon her arrival, she dedicated herself to working in the newly founded hospital, the Hôtel-Dieu de Québec. Throughout her life, Catherine suffered from physical illness and spiritual trials, which she offered for the new colony until her death in 1668 at the age of thirty-six. She was beatified by Blessed Pope John Paul II in 1989.

Our Lady of Lujan (Argentina)

Today the people of Argentina celebrate a feast in honor of their patroness, Our Lady of Lujan, a terra cotta statue of Mary of the Immaculate Conception, made in Brazil and sent to Argentina in May, 1630. According to tradition, the statue was destined for Cordova, but while passing through the small town of Lujan, the wagon carrying the statue suddenly halted, and no efforts of the drivers could induce the oxen to budge. But as soon as the statue was removed from the cart, the animals started off again. It was clear that Our Lady wanted to remain in Lujan! A beautiful basilica, completed in 1865, now houses the shrine, and pilgrims come from all over the country to venerate Our Lady of Lujan. Other sources suggest this feast day is celebrated on December 8 or the Saturday before the fourth Sunday in May. Our Lady of Lujan, pray for us, and for the people of Argentina.

10

OPTIONAL MEMORIAL OF Saint Damien de Veuster, PRIEST 🇺🇸

Joseph de Veuster (1840–1889) was born in Belgium and entered the Congregation of the Sacred Hearts of Jesus and Mary, where he took the name Damien. He professed his vows in 1860. Three years later, although not yet ordained, he was sent to Hawaii and was ordained in Honolulu in 1864. Once he realized that a large number of lepers had been exiled to Moloka'i, Damien asked for and received permission to live among them and minister to them. Moloka'i was a lawless place, and Damien found its residents living in squalor. He helped them build homes, and he provided whatever medical treatment fell within his capability. In 1885, after twelve years of this ministry, Damien realized that he himself had contracted the disease. In spite of this, he continued his work until he was too incapacitated to go on. Adherents of other churches criticized him and spread gossip about his morality, but the author Robert Louis Stevenson defended him in a famous 1890 essay. Damien was canonized by Pope Benedict XVI in 2009. He is the patron saint of victims of leprosy.

12

OPTIONAL MEMORIAL OF Saints Nereus and Achilleus, MARTYRS

Not much is known about Saints Nereus and Achilleus (second century). They must have been important figures because the Roman Christians built a church over their grave in the late fourth century. An inscription composed by Pope Damasus describes them as soldiers who converted to Christianity and were martyred.

OPTIONAL MEMORIAL OF Saint Pancras, MARTYR

Saint Pancras (c. + 304) was brought before Emperor Diocletian, who asked him to sacrifice to the Roman gods. Pancras refused, even when promised wealth and power, and the emperor ordered him to be decapitated. He was only fourteen when he was martyred, in about the year 304.

13

OPTIONAL MEMORIAL OF Our Lady of Fatima

Today the Church honors Mary as Our Lady of Fatima. In 1917, in a tiny, rural town of Portugal, the Blessed Virgin Mary appeared to three shepherd children on the thirteenth day of six consecutive months, beginning on May 13. During these apparitions, the lady urged the children to pray for sinners and above all to pray the Rosary. On October 13, the last of the apparitions, the children were joined by a crowd of around 70,000 people, who witnessed what came to be called "The Miracle of the Sun." Today pilgrimage to the site of the apparitions continues all year round. The largest crowds gather on May 13 and October 13, when up to a million of the faithful come to pray and participate in processions, both during the day and at night, by the light of tens of thousands of candles. Our Lady of Fatima, pray for us.

14

FEAST OF
Saint Matthias, APOSTLE

Before the descent of the Holy Spirit at Pentecost, the eleven remaining Apostles had the task of replacing Judas Iscariot, who had committed suicide after his betrayal of Jesus. They cast lots, and Matthias (first century) was chosen from among the 120 disciples (Acts of the Apostles1:18–26). He was selected as a candidate by the Apostles because he met the following two qualifications: (1) a disciple of Jesus from Jesus' baptism to his Ascension and (2) a witness to Jesus' Resurrection. Tradition has him preaching in Judea and then in Georgia in the Caucasus, where he was crucified. The apocryphal Acts of Andrew and Matthias speak of a mission to evangelize cannibals. Other traditions put him in Ethiopia and in Jerusalem, where he is supposed to have been stoned and beheaded. His symbol in art is an axe, from the legend of his beheading.

15

OPTIONAL MEMORIAL OF
Saint Isidore 🇺🇸

Today we honor Saint Isidore the Farmer (c. 1080–1130), not Saint Isidore of Seville, the Doctor of the Church whose memorial falls on April 4. Isidore the Farmer was born in Madrid to poor parents who sent him to work for a landowner. He was very devout and married a like-minded woman, Maria, who also became a saint. Isidore attended daily Mass and was often late arriving at the fields, but he managed to get his work done nonetheless. He shared the little he had with the poor. He is the patron saint of farmers; it is fitting to remember him in the Northern Hemisphere's agricultural season.

18

OPTIONAL MEMORIAL OF Saint John I, POPE AND MARTYR

Saint John I (+ 526) was a native of Tuscany and was elected pope when quite elderly. Despite his protests, he was sent by the Arian King Theodoric to Constantinople, where he was to convince Emperor Justin to moderate his decree against the Arians. Theodoric threatened reprisals against Orthodox Christians in the West if he failed. When John returned, Theodoric had him arrested on suspicion of conspiring with the emperor. He died in prison of ill treatment.

20

OPTIONAL MEMORIAL OF Saint Bernardine of Siena, PRIEST

Saint Bernardine of Siena (1380–1444) was an Italian Franciscan, a priest, and preacher. He was orphaned young and raised by a pious aunt. While still a student, he helped care for the sick during an outbreak of the bubonic plague, contracted the disease and almost died. Bernardine joined a strict branch of the Franciscans, called the Observants, around 1402. Known as the "apostle of Italy," he preached devotion to the Holy Name of Jesus, popularizing the use of the monogram, I.H.S. and encouraging his hearers to burn unnecessary luxuries in "bonfires of vanities."

21

Optional Memorial of Saint Christopher Magallanes, Priest, and Companions, Martyrs

Saint Christopher Magallanes was a Mexican priest whose years of ministry coincided with an extreme anticlerical era in Mexico. He was falsely accused of promoting rebellion and arrested while on his way to celebrate Mass. Christopher was killed without trial after absolving his executioners, saying, "I die innocent, and ask God that my blood may serve to unite my Mexican brethren." He and his companions died between 1915 and 1928. He was canonized by Blessed Pope John Paul II on May 21, 2000, along with 21 priests and three laymen, also martyred for resisting the anti-Catholic Mexican government of the 1920s.

Optional Memorial of Saint Eugène de Mazenod, Bishop

Charles-Joseph-Eugène de Mazenod (1782–1861) was born in Aix-en-Provence to an aristocratic family that fled to Italy from France during the Revolution. In 1811, Eugène returned to France and was ordained a priest at Amiens. In 1816, he founded the Missionary Oblates of Mary Immaculate, an order founded to serve the poor and restore Catholicism in post-Revolution France. The Oblates subsequently evolved into a missionary and teaching order that did extensive work in Western Canada among the "First Nations." In 1837, Eugène was made bishop of Marseille, succeeding his uncle. Today, his Missionaries of Mary Immaculate serve the Church in over sixty-eight different countries, in North America, South Asia, and Africa.

Our Lady of Vladimir (Russia)

The icon of the Theotokos ("God-bearer"), Our Lady of Vladimir is one of the best-known and best-loved Orthodox icons and has been venerated in Russia for well over a thousand years. By the 16th-century, the Vladimirskaya (as she is known in Russia) was an integral part of Russian faith, history, and culture. The venerated image has been used at the coronations of czars, the elections of patriarchs, and other important ceremonies of state. In December 1941, as the Germans approached Moscow, Russia's atheist ruler Joseph Stalin allegedly ordered that the icon be placed in an airplane and flown around the besieged capital. Within a few days, the German army began to retreat. The image shows the Christ Child tenderly embracing his mother, who looks out at the viewer with an expression of motherly love and concern. Our Lady of Vladimir, pray for us.

22

Optional Memorial of Saint Rita of Cascia, Religious

Saint Rita of Cascia lived in Italy from 1377 to 1457. Against her wishes, her parents arranged for her to marry a man who ended up abusing her. She had two sons with him; both followed their father's bad example. Rita's husband converted toward the end of his life, but he was murdered by an old enemy. Her sons died soon after. Rita was refused entrance to an Augustinian monastery several times because she was a widow, but eventually she was admitted and lived there until her death. She is depicted with a wound in her forehead because she asked to suffer in union with Jesus and was given a wound from a thorn in his crown.

24

SOLEMNITY OF Our Lady, Help of Christians

(Australia / New Zealand)

From the earliest centuries, Mary has been invoked under the title "Help of Christians," especially in times of persecution. When Pope Pius VII was driven from Rome and imprisoned during the Napoleonic wars, the entire Church prayed to Mary on his behalf. He was released and established a solemnity in honor of Mary, Help of Christians, on the anniversary of his return to Rome, May 24, 1814.

Our Lady, Help of Christians is the Patroness of Australia and New Zealand.

OPTIONAL MEMORIAL OF Blessed Louis-Zéphirin Moreau, BISHOP ✤

Blessed Louis-Zéphirin Moreau (1824–1901) was from a large Canadian farming family. A delicate child too frail for farm work, he was fortunately intelligent enough to be sent to be educated. He was ordained to the priesthood in 1846; unfortunately, his theological training was shortened by his ill health. In 1852, he became advisor to the bishops of Saint-Hyacinthe and administered the diocese when the bishops were absent. He earned a reputation for hard work and administrative efficiency and skill. While serving as parish priest, he became concerned about the financial condition of workers, and he established the Union Saint-Joseph, a society that provided protection from unexpected events such as unemployment, accidents, and premature death. In 1876, Louis was consecrated fourth bishop of Saint-Hyacinthe and administered the diocese for twenty-five years. During this time, he built a cathedral, founded two orders of sisters, and worked to support the priests of the dioceses spiritually and intellectually by instituting conferences and retreats for them.

Bishop Moreau's health began to fail around 1896, and he died in 1901. He was beatified by Blessed Pope John Paul II in 1987.

25

OPTIONAL MEMORIAL OF Saint Bede the Venerable, PRIEST AND DOCTOR OF THE CHURCH

The Venerable Bede (673–735), an English Benedictine monk, wrote *The Ecclesiastical History of the English People*, which was his most famous work. Unlike historians who came before him, he did careful research and cited his references.

OPTIONAL MEMORIAL OF Saint Gregory VII, POPE

Saint Gregory VII (c. 1021–1085) was a reformer pope best known for his disputes with the Holy Roman Emperor Henry IV. He fought to prevent the appointment of Church officials by secular authorities and died, saying, "I have loved justice and hated iniquity; therefore, I die in exile."

OPTIONAL MEMORIAL OF Saint Mary Magdalene de' Pazzi, VIRGIN

Saint Mary Magdalene de'Pazzi (1566–1607) was the daughter of a prominent family in Florence. She developed a love of prayer at an early age and began having mystical experiences. Her parents sent her to be educated in a convent but brought her home when they decided she should marry. Fortunately, Mary persuaded them that she had a vocation to be a Carmelite, and they allowed her to return. Her life was marked by prayer, penance, devotion to the Eucharist, and love for the poor.

26

MEMORIAL OF
Saint Philip Neri, PRIEST

Saint Philip Neri (1515–1595) was an Italian priest and founder of the Congregation of the Oratory or Oratorians. Philip was known for his joyful spirit, believing that it is more Christian to be cheerful than melancholy. A well-known figure in the Eternal City, during his lifetime he was known as the "apostle of Rome." Philip was ahead of his time in urging more frequent reception of Holy Communion, and he introduced the Forty Hours' devotion with exposition of the Blessed Sacrament. He was apt to go into ecstasy when celebrating Eucharist, so he had to try to distract himself so he could finish the rites.

27

OPTIONAL MEMORIAL OF Saint Augustine of Canterbury, BISHOP

Saint Augustine, born in the first third of the sixth century, was a Benedictine monk and was named the first archbishop of Canterbury in 598. He was prior of a monastery in Rome when Saint Gregory the Great, after seeing blonde Saxon slaves in the market, chose him to lead a mission to England. Augustine worked in Kent in the south of England, and once he converted King Æthelberht, the rest of Kent followed. He died in 604 and was buried in the abbey church at Canterbury, which became place of pilgrimage. The shrine was destroyed and the relics were lost during the English Reformation.

Infant Jesus of Prague (Czech)

The Infant of Prague is a small statue of the Child Jesus, made in Spain and brought to Bohemia by a young princess who had been given the image as a wedding gift. She presented the statue to the Carmelite fathers in Prague. One day, praying before the statue, one of the Fathers heard a voice say, "The more you honor me, the more I will bless you." Since then, the statue has drawn millions of the faithful from around the world, and replicas of the image are venerated in countless churches. The well-loved image shows Christ as a child, and yet a king; an infant, robed in majesty and crowned with authority. The image of the Infant of Prague reminds us that we have a Lord who rules with gentleness; we have nothing to fear.

31

FEAST OF THE Visitation of the Blessed Virgin Mary

When the angel brought Mary the amazing message that she would be the mother of God's Son, he also brought her some family news: her elderly cousin, Elizabeth, was going to have a baby as well. Immediately, Mary set out to visit her cousin and help her at what must have been a challenging time. When Mary arrived, something amazing happened: the child in Elizabeth's womb leapt up in recognition, and Elizabeth, too, was filled with the Holy Spirit and realized that Mary was carrying God's Son. Even before his birth, John the Baptist was pointing the way to Christ!

We echo Elizabeth's joyful exclamation every time we pray the Hail Mary: "Blessed are you among women, and blessed is the fruit of your womb!" (Luke 1:42). And we echo Mary's response to her cousin, her Magnificat, in the Office of Evening Prayer.

JUNE

Month of June

The sixth month is named after Juno, the Roman goddess of hearth and home. Juno's month was lucky for weddings. In years past, Christian weddings were rarely held during Easter Time. Only on Pentecost did the time of summer weddings begin. After Pentecost the time of summer weddings began. In the Northern Hemisphere, June is the month of the summer solstice.

Month of the Sacred Heart

On the Friday following the Solemnity of the Most Holy Body and Blood of Christ, we celebrate the Solemnity of the Most Sacred Heart of Jesus. Because this solemnity usually falls in June, this month is also known as the "Month of the Sacred Heart." Devotion to the Sacred Heart of Jesus is all about pondering Christ's love and meditating on Christ's suffering.

Images of Saints in June (L to R): Saint Charles Lwanga (June 3), Saint John the Baptist (June 24), Saint Anthony of Padua (June 13).

Father's Day 🇺🇸 🍁
Third Sunday in June

Sonora Louise Smart Dodd of Spokane thought that her father, William Smart, had done a remarkable thing. A veteran of the Civil War, he had raised his six children alone on the family farm in Washington after his wife died in childbirth. When Mrs. Dodd suggested a day for fathers in 1909, she meant it to be a Church service. Mother's Day, which had just come into wide practice, was originally a Church service too. Public interest in establishing Father's Day was strong at once in both the United States and Canada. Father's Day became an official national day in 1966. Father's Day is celebrated around the world—the date of celebration will vary.

SOLEMNITY OF Saints Peter and Paul, APOSTLES (Australia)

Sunday on or after June 29

Please see page 86 for more information.

1

MEMORIAL OF Saint Justin, MARTYR

Saint Justin, also called Justin Martyr (c. 100–165), was born in Judea and raised pagan by parents who were probably Greek or Roman. He studied philosophy, converted to Christianity, and spent his life teaching and writing. Justin is best known for his Apologies and for his Dialogue with Trypho. He fought against the heresy of Marcion, who rejected the Old Testament. Justin's life ended in Rome, where he was martyred under Marcus Aurelius. He is one of the first Christian apologists, and he was one of the first to employ philosophy as a tool toward greater understanding of revelation.

2

OPTIONAL MEMORIAL OF Saints Marcellinus and Peter, MARTYRS

Not much is known of these two early martyrs, who died in 304 AD, except that Saint Marcellinus was a priest, Peter was an exorcist, and they were both martyred under Diocletian. While in prison, they managed to convert the jailer and his family. Pope Damasus honored them with an epitaph. They are mentioned in Eucharistic Prayer I.

3

MEMORIAL OF Saint Charles Lwanga, and Companions, MARTYRS

Saint Charles Lwanga (+ 1886) was a Ugandan catechist who served as a page in the court of King Mwanga II. King Mwanga felt threatened by the presence of missionaries in his country, and he insisted that Christians renounce their faith. After a Massacre of Anglicans in 1885, the head page, Joseph Mukasa, reproached the king, who had him beheaded and arrested his followers. Charles baptized those who were still catechumens, and he and twenty-one others were burnt alive. Although they were not canonized, Paul VI recognized the martyrdom of the Anglican Christians when he canonized Charles and his companions.

5

MEMORIAL OF Saint Boniface, BISHOP AND MARTYR

Saint Boniface (c. 675–754) was an Anglo-Saxon Benedictine monk. He was first sent as a missionary to Frisia, which is in the vicinity of the Netherlands, but he failed because of wars between the local tribes and the Frankish king Charles Martel. Boniface then went to Rome and was commissioned by the pope to evangelize in Germany. He started by chopping down an oak tree dedicated to Thor, and when he was not immediately struck down, the people believed and became Christians. Boniface returned to evangelize the Frisians but was killed by them in 754 AD. He is buried in the cathedral in Fulda.

World Environment Day

The United Nations began this annual observance in 1972 to raise awareness of environmental issues and to encourage environmental action in communities across the planet. Hundreds of thousands of people have responded to the challenge, whether planting trees in Afghanistan or setting up new compost stations in Argentina. Such actions are key at a time when half the world's wetlands and three-quarters of its fish stocks are depleted. Species extinction is occurring at 1000 times the natural rate. This day expresses hope that "every year, everywhere, everyone" can bring about the crucial change that's needed (Press Release, World Environment Day, 2011).

6

OPTIONAL MEMORIAL OF Saint Norbert, BISHOP

Saint Norbert (1080–1134), a subdeacon and canon in the Rhineland, had a conversion experience similar to Saint Paul's, in which he was thrown from a horse during a violent thunderstorm. Following this event he had a change of heart, a growing awareness of the need to renounce the trappings of the world and to preach reform. His preaching led him to the valley of Premontre, where he laid the framework, along with 13 disciples, for a reform movement that became known as the Canons Regular of Premontre, the Premonstratensians, or Norbertines. These Norbertines lived together according to the *Rule of Saint Augustine*, wore a simple white habit, and challenged the clergy through preaching and example to recommit themselves to celibacy and simplicity. Although their message was not always received well among the clergy, more and more young men felt called to join the Norbertines. Because of his extraordinary leadership and reforming spirit, Saint Norbert was appointed archbishop of Magdeburg, Germany.

9

OPTIONAL MEMORIAL OF Saint Ephrem, DEACON AND DOCTOR OF THE CHURCH

Saint Ephrem (c. 300–373) was a Syrian deacon, writer of hymns, and theologian of the fourth century. His hymns were written to provide catechesis, and some even warn against heresies. Over four hundred of them still exist. Pope Benedict XVI has said that Ephrem gives witness to the fact that Christianity is not a European religion but demonstrates the cultural diversity of early Christians.

Saint Columba (*Colum Cille*)

(Scotland)

Saint Columba (c. 521–597), (not to be confused with his contemporary, Saint Columbanus), was an Irish missionary monk who evangelized the Picts in Scotland. He was among the twelve students of Saint Finian who came to be known as the "twelve apostles of Ireland." Because of the Battle of Cúl Dreimhne, which resulted from a dispute over ownership of a manuscript, Columba was exiled to Scotland and told to convert as many people as had died in the battle. Upon arriving in Scotland, he moved until he could no longer see his homeland, Ireland and settled on the island of Iona, which became the base of his mission to the Picts and later developed into a school for missionaries. He attained a reputation for holiness and, as a result, was often looked to as a mediator of disputes. Among his legends are stories of miracles performed to convert the Picts. Saint Columba died on Iona and was buried at the abbey there but was disinterred and is now thought to be buried with Saint Patrick and Saint Brigid at Downpatrick. Saint Columba is a patron saint of Ireland and Scotland, as well as of poets and bookbinders.

11

MEMORIAL OF
Saint Barnabas, APOSTLE

Even though Saint Barnabas (first century) was not one of the original Twelve Apostles, he was given the title of "Apostle" by Saint Luke and the early Church fathers, due to his apostolic endeavors on behalf of Christianity. His original name was Joseph, but the Apostles gave him the surname *Barnabas*, meaning "son of encouragement," probably due to his friendly disposition. Together with Saint Paul, he extended the missionary efforts of the Church beyond Jerusalem to Antioch, and after much success moved on to other places throughout Asia Minor. After parting ways with Saint Paul over issues regarding circumcision and the Mosaic law, Saint Barnabas embarked on further missionary journeys with John Mark (see Acts of the Apostles 15:36–40). Tradition indicates that Saint Barnabas was stoned to death, and his remains were taken to Constantinople where a church stands in his honor.

13

MEMORIAL OF **Saint Anthony of Padua**, PRIEST AND DOCTOR OF THE CHURCH

Saint Anthony of Padua (1195–1231), a member of a noble Portuguese family, joined the Canons Regular of Saint Augustine at a young age, but later joined the Franciscans to engage in missionary work. Although his missionary dreams were halted due to illness, he received public acclaim for his preaching style, which led to the conversion of many from heresy, earning him the title "the Hammer of the Heretics." He had the privilege of meeting Saint Francis of Assisi in person and was later elected provincial of Northern Italy. His writing is extensive, especially in the area of sermons; therefore, he was named a Doctor of the Church. People invoke his name when trying to find lost items. This comes from the story in the saint's biography when a young novice took Anthony's Psalter, but returned it in a hurry when the angry saint appeared to him in a vision!

14

Flag Day 🇺🇸

Today, as the foremost symbol of the United States of America is honored around the nation, one observance will take place at 239 Arch Street in Philadelphia, historic home of seamstress Betsy Ross. A young widow at the time of the Revolutionary War, she was asked by General George Washington to turn his rough design of 13 stars and 13 stripes into a flag. That design has changed many times as 13 colonies have grown into 50 states. However, the flag's colors have continued to stand for values of courage (red), purity (white), and vigilance and justice (blue). In 1949 the date June 14 was designated a national holiday to honor the flag. So all across the United States of America, scout troops and veterans groups will join in flag-raising ceremonies as marching bands render "The Star-Spangled Banner."

19

OPTIONAL MEMORIAL OF Saint Romuald, ABBOT

Saint Romuald (c. 950–1027) was born in Ravenna and led a self-indulgent life as a young man, but when he saw his father kill an opponent in a duel, he fled to a monastery. Romuald yearned for a stricter life than he found there, and so he withdrew to become a hermit. Eventually, he founded the Camaldolese branch of the Benedictine family, integrating community life with the solitary life. His monks live and work in individual hermitages but come together to celebrate Eucharist and the Liturgy of the Hours.

20

Saint Alban (England and Wales), Saint Julius, Saint Aaron (Wales)

Saint Alban (died c. 304) is the first martyr of Britain. The account of his martyrdom is in the *Ecclesiastical History of Saint Bede*. Alban was a pagan living in the regions of Hertfordshire, in the town now known as Saint Alban. During a time of persecution, a priest took refuge with Alban, and Alban was so impressed by him that he was baptized. When a search party came for the priest, Alban dressed himself in the priest's cloak and gave himself up in his place. When he was brought before the governor, Alban adhered to his new-found faith and refused to sacrifice to the gods. Alban was scourged, and when that had no effect, the governor ordered him to be beheaded. The Abbey of Saint Alban was founded near the site of the execution. Saint Alban is the patron saint of converts, refugees, and torture victims and is also venerated by the Anglican Communion and Eastern Orthodox Church.

Saints Julius and Aaron (died c. 304 AD) were executed under Diocletian. By tradition, they are mentioned with Saint Alban as early martyrs of Britain. According to Saint Gildas the Wise, they were "citizens of Caerleon" in Wales and were executed there.

21

MEMORIAL OF Saint Aloysius Gonzaga, RELIGIOUS

Saint Aloysius Gonzaga (1568–1591) was born to a noble family in Italy who destined him for the military. While recovering from an illness, he read the lives of the saints and spent time in prayer. As a result, Aloysius decided to dedicate himself to God as a Jesuit. Most of his family was against it, but he joined anyway, making his vows in 1587. In 1591, the plague broke out in Rome. Aloysius volunteered to care for the victims and became sick himself. He recovered, but his health was broken, and he died within a few months. Many schools are named for him because he is the patron saint of Catholic youth.

Summer Solstice

On this day the sun is at its highest in the Northern Hemisphere. It's the official beginning of summer and an ancient day of celebration. In places north of the Arctic Circle, called "the land of the midnight sun," the sun never sets during the days near the summer solstice. In most of northern Europe, these are called "the days that never end" because dawn begins before the evening twilight has faded. The sky is never completely dark. Many ancient peoples made today one of their great feasts. People lit huge bonfires during these shortest nights of the year to announce the official change of seasons. Some sort of protection at this time of year seemed especially important because spirits were thought to wander about during festival times. As European nations became Christian, the solstice traditions became associated with the birth of Saint John the Baptist (June 24), called Midsummer Day because it is midway between the vernal and autumnal equinoxes.

22

OPTIONAL MEMORIAL OF Saint Paulinus of Nola, BISHOP

Saint Paulinus of Nola (c. 354–431) was raised in a family of wealthy politicians in Bordeaux. His interests were varied: everything from practicing law to writing poetry, from traveling to governing. After the death of a newly born son, he and his wife, Therasia, gave away the family fortune to the poor and to the Church. Saint Paulinus and Therasia moved to Italy where they began to live, along with some other friends, a life of prayer and service. They lived in a two-story building in which the first floor provided a place of rest for the wayward and the lost, and the second floor was their place of residence based on the rhythms of monasticism. Gaining a reputation for holiness, Saint Paulinus was ordained a priest and was eventually made a bishop of Nola.

OPTIONAL MEMORIAL OF Saints John Fisher, BISHOP, and Thomas More, MARTYRS

Saint John Fisher (1469–1535) and Saint Thomas More (1478–1535) lived during a time of great upheaval and reformation. Both were friends and consultants to King Henry VIII, and both were executed because they would not declare the king's supremacy over the Church. Saint John Fisher, born in Yorkshire, was an astute scholar recognized for his profound insight into the complex questions of life. He held many positions of esteem, including a tutor to the young Henry VIII, Chancellor of Cambridge University, and bishop of Rochester.

Saint Thomas More, born in London, was a family man characterized by a deep affection for his wife and three daughters. He, too, held many powerful positions in the Church and in society; in particular, a Parliament lawyer, Speaker of the House of Commons, and Chancellor of England.

24

SOLEMNITY OF the Nativity of Saint John the Baptist

Today we commemorate the birth of Saint John the Baptist, the only person besides Jesus and Mary whose birthday is celebrated on the Church calendar. John is the forerunner of Jesus, as we hear in the Benedictus, the prophetic canticle that John's father, Zachary, proclaimed: "And you, child, will be called prophet of the Most High, for you will go before the

Lord to prepare his ways, to give his people knowledge of salvation to his people by the forgiveness of their sins . . ." (Luke 1:76–77).

This is an ancient solemnity, reaching back to the fourth century, though the date of the celebration varied in East and West. In the East, the birth of the forerunner was celebrated on the day after Epiphany, January 7, because of the association with the baptism of the Lord. In the West, it was celebrated on June 24, in keeping with Luke 1:36, which notes that Elizabeth was six months pregnant at the time of the Annunciation of the Lord. It is not by coincidence that the birth of John the Baptist falls shortly after the summer solstice (June 21), while that of Christ is after the winter solstice (December 22). In the northern hemisphere, June 21 is the longest day of the year; after that, the days will get shorter and shorter. After the winter solstice, the days will gradually increase in length. Saint Augustine drew a connection between this cosmic pattern and the saint we honor, who said "he must increase, but I must decrease" (John 3:30).

27

MEMORIAL OF Saint Cyril of Alexandria, BISHOP AND DOCTOR OF THE CHURCH 🇺🇸

As the patriarch of Alexandria, Saint Cyril of Alexandria (376–444) was an avid defender of the faith; therefore, he was no stranger to conflict. He found himself at odds with Nestorius, the archbishop of Constantinople, who taught that the Blessed Virgin is the mother of Christ (*Christotokos*) not the Mother of God (*Theotokos*). Saint Cyril presided over the First Council of Ephesus (431), which condemned this particular belief, known as Nestorianism, as heresy and proclaimed Mary as the Mother of God. The Council of Chalcedon (451)

based its teachings regarding the two natures of Christ on the thought of Saint Cyril. Due to the breadth of his writing on the Incarnation and the dignity of the human person, he was declared a Doctor of the Church.

OPTIONAL MEMORIAL OF Blessed Nykyta Budka and Vasyl Velychkowsky, BISHOPS AND MARTYRS 🍁

After studies in Vienna and Innsbruck, Blessed Nykyta Budka received his PHD in Theology and was ordained a priest in 1905. After his consecration as bishop, he became the first leader of the Greek Catholic Church in Canada but he lacked organizational skills. A trip to Rome to report on conflicts in the Canadian Church led to his resignation and reassignment. He was arrested by the Soviets in 1945 and sentenced to eight years in a concentration camp where he died a martyr in 1949.

Blessed Vasyl Velychkovsky, a Ukrainian priest of the Byzantine Rite, was arrested by Communist secret police and served ten years at hard labor before his sentence was commuted. In 1963, he was secretly consecrated the archbishop of Moscow. Suffering from a heart disease, Velychkovsky was deported to Winnepeg, Canada, where he died.

28

MEMORIAL OF Saint Irenaeus, BISHOP AND MARTYR

Saint Irenaeus (c. 125–202) was the bishop of Lyons, France, a disciple of Saint Polycarp of Smyrna, and one of the first Christian theologians. His best known work, *Against Heresies*, is an attack on the gnostics, who claimed to have a secret oral tradition from

Jesus. Irenaeus refutes them by pointing out that we know who the bishops are back to the Apostles, and that none of them were gnostic. He is an early witness to the recognition of the four accounts of the Gospel, to the unique importance of the Bishop of Rome, and to the apostolic succession—the handing on of ecclesial authority from the Apostles themselves.

29

MEMORIAL OF Saints Peter and Paul, APOSTLES

Today we commemorate Saints Peter and Paul, martyred on this date around the year 64 AD during Nero's persecution following the Great Fire of Rome. Tradition says that Peter fled Rome to avoid arrest and saw Jesus on the road. "Where are you going, Lord," Peter asked. Jesus replied, "I am going to Rome to be crucified again." Peter turned back and was crucified upside down because he felt unworthy to meet his death the same way as Christ. Paul was arrested in Jerusalem and was sent to Rome, where he was placed under house arrest. He was slain by beheading, because as a Roman citizen he could not be subjected to the indignity of crucifixion.

30

OPTIONAL MEMORIAL OF THE First Martyrs of the Holy Roman Church

Today we commemorate the martyrs who died between the years 64–68 AD, around the same time as Saints Peter and Paul. The emperor Nero was accused of starting the Great Fire of Rome, and to divert attention from himself and satisfy his appetite for cruelty, he turned the blame on the Christians in Rome. They were rounded up and killed by various means: by crucifixion, by being fed to wild animals, and by being burned as torches to provide light for parties. The Roman historian Tacitus provides an independent record of their torture and death.

Venerable Pierre Toussaint

Venerable Pierre Toussaint (1766–1853), a Haitian slave, came to New York City, where he embarked on a successful career as a hairdresser. His extraordinary talent began attracting clientele from the upper echelon of the city. Due to his financial success, he was able to purchase his own freedom and the freedom of Marie Rose Juliette, a Haitian slave whom he loved and planned to marry. Rather than squandering their wealth on frivolity and opulence, Venerable Pierre and his wife cared for the poor and sick of New York City as well as opened their home as a shelter for orphans. Along with offering shelter, Venerable Pierre and his wife would provide an education for the orphans and abandoned so they could eventually secure steady and fair employment. Toussaint died on this date in 1853. His cause for beatification is still pending.

July

Month of July

The seventh month is named after Julius Caesar. He was a Roman general and politician who was assassinated in the year 44 BCE, on the Ides of March, March 15. Julius Caesar had ordered that the calendar be reformed. The Roman mathematicians came up with a calendar that is almost identical to the one we use today. It is called the Julian calendar (see January 7) in honor of Julius Caesar.

Month of the Precious Blood

July is the month of the Precious Blood of Christ. "As we now approach the feast and month devoted to honoring Christ's Blood—the price of our redemption, the pledge of salvation and life eternal— may Christians meditate on it more fervently, may they savor its fruits more frequently in sacramental communion." So wrote Pope John XXIII, in his apostolic letter, *Inde a Primus*, encouraging devotion

Images of Saints in July (L to R): Blessed Kateri Tekakwitha (July 14), Saint Maria Goretti (July 6), Saint Mary Magdalene (July 22).

to the Precious Blood of Christ, June 30, 1960. Devotion to Christ's Precious Blood owes much to Saint Gaspar del Bufalo, the founder of the Missionaries of the Precious Blood, but it has its roots in Scripture. Remember, writes Saint Peter, that "you know that you were ransomed from the futile ways inherited from your ancestors, not with perishable things like silver or gold, but with the precious blood of Christ, like that of a lamb without defect or blemish" (1 Peter 1:18–19). In the Precious Blood of Christ is healing and forgiveness. "This blood," marveled Saint Thomas Aquinas, "that but one drop of has the power to win / All the world forgiveness of its world of sin."

Parents' Day 🏴

Fourth Sunday of July

> This day is a relatively new observance, established by Congressional Resolution and signed into law by President Bill Clinton in 1994 as a perennial day of commemoration. Its purpose is to recognize, uplift, and support the role of parents in the rearing of children, our most precious resource. A year-long process leading up to this day allows people around the United States of America to nominate persons they consider to be exemplary parents. From this list, "Parents of the Year" are chosen to serve as role models for parents around the country. However, this day is also a time set aside for all parents to honor their children and to recommit themselves to show the highest standards of unconditional love toward those children. Countries such as Canada, India, and South Korea also observe a form of Parents' Day.

1

OPTIONAL MEMORIAL OF Blessed Junípero Serra, PRIEST 🏴

Blessed Junípero Serra (1713–1784) was a Spanish Franciscan friar, best known for founding the string of twenty-one missions that stretch from San Diego to Sonoma, California. Junípero was born in Majorca and at the age of sixteen entered the Franciscans. After completing his theological studies, he served as professor of philosophy at Majorca before volunteering for the missions in the New World. Upon arrival, he went to Mexico City to dedicate his mission at the shrine of Our Lady of Guadalupe. Serra founded his first mission at San Diego in 1769, and worked his way up the coast along El Camino Real, making converts as he went. In spite of a leg injury he suffered at the beginning of his ministry, he traveled on foot whenever possible, eventually covering 24,000 miles. The chapel at Mission San Juan Capistrano is believed to be oldest standing building in California, and it is the only mission left where Serra is known to have celebrated the liturgy. He was beatified by Pope John Paul II in 1988.

Saint Oliver Plunkett, Bishop

(Ireland)

Saint Oliver Plunkett (1625–1681) was the Catholic archbishop of Armagh during a period of persecution. He was born into a prominent family and was sent to Rome to study for the priesthood, where he remained to escape from the persecution that Oliver Cromwell started in 1649. Once it let up, he returned to Ireland and was made archbishop of Armagh in 1657. Plunkett worked to reorganize the Church, which was staggering after the years of persecution, and founded schools to educate the clergy. In 1678, he was rounded up in the persecution that resulted from "Popish Plot" concocted by Titus Oates. False witnesses testified that he was working for a French invasion. Oliver Plunkett was found guilty of high treason in London, and on July 1, 1681, he was the last Catholic martyr to be hanged, drawn, and quartered at Tyburn. He was canonized by Pope Paul VI in 1975, the first new Irish saint in almost seven hundred years. He is the patron saint of peace and reconciliation in Ireland.

Canada Day 🍁

The strains of "O Canada," the stirring anthem of that nation, will resound many times today as its citizens celebrate their nationhood. On this day in 1867, the British North American provinces officially joined together under the name of Canada. So today is the equivalent in Canada of Independence Day in the United States of America. It is a Canadian national holiday marking the start of summer. Parades, picnics, clean-up projects, and, of course, fireworks will happen everywhere. In Ottawa, Ontario, the nation's capital, a resounding noon show features Canadian performers who have achieved worldwide fame. Some observances elsewhere feature aboriginal elders and chiefs speaking about the traditions of the First Nation—the peoples who lived in Canada before the arrival of Europeans.

It used to be said that the sun never set on the British Empire because Britain held lands all over the world. Even after the United States fought for its independence, the sun still shone on British soil in North America for nearly 100 years. Then, on July 1, 1867, the provinces of New Brunswick, Nova Scotia, Ontario, and Quebec joined together to form their own government. Now the country of Canada has ten provinces and two territories. Canada Day (also called Dominion Day) will be celebrated all over the vast nation today. A jazz festival in Montreal, a gold panning competition in the Rocky Mountains, and even a rubber duck race on the Yukon River will be held, along with fireworks, parades, and family reunions.

Since 1959, Windsor, Ontario, and Detroit, Michigan have celebrated their countries' independence days with the International Freedom Festival. It's held on the days between Canada Day and Independence Day. The Detroit River, which separates the cities, is the site of a spectacular fireworks display.

3

FEAST OF
Saint Thomas, APOSTLE

Saint Thomas (first century), also called "Didymus" or "the Twin" (John 11:16) was one of the Twelve Apostles. He is remembered for doubting the Resurrection of Christ: "Unless I see the mark of the nails in his hands, and put my finger in the mark of the nails and my hand in his side, I will not believe." The following week, Thomas was with the Twelve, when Jesus appeared and chided him for his lack of faith: "Have you believed because you have seen me? Blessed are those who have not seen and yet have come to believe" (John 20:25–29). After seeing the risen Jesus alive, Thomas exclaimed "My Lord and my God!" (John 20:28). According to tradition, Thomas is the only apostle who went outside the borders of the Roman Empire to evangelize. Although there is a Gospel account attributed to him, it is not accepted in the canon of scripture, and is, in fact, of gnostic origin. The people of Kerala in South India fervently believe that it was Thomas who evangelized them. He is represented in art with a spear, the instrument of his martyrdom. He is the patron saint of architects and builders, and of India, where today is a solemnity.

4

Independence Day 🇺🇸

Imagine flying over the United States in a small private plane at twilight tonight. You could watch fireworks going off beneath you in all directions, as every town celebrates the birthday of the nation. They celebrate because on this day in 1776, the *Declaration of Independence* was announced publicly. The Declaration was basically a list of the reasons why the 13 colonies had broken ties with their mother country, Great Britain. It was written by a committee headed by Thomas Jefferson. It stated that all people have a right to life, liberty, and the pursuit of happiness. By the time the Declaration was produced, the Revolutionary War had already been going on for some months. It would take eight years for the colonists to win the independence they prized so greatly.

Traditional celebrations for Independence Day include torchlight parades, bell ringing, picnics, family reunions, band concerts, and, of course, fireworks. It's a time for fun and a time for reflection, too. People give thanks today for a beautiful country and for a system of government that is admired all over the world.

Our bright celebrations this day are done in the hope that one day all will be free, that one day the earth itself will shine with liberty.

OPTIONAL MEMORIAL OF Saint Elizabeth of Portugal 🍁

Saint Elizabeth of Portugal (1271–1336) was the grandniece of Saint Elizabeth of Hungary and is known by the Spanish version of her name, Isabel. When very young, she was married to the King of Portugal. Elizabeth had been raised to be devout, but at her husband's court, she found much corruption and immorality. In spite of this, she managed to continue her life of prayer, penance, and devotion to the care of the sick. This caused resentment in the court, which Elizabeth bore quietly. After her husband, the king, died, she went to live in a convent of Poor Clares that she had founded, and she took the habit of a Third Order Franciscan. Throughout her life she was well known for her peacemaking skills, most importantly when she prevented a war between Portugal and Castile in 1336. The exertion weakened her health, and she died soon after and is buried at Coimbra. Elizabeth of Portugal is a patron saint of Franciscan Tertiaries.

5

OPTIONAL MEMORIAL OF Saint Anthony Zaccaria, PRIEST

Saint Anthony Mary Zaccaria (1502–1539) was from Cremona, Italy. He was born into a noble family, and dedicated himself to the Lord from a young age. He studied philosophy, went to study medicine at the University of Padua, and practiced for three years before deciding to become a priest. Anthony had already done so much study that he was ordained quickly, in 1528. He founded three religious orders: the Barnabites or Clerics Regular of Saint Paul—the first order named for Saint Paul—the Angelic Sisters of Saint Paul for nuns, and a lay community. The three groups worked together to reform society. Because of the implied criticism of abuses in the Church, Anthony was investigated for heresy twice, but was acquitted both times. In addition to founding the Barnabites, he popularized the forty-hour devotion of exposition of the Eucharist. In 1539, he became ill with a fever, and because his health had been undermined by his penitential practices, he died at the age of thirty-seven. Anthony is the patron saint of his order, the Barnabites and is represented in art wearing a cassock and with a lily, a cross, or a symbol of the Eucharist. Today the Barnabites can be found in sixteen countries, including Italy, the United States, Brazil, and Afghanistan.

Optional Memorial of Saint Elizabeth of Portugal

Please see page 90 for more information.

Optional Memorial of Saint Maria Goretti, VIRGIN AND MARTYR

Saint Maria Goretti (1890–1902) is one of the youngest saints to be canonized. She died of stab wounds after she resisted a rapist. Maria came from a poor Italian family. They lost their farm and a few years later, her father died of malaria. In spite of their hard existence as farm laborers, the family was close-knit and devout. By 1902, the family was sharing a building with another family of farm workers, one of whom was Alessandro Serenelli, who made it a habit to sexually harass Maria. One day, finding her alone, he threatened to kill her if she did not submit to him. Maria protested that what he asked was a mortal sin. Alessandro choked, and then stabbed her, leaving her bleeding to death. She was taken to the hospital, but she could not be saved and died forgiving her murderer. Shortly after Maria died, Alessandro was arrested, charged with her murder, and sentenced to twenty years in prison. He remained unrepentant until Maria appeared to him in a dream. Upon his release, he went to Maria's mother and asked for forgiveness. Eventually he became a Capuchin lay brother and was present at Maria's canonization in 1950, as was her mother. Maria Goretti is the patron saint of rape victims and teenage girls and is shown in art dressed as a peasant farmer, holding lilies. Her story has prompted thought on the broader meaning of chastity, integrating sexual purity with personal integrity, and self-determination.

9

Optional Memorial of Saint Augustine Zhao Rong, PRIEST AND MARTYR AND HIS COMPANIONS, MARTYRS

Between 1648 and 1930, 87 Chinese Catholics and 33 Western missionaries, some of whom were Dominicans, Franciscans, Salesians, Jesuits, and Vincentians, were martyred for their ministry or for refusing to renounce their Christian faith. Many of the Chinese converts were killed during the Boxer Rebellion, a xenophobic uprising during which many foreigners were slaughtered by angry peasants. Augustine Zhao Rong was a Chinese diocesan priest who was tortured and killed in 1815, after the Emperor Kia-Kin issued decrees banning Catholicism. Augustine Zhao Rong and the other Chinese martyrs were canonized in 2000 by Pope John Paul II.

Our Lady of the Rosary of Chiquinquira (Colombia / Venezuela)

There are several stories about the origins of the image of Our Lady of the Rosary of Chiquinquira in Venezuela. One of them tells of how, in 1709, an elderly washerwoman named Maria Cardenas was busy washing clothes as usual, when she saw a plank of wood floating towards her on the lake. She pulled the plank out of the water and took it home. Only then did she see an image of the Virgin and Child, miraculously imprinted on the wood. Today the street where Maria Cardenas once lived is called *El Milagro* ("the Miracle"), and on the site of her home is a large basilica honoring Our Lady. The image, which shows the Virgin holding the Child Jesus, with Saint Andrew on her left and Saint Anthony on her right, is venerated by thousands of pilgrims each year.

11

MEMORIAL OF
Saint Benedict, ABBOT

Saint Benedict of Nursia (c. 480–c. 550) was born north of Rome in Umbria. While studying in Rome, surrounded by self-indulgent companions, he decided to pursue a life as taught in the Gospel and withdrew to Enfide. On the advice of an elderly monk, Romanus of Subiaco, he became a hermit for three years. His reputation for holiness grew in the surrounding area, and the monks of Vicovaro begged him to come be their superior. Unfortunately, the monks were not inclined to follow Benedict's austere example, and they twice tried to kill him, once with poisoned bread and then with poisoned wine. Both times he was saved by miraculous intervention. Benedict's reputation grew, and after leaving Vicovaro, he found himself surrounded by so many followers that he was able to found twelve monasteries in the area of Subiaco. Eventually, Benedict built an abbey on the summit of Monte Cassino. Much of what we know of his life comes from Book Two of the *Dialogues of Gregory the Great*. Benedict is best known for his *Rule*, which is known for its wisdom and adaptability; communities both of men and of women have followed it since the sixth century to this day. For his influence, he is known as the Father of Western Monasticism and is a patron saint of Europe, venerated by Catholics and non-Catholics alike. Benedict is represented in art with symbols associated with the attempted poisonings at Vicovaro, such as a broken cup and a raven, or dressed as a monk, holding a crozier and his *Rule*. During his lifetime, Benedict predicted that his abbey on Monte Cassino would be destroyed. The first time was a few years after his death, when the Lombards invaded; most recently, it was destroyed by Allied bombs during World War II. On the Roman Calendar, Benedict is celebrated on July 11, which is the anniversary of his relics supposedly being moved to the monastery of Saint Benoît-sur-Loire in northern France. He is also celebrated on the anniversary of his death, March 21. It is possible that Benedict was descended from Jews deported from Palestine by the Romans after the fall of Masada—the part of Italy where he is from is known to be an area where deported Jews were resettled, and his name, "Benedict," is the Latin translation of a common Jewish name, "Baruch."

12

John Jones, Priest and Martyr
(Wales)

John Jones (+ 1598) is one of the Forty Martyrs of England and Wales, who were killed during the English Reformation. While the date of his birth is not known, we do know he was born in Clynnog Fawr, Wales, into a family of Welsh recusants (that is, those who remained faithful to Roman Catholicism in spite of the Reformation and subsequent persecutions). He entered a Franciscan friary at Greenwich, but when it was dissolved in 1559, he went to France and made his vows at Pontoise. Later, he moved to Rome and joined a stricter branch of the Franciscans. In 1591, he asked to be sent back to Britain, where he arrived in 1592. He worked throughout the country and became provincial of the Franciscans left in England. In 1596, he was arrested by Richard Topcliffe, a notorious "priest catcher," who tortured him before turning him over to be imprisoned. On July 3, 1598, he was tried and convicted of high treason and sentenced to be hanged, drawn, and quartered. His butchered remains were displayed on the roads to Newington and Lambeth. John Jones was canonized in 1970 by Pope Paul VI. He is sometimes known as John Buckley or John Griffith.

13

OPTIONAL MEMORIAL OF
Saint Henry

Saint Henry II (972–1024) was a German king and Holy Roman Emperor, the only German king to be canonized. Henry had considered becoming a priest, but when his father died, he inherited his father's title of Duke of Bavaria. He became King of Germany in 1002 and married Cunegunda, who is also a saint. He had a reputation for being learned and pious, and was a positive influence in Church–state relations. At that time, secular authorities appointed bishops and often selected their political allies. Henry appointed bishops who would be good pastors, and supported them in their work. Although he waged many wars, he was not the aggressor but fought only to protect his borders and preserve peace. Henry is a patron saint of Benedictine oblates and is invoked against infertility, for he and his wife were childless.

14

OPTIONAL MEMORIAL OF
Saint Camillus de Lellis 🍁

Laying aside a life of violence and gambling, Saint Camillus de Lellis (1550–1614) was ordained a priest and later founded the Order of Clerks Regular Ministers to the Sick (the Camillians), a religious order dedicated to the sick, especially those afflicted with the plague. Whether they were ministering in a hospital or tending to the wounded on the battle-field, the Camillians were easily identified by their black habit with a large red cross on the breast. Saint Camillus implemented many innovative approaches to hospital care, including proper ventilation, suitable diets, and isolation of people with infectious diseases. He is also credited with inventing field ambulances and military hospitals. Along with Saint John of God, he is patron saint of hospitals, nurses, and the sick.

MEMORIAL OF Blessed
Kateri Tekakwitha, VIRGIN 🇺🇸

Please see page 62 for more information.

15

MEMORIAL OF
Saint Bonaventure, BISHOP AND DOCTOR OF THE CHURCH

Saint Bonaventure (1221–1274), scholastic theologian and philosopher, was born in Italy and joined the Franciscans in 1243. He studied theology at Paris with his great contemporary, Thomas Aquinas. After teaching for a time, he was chosen minister general of the Franciscans in 1257, at a time when the order suffered from divisions, which he was able to do much to heal. Later, he was named cardinal bishop of Albano. Bonaventure was declared a Doctor of the Church in 1588 by Pope Sixtus V and is called the "Seraphic Doctor" because his love of God is so evident, even in his philosophical writings. When the Council of Lyons was called to bring the Greek and Latin churches back together, Bonaventure went at the request of Pope Gregory X, but he died before the Council's work was finished, receiving the Sacrament of the Sick from the pope himself. Saint Bonaventure is shown in art dressed in a Franciscan habit and wearing a cardinal's hat.

16

OPTIONAL MEMORIAL OF
Our Lady of Mount Carmel

Mount Carmel is part of a mountain range in northern Israel, significant to Christians for its biblical association with the prophet Elijah (see 1 Kings 18). In the twelfth century, the Carmelites were founded at a site that is supposed to have been Elijah's cave and soon built a monastery there. For this reason, the Carmelites honor the Blessed Virgin Mary under the title Our Lady of Mount Carmel. The English Carmelite, Saint Simon Stock (feast day, May 16), is believed to have been given the brown scapular by Our Lady, and those who wear it believe they can be sure of her help at the hour of their death.

Our Lady of Carmel of Maipú (Chile)

Today the people of Chile celebrate their patroness, Our Lady of Mount Carmel. The statue, which dates from 1785, has become an icon of the struggle for independence of the people of Chile. In 1818, when Chile was at war with Spain, the people prayed to Our Lady and the leaders vowed to build a church in her honor at the site of their victory over the Spanish. On April 5, the Chilean forces defeated the Spanish at Maipu, and before the year was out, the first stone of the sanctuary was laid. The present church was completed in 1974.

18

OPTIONAL MEMORIAL OF Saint Camillus de Lellis, PRIEST 🇺🇸

Please see page 93 for more information.

20

OPTIONAL MEMORIAL OF
Saint Apollinaris, BISHOP AND MARTYR

Not much is known about Saint Apollinaris (dates unknown) except that he was from Antioch, a Syrian, and the first bishop of Ravenna. Tradition says he was appointed bishop by Saint Peter himself. Apollinaris was exiled with his people during the persecution of Emperor Vespasian. As he left the city, he was pointed out as the leader of the Christians. He was tortured and executed with a sword. Saint Apollinaris is a patron saint of those suffering from epilepsy or gout and is shown in art with a sword, the instrument of his martyrdom.

21

OPTIONAL MEMORIAL OF Saint Lawrence of Brindisi, PRIEST AND DOCTOR OF THE CHURCH

Saint Lawrence of Bridnisi (1559–1619) was born at Brindisi in what was then the Kingdom of Naples. He joined the Capuchins and was sent to be educated at University of Padua. Lawrence was known for his intelligence, and he became fluent in most Europeans and Semitic languages. It was said that he knew the entire Bible in the original languages. His known writings comprise eight volumes of sermons, two treatises on oratory, commentaries on Genesis and Ezekiel, and three volumes of religious polemics annotated in Greek and Hebrew. He was canonized by Pope Leo XIII in 1881 and was proclaimed a Doctor of the Church in 1959 by Pope John XXIII. Saint Lawrence is the patron saint of the city of

Brindisi and is depicted leading an army against the Turks, bearing the child Jesus, because of his role in battle against the Ottoman Empire.

22

MEMORIAL OF
Saint Mary Magdalene

Saint Mary Magdalene (first century) was one of the followers of Jesus and one of the few witnesses of his Crucifixion and burial. At dawn on the third day, she went to anoint the body and was the first to see the empty tomb. She immediately ran to tell Peter and John (see John 20:1–2)—for this reason, she has been called the "apostle to the Apostles" by Saint Bernard of Clairvaux, among others. One tradition puts her in Ephesus after the Ascension, but the French believe she sailed to Marseilles in a small boat, accompanied by her brother Lazarus, and lived in a cave doing penance for the rest of her life.

23

OPTIONAL MEMORIAL OF
Saint Bridget, RELIGIOUS

Saint Bridget of Sweden (1303–1373) was a mystic and the founder of the Bridgettines. She was happily married to a Swedish lord and had eight children, one of whom was Saint Catherine of Sweden. The couple went on pilgrimage to Santiago de Compostela in the early 1340s, and Bridget's husband died soon after their return. Bridget had a series of visions that heavily influenced the way the nativity is represented in art: Mary is blond-haired, and Jesus is not born naturally but arrives as a beam of light, so that she is able to kneel immediately with Saint Joseph to adore

him. Saint Bridget is a patron saint of Europe and of widows, and is shown in art bearing a pilgrim's staff and bag, or wearing a crown.

Saint Philip Evans and Saint John Lloyd, Priests and Martyrs (Wales)

Saints Philip Evans (1645–1679) and John Lloyd (+1679), both priests, are among the Forty Martyrs of England and Wales who died during the persecution of Catholics that resulted from the English Reformation. Philip Evans was a Jesuit who returned to Wales after Ordination. John Lloyd was a diocesan priest who had to leave Great Britain to be educated but returned in spite of the danger. The two priests were arrested during the scare that followed the false plot dreamed up by Titus Oates. Both were executed on July 22, 1679 and were canonized in 1970 by Pope Paul VI.

24

OPTIONAL MEMORIAL OF Saint Sharbel Makhlūf, PRIEST

Saint Sharbel Makhlūf (1828–1898) was a Maronite Catholic monk and priest in Lebanon. He joined the monastery of Saint Maron at 23, and after living in community became a hermit from 1875 to his death. His reputation for holiness drew visitors who sought a word of wisdom or blessing. Sharbel observed a strict fast and had great devotion to the Eucharist. Although dedicated to his life as a hermit, he always willingly went out to perform priestly ministry in local villages when requested. Sharbel died on Christmas Eve 1898, after becoming ill while celebrating Eucharist. He was canonized in 1977.

25

FEAST OF Saint James, APOSTLE

Today we celebrate Saint James "the Greater" (first century), not to be confused with Saint James "the Lesser," the Apostle who later became the first bishop of Jerusalem and is thought to be the author of the letter that is part of the New Testament.

The Saint James we honor today is the brother of the Apostle John, one of the "Sons of Thunder" (Mark 3:17) who were privileged witnesses of some of Jesus' greatest signs: the raising of the daughter of Jairus from the dead, the Transfiguration, and the agony in the garden. James was the first Apostle to suffer martyrdom and the only one to have his death recorded in the Acts of the Apostles. According to legend, his friends carried his remains away in a rudderless boat that drifted all the way to Spain. Many centuries later, they were discovered, and a great cathedral was built over the spot (Santiago de Compostela), which became one of the most popular pilgrimage destinations of the Middle Ages. To this day, hundreds of thousands of pilgrims make their way to that remote corner of Spain to venerate the relics of Saint James. He is depicted in art dressed as a pilgrim with a scallop shell on his hat, the way pilgrims to Compostella dress. He is venerated as the patron saint of Spain, Nicaragua, and Guatemala.

26

MEMORIAL OF Saints Joachim and Anne, PARENTS OF THE BLESSED VIRGIN MARY

The tradition of Saints Joachim and Anne (first century) is not scriptural but comes mostly from the apocryphal Protoevangelium of James. It became popular in the thirteenth century when Jacobus de Voragine retold the story in his *Golden Legend*, which was very popular in the Middle Ages. The story of the conception of Mary echoes that of Samuel (see 1 Samuel 1:20): Joachim and Ann are a childless couple who pray to have children and promise to dedicate their child to God. Each is told by an angel that they will conceive, and afterward they meet at a gate of Jerusalem and embrace in joy. This event has been depicted in art by artists such as Dürer and Giotto.

Today is a feast in Canada. The proper title in Canada is the Feast of Saint Anne, Patron of the Province of Quebec, and Saint Joachim, Parents of the Blessed Virgin Mary.

29

MEMORIAL OF Saint Martha

Saint Martha was the sister of Lazarus and Mary, friends of Jesus. She appears to have been a practical-minded woman, for she seems to have organized the dinner in Luke 10:38–42, and she protests when Jesus commands that the stone be rolled from the entrance to her brother's tomb after he'd been dead for three days. At the same time, however, she is one of the few in the Gospel to profess her faith in Jesus as the Messiah: "Yes, Lord, I believe that you are the Messiah, the Son of God, the one coming into the world" (John 11:27). The Golden Legend records the tradition that Martha, with her sister, Mary, and brother, Lazarus, fled Judea after the death of Jesus and landed at Marseilles. Martha is supposed to have traveled to Avignon, where she converted many to Christianity. Saint Martha is shown in art bearing the tools of a housekeeper—keys or a broom—and is a patron saint of domestic servants, homemakers, cooks, and single laywomen.

Venerable Nelson Baker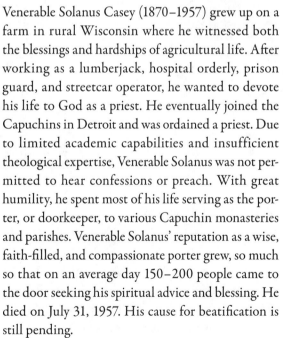

After fighting in the Civil War and establishing a successful business, Venerable Nelson Baker (1842–1936), a New York native, decided to become a priest. While serving as superintendent of Limestone Hill Institutions, consisting of a parish and orphanage, he founded the Association of Our Lady of Victory to provide financial support to charitable organizations. With the help of the Association and many other faith-filled people, Venerable Nelson launched many initiatives, including an infant home, orphanage, hospital, elementary school, high school, home for unwed mothers, nurses' home, and the building of a minor basilica. Due to these many charitable endeavors, Venerable Nelson is remembered as building the "city of charity" in Lackawanna, New York.

Reverend Nelson died on this day in 1939. His cause for beatification is still pending.

30

OPTIONAL MEMORIAL OF Saint Peter Chrysologus, BISHOP AND DOCTOR OF THE CHURCH

Not much is known about Saint Peter, who lived from approximately 380 to 450. He was bishop of Ravenna from about the year 433. One hundred and seventy-six of his homilies survive, brief and to the point, in which he explains the Incarnation, the Creed, and the major heresies of his day. He was given the name Chrysologus, or "golden-worded," for his eloquent preaching.

31

MEMORIAL OF Saint Ignatius of Loyola, PRIEST

Saint Ignatius of Loyola (1491–1556) was the founder and first Father General of the Society of Jesus, or Jesuits, and author of the *Spiritual Exercises.* Born in the Basque region of Spain, he joined the army and was severely wounded in battle. While recovering, he read a life of Christ and lives of the saints, and decided to emulate them. He laid his military equipment before a statue of Mary at the Benedictine Abbey of Montserrat, and spent several months in a cave near Manresa. After making a pilgrimage to the Holy Land, he enrolled at the University of Paris, and he gathered six companions who would become the first Jesuits.

Venerable Solanus Casey

Venerable Solanus Casey (1870–1957) grew up on a farm in rural Wisconsin where he witnessed both the blessings and hardships of agricultural life. After working as a lumberjack, hospital orderly, prison guard, and streetcar operator, he wanted to devote his life to God as a priest. He eventually joined the Capuchins in Detroit and was ordained a priest. Due to limited academic capabilities and insufficient theological expertise, Venerable Solanus was not permitted to hear confessions or preach. With great humility, he spent most of his life serving as the porter, or doorkeeper, to various Capuchin monasteries and parishes. Venerable Solanus' reputation as a wise, faith-filled, and compassionate porter grew, so much so that on an average day 150–200 people came to the door seeking his spiritual advice and blessing. He died on July 31, 1957. His cause for beatification is still pending.

August

Month of August

The eighth month is named after Augustus Caesar, who was emperor at the time of the birth of Jesus. Augustus was the first Roman emperor. In the Northern Hemisphere, this month marks the fullness of summer. The worship of the Church during August reflects summer's abundance in celebrating the Feast of the Transfiguration of the Lord and the Solemnity of the Assumption of the Blessed Virgin Mary .

Month of the Immaculate Heart

The month of August is dedicated to the Immaculate Heart of Mary. The memorial of the Immaculate Heart of Mary takes place on the day after the Solemnity of the Sacred Heart of Jesus, usually in June, but in this month when we celebrate Mary's Assumption (August 15) and her Coronation or Queenship (August 22), we also give honor to her Immaculate Heart. There are many prayers to the

Images of Saints and Feasts in August (L to R): Saint Augustine (August 28), Transfiguration of the Lord (August 6), Saint Maximilian Mary Kolbe (August 14).

Immaculate Heart of Mary. Here is one short enough to memorize and pray every day during this special month:

> O Immaculate Heart of the Blessed Virgin Mary, obtain for me from Jesus a pure and humble heart.

1

MEMORIAL OF Saint Alphonsus Mary Liguori, BISHOP AND DOCTOR OF THE CHURCH

Following a successful career as a lawyer, Saint Alphonsus Mary Ligouri (1696–1787) lost a legal case. He believed this to be a sign from God that he should change his life and study for the priesthood. At the suggestion of a bishop friend, he founded the Congregation of the Most Holy Redeemer, also known as the Redemptorists, a community of priests dedicated to preaching, hearing confessions, and administering the sacraments. One of his most important contributions to the Church is his prolific writing in the area of moral theology. Also included among his writings are many devotional works regarding Mary and the saints. He influenced the Church not only through his writings, but also through his leadership as a bishop. Due to his many accomplishments, he was declared a Doctor of the Church and is recognized as one of the greatest moral theologians in Church history.

1–6

FEAST OF THE Savior of the World (El Salvador)

El Salvador means "The Savior," and the full name of El Salvador's capital city is *La Ciudad de Gran San Salvador*, "The City of the Great Holy Savior." A monument to Christ standing in the center of the city has become an emblem for the entire nation. The statue shows Christ standing on the globe, with one hand extended in blessing over the world, while the other hand points upwards. The monument is a reminder to the people of El Salvador that Christ is the Lord of heaven and earth; and that we must live on earth in a manner worthy of our heavenly destiny. During the week preceding August 6, the city of San Salvador has a great festival honoring their patron.

2

Our Lady of the Angels (Costa Rica)

Our Lady of the Angels, *Nuestra Señora de los Ángeles*, is a three-inch-high stone statue of the Virgin Mary holding the infant Jesus. The story is told that a poor woman named Juana Pereira found the small statue on a rock and took it home with her. The next morning the statue had disappeared, but Juana discovered it again on the same rock. She took the statue to the priest who put it under lock and key; nevertheless, the next morning, the statue was back in its place on the rock! Clearly, the Virgin wanted to remain there, and eventually a great basilica was erected over the spot. Because of the dark color of the stone, this image of Mary is affectionately called La Negrita. She is the Patroness of Costa Rica, and is especially loved by the poor. Each August, more than a million people go on pilgrimage to the shrine, some making the last stage of the journey on their hands and knees. Our Lady of the Angels, pray for us, and for the people of Costa Rica.

OPTIONAL MEMORIAL OF Saint Eusebius of Vercelli, BISHOP

Saint Eusebius (+ 371) was born in Sardinia. He was made the first bishop of Vercelli, probably in the 340s, and formed his clergy into a monastic community. At the 355 Synod of Milan, he refused to condemn

Athanasius for opposing the Arian heresy, which undermined belief in the full divinity of Christ. As a result, he was exiled to Syria, to Cappadocia, and later to Egypt. When he was finally allowed to return from exile, he joined Athanasius at a synod that affirmed the divinity of the Holy Spirit and urged merciful treatment of repentant bishops who had signed Arian creeds. Once he returned to Vercelli, he joined Hilary of Poitiers to defeat the Arian heresy in the West. He died in 371 but was probably not martyred.

OPTIONAL MEMORIAL OF Saint Peter Julian Eymard, PRIEST

Saint Peter Julian Eymard (1811–1868) was a French Catholic priest, who founded two religious orders, the Congregation of the Blessed Sacrament and, for women, the Servants of the Blessed Sacrament. Originally rejected as a candidate for the priesthood because of poor health, he was eventually ordained for the Diocese of Grenoble and later joined the Marist Fathers. Peter Julian Eymard worked tirelessly to encourage frequent reception of Holy Communion and has been called the "apostle of the Eucharist." He was a friend of his contemporaries, Saint Peter Chanel and Saint John Vianney, and advised the sculptor Auguste Rodin not to give up art to become a lay brother in his Congregation.

3

Saint Germanus of Auxerre, Bishop (Wales)

Saint Germanus of Auxerre (c. 380–c. 448) was born in Gaul to noble parents and practiced law before becoming a priest and being ordained bishop of Auxerre by his predecessor, Saint Amator. The bishops of Gaul selected him to visit Britain shortly after the Romans left, in order to combat the heresy of Pelagianism, which denied that original sin had

corrupted human nature, and that we can choose between good or evil without grace. He is supposed to have led an army of Britons to victory against an army of Picts and Saxons. Germanus later returned to the Continent and died in Ravenna. Because he visited Cornwall and Wales, he is venerated there, and he is credited with the founding of the diocese of Sodor and Mann on the Isle of Man.

4

MEMORIAL OF Saint John Mary Vianney, PRIEST

The suppression of the Church during the French Revolution (1786–1759) resulted in an unchurched and ignorant generation. Saint John Mary Vianney desired to draw these lost souls back to the Church and re-educate them in their faith. As the *curé* (parish priest) of the isolated village of Ars, he began by living a life of austerity and mortification, and brought catechesis and the sacraments, especially the Sacrament of Reconciliation, back to the people. His reputation for holiness spread throughout France—so many wished to see the *Curé d'Ars*, that one could wait over a week to see him, and it was said that if all priests were like him, everyone in France would be Catholic. Saint John Vianney is the patron saint of priests, especially those who work in parishes.

5

OPTIONAL MEMORIAL OF THE Dedication of the Basilica of Saint Mary Major

Today the Church celebrates the dedication of the Basilica of Saint Mary Major, *Santa Maria Maggiore*, in Rome, the oldest church in the West dedicated to the Blessed Virgin Mary. At the Council of Ephesus in 431, Mary was acclaimed not only as the mother of Jesus, but as the Mother of God. Following the Council, Pope Sixtus III dedicated this basilica to the honor of Mary, Mother of God.

A wonderful legend is associated with this great church. Tradition tells us that on August 5, in the hottest days of the Roman summer, a miraculous snow fell on the Esquiline Hill in Rome, marking the spot where Mary wanted a church built in her honor. It was thus that Mary came to be venerated here as Our Lady of the Snows.

This great church houses the oldest image of the Virgin and Child in Rome, known as the *Salus Populi Romani*, "Salvation of the people of Rome." Perhaps the most-visited place in the basilica is the crypt of the Nativity, where the faithful venerate the relics of the manger in which Mary laid the infant Jesus.

OPTIONAL MEMORIAL OF Blessed Frédéric Janssoone, PRIEST 🍁

Blessed Frédéric Janssoone (1838–1916) was born in Flanders to a family of wealthy farmers, the youngest of thirteen children. When his father died, he left school to help support his family, even though he was only nine years old. When his mother died in 1861, he realized that he was called to be a religious and, after considering the Trappists, joined the Franciscans. After Ordination, he was sent to the Holy Land where he ministered to pilgrims and revived the custom of making the Stations of the Cross in the streets of Jerusalem. In 1881, Frédéric was sent to Canada to raise funds for the Holy Land mission, and in 1888, he returned to minister there for the rest of his life. He was instrumental in strengthening the Franciscan presence in Canada, especially by encouraging the growth of the Third Order and writing and distributing Catholic literature. He built the shrine to Our Lady at Cap-de-la-Madeleine in the diocese of Trois-Rivières. Blessed Frédéric was a friend of Saint André Bessette, who testified to his holiness. He was beatified by Pope John Paul II in 1988.

Our Lady of Copacabana (Bolivia)

In Bolivia today, Mary is venerated under the title of Our Lady of Copacabana. This image of the Virgin and child dates from the late 16th century and has a remarkable history. Some Inca fishermen, caught in a storm on Lake Titicaca, prayed to the Virgin, who appeared to them and led them safely to shore. To express their gratitude, they built a chapel, and wanted to place in it a statue of the Virgin. They asked an Inca sculptor, Francisco Tito, to create the image of the Mother of God for the new chapel. He brought his first effort, in clay, to the priest, but he deemed it too clumsy to be placed in the church. Not discouraged, Francisco Tito began to study wood carving. At last, he succeeded. The statue he carved stands about four feet high. Mary and Jesus have Inca features, and Mary even wears the garb of an Inca princess. The image was first venerated on February 2, in 1583, and ever since a steady stream of pilgrims have visited the shrine. The original image never leaves the sanctuary, but a copy has been made for processions that draw thousands of the faithful every year. Our Lady of Copacabana, pray for us, and for the people of Bolivia.

FEAST OF THE Transfiguration of the Lord

Today, the Church recalls the Transfiguration of the Lord, which is recorded in all three synoptic Gospels. In the East, this special feast was observed as long ago as the fifth century, though it took a little longer to become part of the Roman liturgical calendar, and was not universally celebrated until 1457.

Matthew, Mark, and Luke all recount the same sequence of events: Jesus tells his disciples about his coming Passion—how he must be put to death and rise again before entering his glory, and the disciples are scandalized. How could the long-awaited

Messiah suffer rejection and death? A few days later, Jesus takes Peter, along with James and John, and goes up a mountain to pray. As he prays, his appearance changes. His face shines "like the sun," and even his clothes are "dazzling white, such as no one on earth could bleach them" (Mark 9:3). And suddenly Moses and Elijah are there with him, and the voice of God is heard. No wonder the disciples are stunned and frightened, and Peter blurts out, "Rabbi, it is good for us to be here" (Mark 9:5). Peter wants to cling to this vision of Christ in his glory forever. But suddenly, the vision is over, and Jesus is there alone.

Jesus' Transfiguration and his Passion are closely intertwined. Moses and Elijah speak to him of his "exodus," his Passion, which is the sacrifice that fulfills all the precepts of the Law, the mystery foretold by the Prophets. Jesus gives his disciples this glimpse of his glory for a reason: so that when the Cross comes, they will not lose heart. When they come down from the mountain, Jesus warns the three not to tell anyone what they have seen, "until after the Son of Man had risen from the dead" (Mark 9:9). The Transfiguration and the Passion of Jesus are part of the same mystery: the only way to glory is through the Cross.

"These are the divine wonders we celebrate today," says an ancient homily for this feast. "This is the festival of Christ that has drawn us here. Let us listen, then, to the sacred voice of God so compellingly calling us from on high, from the summit of the mountain, so that with the Lord's chosen disciples we may penetrate the deep meaning of these holy mysteries, so far beyond our capacity to express" (Saint Anastasius of Sinai, Liturgy of the Hours, volume IV, p. 1286).

Hiroshima Memorial Day

Hiroshima, Japan, is a thriving city of shipyards and factories. Along one of its seven rivers sits a building once used to display Japanese products. Now, half-destroyed, the building has become known as the Atomic Dome. It serves as an eerie reminder of what happened on this day in 1945. That was when the first atomic bomb ever used on an inhabited area was dropped on Hiroshima. At that time the city was built mostly of wood. After the explosion, the few structures made of concrete, like the Atomic Dome, stood in a wasteland. No one knew if grass would grow again in Hiroshima or if humans could ever safely live there. Many people were killed outright by the explosion. Many more died slowly because of radiation sickness. A large group of survivors have suffered throughout their lives with health problems. They are called *hibakusha*—explosion-affected people.

The Atomic Dome is now surrounded by a peace park. All day today the park will be filled with people. Services begin at 8:15 in the morning, when survivors and their children will say a silent prayer for peace. Later, all will gather at the Cenotaph, a monument bearing the names of all who died because of the bomb. After dark, children will set paper lanterns afloat in the Ohta River. Each lantern bears the name of someone who has died. As the children float their lanterns, they will sing, "So long as this life lasts, give peace back to us, peace that will never end."

This day is a time for all citizens of the world, to join in heartfelt prayer and work for lasting peace. Pope John Paul II said when he visited Hiroshima, "In the past it was possible to destroy a village, a town, a region, even a country. Now the whole planet has come under threat."

7

OPTIONAL MEMORIAL OF
Saint Sixtus II, POPE, AND COMPANIONS, MARTYRS

Saint Sixtus II was pope for less than a year, from August 30, 257, to August 6, 258. He restored relations with the African and Eastern churches, which had been broken off over the question of heretical Baptism. Pope Sixtus, along with several deacons, was one of the first victims of the persecution begun by the emperor Valerian in 258. He is referred to by name in Eucharistic Prayer I.

OPTIONAL MEMORIAL OF
Saint Cajetan, PRIEST

Saint Cajetan—not to be confused with Thomas Cardinal Cajetan—was born in 1480 and founded the Order of the Clerics Regular, or Theatines, which was canonically erected by Clement VII in 1524. The idea behind the Order was to combine the spirit of monasticism with active ministry. He died in 1547. He is a patron saint of workers, gamblers, and the unemployed, and is especially venerated in Argentina.

MEMORIAL OF
Saint Dominic, PRIEST

Saint Dominic (c. 1170–1221), a contemporary of Saint Francis of Assisi, founded a mendicant order of men (those who rely on the charity of others), called the Order of Preachers or Dominicans, to preach against theological error. One of the pressing issues facing the newly established Order was the Albigensian heresy, claiming that matter, specifically the body, is evil. In order to fight against this heretical thinking, the Black Friars, as they were commonly known because of the color of the cape they wore over their white habit, went from town to town preaching the goodness of the body. In order to preach sound doctrine with clarity, Saint Dominic exhorted his sons to engage in rigorous academic study. He eventually started a contemplative female branch of the Dominicans to support the apostolate of the men through prayer.

OPTIONAL MEMORIAL OF
Saint Teresa Benedicta of the Cross, VIRGIN AND MARTYR

Saint Teresa Benedicta of the Cross was born Edith Stein at Breslau in 1891 into an observant Jewish family, but by the time she reached her teens, she had become an atheist. She went on to study philosophy and received her doctorate at Freiburg under the philosopher Edmund Husserl but left her university career to teach at a girls' school when Husserl did not support her further studies. Influenced by her study of scholastic theology and spirituality, she became a Catholic in 1922. In 1932, she became a lecturer at Munster, but anti-Semitic laws passed by the Nazis forced her to resign, and she entered the Carmel at Cologne in 1933. In an attempt to protect her from the Nazis, she was transferred to a Carmel in the Netherlands, but when the Dutch bishops condemned Nazi racism, the Nazis retaliated by arresting Jewish converts. Edith, along with her sister Rosa, who had also become a Catholic, was deported to Auschwitz and died in the gas chamber on August 9, 1942. She was canonized by Pope John Paul II in 1998.

Nagasaki Memorial Day

Today marks the second time in history that a nuclear weapon was used in war. The bomb was dropped in 1945 on the city of Nagasaki in Japan. Nagasaki is a port city on the west coast of the island of Kyushu. The first nuclear explosion, three days earlier, destroyed the Japanese city of Hiroshima. The bomb dropped on Nagasaki destroyed almost two square miles in the heart of the city, where its medical centers were located. So just at the time when there were large numbers of injured people, the doctors and hospitals to care for them were gone. Each time a nuclear weapon is tested, the citizens of Nagasaki send a letter of protest. In 1980, they issued the Nagasaki Peace

Declaration. It points out that the world's nuclear stockpile could now destroy humanity several times over. It asks the nations to pray for peace, to stop the buildup of nuclear weapons, and to end the arms race. It says that "unless this dangerous course is reversed, no true peace or progress will ever be attained on earth."

In 1983 the American Catholic bishops sent out a letter on the nuclear arms race. They used the Scriptures, traditional Church teachings and the experience of peacemakers in forming their judgments. The result of their work is called *The Challenge of Peace: God's Promise and Our Response*. In this letter the bishops say "Peace, like the kingdom of God itself, is both a divine gift and a human work. We are called to be a church at the service of peace."

10

FEAST OF Saint Lawrence, DEACON AND MARTYR

Saint Lawrence (+ 258) was one of seven deacons of ancient Rome martyred under Emperor Valerian in 258. Tradition says that he was deacon to Pope Saint Sixtus II. According to Saint Ambrose, Lawrence met the pope being taken to execution and is supposed to have said, "Where are you going without your deacon?" Sixtus prophesied that he would follow in three days. Lawrence is said to have been martyred by being cooked alive on a grill. He is portrayed in art holding a gridiron, the instrument of his martyrdom, and wearing a dalmatic, the vestment of a deacon. Saint Lawrence is a patron saint of the city of Rome and of comedians because of the quip he is reputed to have made to his executioners: "Turn me over; I'm done on one side."

11

MEMORIAL OF Saint Clare, VIRGIN

Saint Clare of Assisi (c. 1193–1253) was one of first followers of Saint Francis of Assisi and the foundress of the Poor Clares. Her parents wanted her to marry a rich man, but she fled and Francis received her into religious life. She remained close to Francis and cared for him in his illnesses. After Francis died, Clare fought to maintain the unique spirituality of the Poor Clares, and is the first woman known to have written a monastic rule. She is depicted holding a monstrance, ciborium, or pyx because of a tradition that she warded off invaders in 1234 by displaying the Blessed Sacrament. Her sister, Agnes of Assisi, followed her into religious life and is also a canonized saint. Saint Clare is a patron saint of those afflicted with eye diseases.

12

OPTIONAL MEMORIAL OF Saint Jane Frances de Chantal

Saint Jane Frances de Chantal (1572–1641) was born in Dijon, France. She was happily married with six children, when her husband was killed in a hunting accident. She begged God to send her a spiritual guide, and shortly thereafter she met Francis de Sales. In 1610, she founded the Order of the Visitation of Mary, a community of nuns unique at the time for accepting widows and moderating austerities so they could adapt to community life. Although she was careful to make arrangements for her children before leaving them, they caused her great suffering. Saint Jane Frances is known for her spirit of renunciation and union with God's will and is the patron saint of parents who have been separated from their children.

13

OPTIONAL MEMORIAL OF Saints Pontian, POPE, AND HIPPOLYTUS, PRIEST, MARTYRS

Little is known about Saint Pontian (c. + 236), save that he was pope from 198 or 199 to 236. After the schism of Saint Hippolytus ended, Emperor Maximinus exiled Pontian to the Sardinian mines, where he died.

Saint Hippolytus (c. 170–c. 236) was a prolific writer and probably a disciple of Irenaeus. He wrote the *Refutation of All Heresies* and exegeses of the Song of Songs and Daniel, but he is best known as a possible author of the *Apostolic Tradition*, an invaluable source of information on customs and liturgy during the first centuries of the Church. Ironically, Hippolytus shares this day with Pope Pontian, against whom he led a schism.

14

MEMORIAL OF Saint Maximilian Mary Kolbe, PRIEST AND MARTYR

Saint Maximilian Maria Kolbe (1894–1941) was a Polish Franciscan who volunteered to die in place of a stranger in Auschwitz. From an early age, Maximilian had a strong devotion to the Virgin Mary, and in 1907, he entered the Conventual Franciscans, along with his brother. He was sent to study at the Pontifical Gregorian University in Rome, and seeing anti-Catholic demonstrations, he decided to form the Militia Immaculata. He was innovative in his use of modern media, especially printing technology and radio, for catechesis, publishing first a monthly magazine, and then a daily

newspaper that soon had the widest circulat[ion] Poland. During the 1930s, he started a missi[on] Japan and built a monastery in Nagasaki that [was] one of the few buildings left undamaged by t[he] atomic bomb dropped at the end of World War II. Because he hid Jews from the Nazis in his monastery in Poland, the Gestapo arrested Maximilian, and eventually he was transferred to Auschwitz. When three prisoners escaped, the camp commandant selected ten men to die by starvation. One of the men cried out, "My wife! My children!" and Maximilian volunteered to take his place in the bunker. He survived for two weeks, outliving the others, dying only when the guards injected him with carbolic acid. Saint Maximilian Kolbe was canonized by Pope John Paul II in 1982. He is a patron saint of journalists, amateur radio operators, and of prisoners, and he is often depicted wearing the striped uniform of a death-camp inmate.

Venerable Michael J. McGivney

Venerable Michael J. McGivney (1852–1890), the oldest child of Irish immigrants, grew up in Waterbury, Connecticut where he witnessed and experienced impoverished conditions. Due to financial need within his family, he left school at the age of thirteen to pursue work in the brass mills of Waterbury. At the age of sixteen, he decided to pursue his lifelong dream of becoming a priest, but his father died soon after he began his studies, which placed the family in dire financial need. He returned home for a period of time to help support the family but was eventually ordained a priest. With a group of fervent parishioners, he founded the Knights of Columbus, a fraternal society for Catholic men that promotes the Catholic faith, supports priestly and religious vocations, performs charitable works, and provides various life insurance programs. Reverend Michael died on August 14, 1890. The cause for his beatification is still pending.

15

THE Assumption
~~~~~ssed Virgin Mary

~~~~~ of the Assumption of the Blessed Virgin ~~~~~ was proclaimed in 1950, but this observance ~~~~~ been celebrated on this day from the middle of the fifth century. On this solemnity, we profess our belief that Mary has gone before us, body and soul, into heaven. For her, the resurrection of the dead has taken place already. And thus the Assumption is technically an "Easter feast." As Pope Benedict said in his homily for this day (2008), "The Solemnity of the Assumption of the Blessed Virgin Mary, the oldest Marian Feast, returns every year in the heart of the summer. It is an opportunity to rise with Mary to the heights of the spirit where one breathes the pure air of supernatural life and contemplates the most authentic beauty, the beauty of holiness. The atmosphere of today's celebration is steeped in paschal joy."

Our Lady of La Vang (Vietnam)

From 1798–1801, there was a severe persecution of Christians in Vietnam. During this persecution, a group of Christians took refuge in the rain forest of La Vang. Conditions were extremely difficult, and many were ill. One night as they gathered in prayer, a beautiful lady appeared to them, surrounded with light. She wore traditional Vietnamese dress and held a child in her arms. The lady told them not to be afraid, but to boil leaves from the trees around them for medicine and to trust in God. The witnesses realized that they had seen the Blessed Virgin Mary with the infant Christ. After the persecutions ended, people continued to come to that place to pray, and by 1820 a chapel had been built on the spot. Today, Our Lady of La Vang is venerated as the Patroness of Vietnam, and her shrine draws thousands of pilgrims each year. On this Solemnity of the Assumption of the Blessed Virgin Mary, the people of Vietnam

remember how Mary came to help them in their hour of need. Our Lady of La Vang, pray for us, and for the people of Vietnam.

16

OPTIONAL MEMORIAL OF
Saint Stephen of Hungary

Saint Stephen (+ 1038) is thought of as the founder of the kingdom of Hungary, was its first king, and established Christianity there. According to legend, he was baptized by Saint Adalbert of Prague. Hungarians believe that Pope Silvester II sent Stephen a jeweled gold crown, along with a letter recognizing him as king. This crown is venerated by the people of Hungary, although the Crown of Saint Stephen that we have today probably dates from the twelfth century. Saint Stephen discouraged the practice of pagan customs, brought priests in to serve as missionaries, and founded several dioceses. He had hoped to retire and lead a life of prayer and contemplation after handing the kingdom to his son, Emeric, but Emeric died young, breaking his father's heart. Stephen ruled until his death in 1038 on August 15, the celebration of the Assumption of the Blessed Virgin Mary. As he died, he asked Mary to look after the people of Hungary as their queen. Stephen was the first canonized "confessor king," a new category, and is venerated as the patron saint of Hungary. He is also the patron saint of kings, masons, and children who are dying.

19

OPTIONAL MEMORIAL OF
Saint John Eudes, Priest

Saint John Eudes (1601–1680), a successful preacher in France, cared for plague victims on both a physical and spiritual level. In light of the Protestant Reformation, he felt that the academic and spiritual training of priests needed to be strengthened; therefore, he established a society of diocesan priests: the Congregation of Jesus and Mary, commonly called the Eudists. Their sole purpose was directed toward the foundation of new seminaries where future priests would be equipped with the necessary tools to respond pastorally to the turbulent times. He eventually established a religious community of women, the Congregation of Our Lady of Charity of the Refuge, dedicated to the rehabilitation of prostitutes.

20

Memorial of
Saint Bernard, Abbot and Doctor of the Church

Saint Bernard (1090–1153) joined the Cistercian Abbey at Citeaux, known for its strict and austere way of life. Within a short time he was noticed for his leadership; hence, he was appointed abbot of a new monastery at Clairvaux. His monastic vision at Clairvaux led to the foundation of several monasteries throughout France, Britain, and Ireland. In the solitude he wrote numerous theological and spiritual classics, including his treatise *On Loving God*, 86 sermons on the Song of Songs, and a major work *On Consideration*, a reflection on papal spirituality. Saint Bernard had a special devotion to Mary, earning him the titles "Our Lady's faithful chaplain" and "Mary's harper." Due to his abundant writing and influence upon the Church, he was declared a Doctor of the Church.

21

Memorial of
Saint Pius X, Pope

Saint Pius X (1835–1914) was born Giuseppe Sarto in Riese, Italy. He grew up poor but was able to attend seminary on a scholarship. As pope he was a reformer but at the same time conservative in matters of theology. He published the first Code of Canon Law, which gathered the laws of the Church into one volume. His early pastoral experience influenced him to encourage frequent reception of communion, his lasting legacy. He reformed the liturgy, especially the breviary (Liturgy of the Hours) and encouraged the use of Gregorian chant, replacing the ornate Baroque and Classical compositions that were commonly used. Pius X lowered the "age of reason" from twelve to seven, making it possible for younger children to receive the Eucharist. It is said that the onset of World War I caused him so much distress that he died in 1914, as the war began. Pius X is a patron saint of first communicants for his role in lowering the age of first Holy Communion.

Our Lady of Knock (Ireland)

August 21, 1879, was an ordinary day in Knock, County Mayo, Ireland. It was raining, and most people were inside. But a few who walked past the village church beheld a remarkable sight. Against the outside wall of the church, they saw a vision of Mary, wearing a crown that shone as if made of fire, flanked by Joseph and John the Evangelist. To her left was an altar surmounted by a large cross, and at the foot of the cross, the Lamb of God. Behind the altar, angels knelt in adoration. The apparition lasted about two hours, and the witnesses, who ranged in age from five to seventy-five, stayed there throughout, praying the Rosary together. The apparitions recurred three more times in the next few months, always in the same way. The site of the apparition rapidly became a very popular shrine. An airport was even built near the site to accommodate the pilgrims! Our Lady of Knock, pray for us, and for the people of Ireland.

22

MEMORIAL OF THE Queenship of the Blessed Virgin Mary

Today's Memorial of the Queenship of the Blessed Virgin Mary is a relatively new one on the Catholic calendar, established by Pope Pius XII in 1954. But its roots reach deep into our Catholic tradition. The early Church Fathers recognized that the Mother of Christ, the King, is herself a Queen. Through the centuries, artists have loved to paint the humble Virgin, crowned by the Holy Trinity amid the glories of heaven. In the Litany of Loreto, we call upon Mary as Queen of Angels, Queen of all saints, Queen conceived without sin, Queen assumed into heaven, Queen of the rosary, Queen of peace. Mary is our Queen, but she is also our Mother. And in the words of Saint Thérèse, the Little Flower, "She is more Mother than Queen."

23

OPTIONAL MEMORIAL OF Saint Rose of Lima, VIRGIN

During Saint Rose of Lima's (1586–1617) brief life, people noticed her physical beauty, declaring her *como una rosa* ("like a rose"), but the beauty of her soul far surpassed her physical appearance. Saint Rose longed to live solely for God, so she renounced the institution of Marriage by claiming Christ as her spouse. Basing her life upon Saint Catherine of Siena, she lived a penitential life, setting up an infirmary in the family home to care for impoverished children and the sick. She gained popularity due to

her selfless service to the needy. As the first canonized saint of the Americas, she is the patron saint of South and Central America, the Philippines, and the West Indies.

24

FEAST OF Saint Bartholomew, APOSTLE

Not much is known about Saint Bartholomew (first century) other than the fact that he was one of the Twelve Apostles. He is also mentioned in the Acts of the Apostles as one of the disciples waiting for the descent of the Holy Spirit. According to a second-century Alexandrian teacher Pantaenus, an early Christian community in India claims Saint Bartholomew as its founder. Tradition states that he preached throughout Persia, Mesopotamia, Lycaonia, and Phrygia. It is believed that he was skinned alive and beheaded at Albanopolis, on the west coast of the Caspian Sea. He is patron saint of tanners due to the loss of his skin during his martyrdom.

25

OPTIONAL MEMORIAL OF Saint Louis

Becoming King of France at the age of twelve, Saint Louis (1214–1270) imbued French culture with a deep sense of divine justice. Although he enjoyed the finer things in life, including good wine and food, he never lost sight of the poor. It was not uncommon for him to feed the less fortunate from his own table, but he felt this was not enough, so he provided homes for them. Even with the many constraints upon his time, he managed to spend several hours a day in prayer.

OPTIONAL MEMORIAL OF Saint Joseph Calasanz, PRIEST

The priest Saint Joseph Calasanz (1556–1648) formed a religious order, the Clerks Regular of the Pious School, to set up free schools for the education of poor children. He believed that education would free the young from the dismal life of the slums, ending the cycle of poverty, by giving them the necessary skills to build a brighter future. During the plague of 1595 he ministered to the sick with Saint Camillus de Lellis.

26

Blessed Dominic of the Mother of God, Priest (England)

Blessed Dominic of the Mother of God (1792–1849) was an Italian Passionist and theologian. After his Ordination in 1818, he felt called to work for the conversion of England. In 1840, the head of the English mission, Bishop Wiseman, asked Dominic to make a Passionist foundation in England. In 1845, he received John Henry Newman into the Church, which Newman relates in his *Apologia pro Vita Sua*. Although he is best known for bringing Newman into the Church, Blessed Dominic is remembered for his work to bring Catholicism back to England. He was beatified by Pope Paul VI in 1963, during the Second Vatican Council.

Saint Ninian, Bishop (Scotland)

Saint Ninian lived in the fourth and fifth centuries, and was a missionary to the Picts in what is now Scotland. Very little is known of his life—one of the first accounts is by Saint Bede, writing in the eighth century. According to Bede, Saint Ninian was a Briton who studied for the priesthood in Rome. Some legends say that he traveled to Ireland after converting the Picts in Scotland and died there in 432.

Our Lady of Częstochowa (Poland)

For the people of Poland, the image of Our Lady of Częstochowa, is more than an object of veneration; she is a part of their history and their national identity. Blessed Pope John Paul II was deeply devoted to this image of Our Lady. He prayed before this image on his first visit to his homeland as pope, in 1979, saying: "If we want to know how . . . history is interpreted by the heart of the Poles, we must come here, we must attune our ear to this shrine, we must hear the echo of the life of the whole nation in the heart of its Mother and Queen." Nearly twenty years later, standing again before the image of Our Lady of Częstochowa, the pope recalled the words of an ancient Polish hymn:

> O Mother Divine,
> O Virgin by God glorified,
> Mother elect, to us send
> Your Savior Son.
> O Son of God, by your Baptist,
> Hear our voices,
> Fulfill our human thoughts.

Saint David Lewis, Priest and Martyr (England / Wales)

Saint David Lewis (1616–1679) is one of the Forty Martyrs of England and Wales who suffered during the English Reformation. He was raised as a Protestant but converted to Catholicism at the age of sixteen and went to study for the priesthood in Rome. After Ordination, he entered the Jesuits. In 1678, he was arrested for celebrating the Mass, accused of high treason, and executed by hanging.

27

MEMORIAL OF **Saint Monica**

Saint Monica (c. 331–387) knew the pain of disappointment, an unfaithful husband named Patricius who drank too much, and a promiscuous son, Saint Augustine of Hippo, who lived an immoral youth. Through patience and love, her husband had a change of heart, choosing to become a Christian. Saint Augustine's conversion was a much more difficult task. Saint Monica prayed constantly and fasted daily, but nothing seemed to work, so she consulted Saint Ambrose, bishop of Milan, for guidance. Through the intervention of God the two of them managed to lead Saint Augustine to the waters of Baptism. Saint Monica exemplifies that unconditional love and persistence are portals for God's saving grace.

28

MEMORIAL OF **Saint Augustine,** BISHOP AND DOCTOR OF THE CHURCH

Saint Augustine of Hippo (354–430) is one of the four great Latin Fathers of the Church. Augustine was born in North Africa in present-day Algeria. His mother was Saint Monica and his father, Patricius, a pagan. Augustine showed early promise as a scholar, but he disappointed his mother by espousing Manicheism (gnostic religion) and leading a hedonistic life (a life devoted soley to pleasure), even living with a mistress with whom he had a child. Eventually, due to Monica's prayers, he decided to become a Christian and was baptized by Saint Ambrose in Milan. He became a priest, and later, the bishop of Hippo. Augustine was a prolific writer and is credited with writing one of the first autobiographies, his *Confessions.* His books, homilies, and letters are a rich source of theological insight still mined

today by students of every Christian denomination or ecclesial community.

Saint Moses the Black

Saint Moses the Black (c. + 405) was a monk and priest in Egypt during the era of the desert fathers and mothers. Early in his life, he was a thief and a murderer, but after hiding from the authorities with a group of monks, he underwent a conversion and joined a community at Skete. Some of the famous sayings of the Desert Fathers are attributed to him. For example, when summoned to a meeting to discuss the faults of one of the brothers, Moses came bearing a leaking jug filled with sand. When asked why, he said, "My sins run out behind me and I do not see them, but today I come to judge the faults of another." In one account of his death, Moses is said to have died at the hands of bandits who were attacking the monastery.

29

MEMORIAL OF **the Passion of John the Baptist**

"I tell you, among those born of women, no one is greater than John," Jesus told the crowds (Luke 7:28). John the Baptist, the forerunner, came to prepare the way of the Lord, and he did that from the first moments of his life. In his mother's womb, he leapt for joy at the nearness of the Lord. He preached repentance to the people, preparing them for the coming of the Kingdom, and baptizing them with water so that they might be prepared to receive baptism "with the Holy Spirit and with fire." Even in his death, John prepared the way for the Lord. He boldly told Herod that he was violating the Law in taking his brother's widow as his wife, and Herod had him arrested and imprisoned and then executed. Even in his martyrdom, he prepared the way of the Lord, pointing to the way of the cross.

September

Month of September

September is the ninth month, but the word *September* actually means "seventh month." Before the time of Julius Caesar the Roman year had ten months. The first month was March, which made September the seventh month. There was no January or February on the calendar. Calendars were used mainly by farmers, who weren't interested in keeping track of time during winter, when there was little to

do. So during winter people lost track of days until their leaders announced the start of a new year each spring. Julius Caesar reformed the calendar. Winter months were added. Now the year began on the first of January, not March. But the old names for the months continued to be used. Many ancient calendars have the year beginning in spring. For instance, the Jewish people mark the first month of their religious year in early springtime, near the vernal

Images of Saints in September (clockwise from top left): Saint Matthew (September 21), Saints Michael, Gabriel, and Raphael, Archangels (September 29), Nativity of the Blessed Virgin Mary (September 8).

equinox. (The Jewish New Year [Rosh Hashanah], however, begins on the first day of the seventh month.) In the Byzantine Christian calendar, September is the first month of the liturgical year.

Month of Our Lady of Sorrows

On September 15, the Church observes a memorial honoring Mary as Our Lady of Sorrows. "And a sword will pierce your own soul, too," Simeon told Mary when she presented the child Jesus in the Temple forty days after his birth (Luke 2:35). That prophecy was fulfilled when Mary stood at the foot of her Son's Cross, sharing his bitter suffering. During this month of September, we honor Mary under the title, Our Lady of Sorrows. This month, let us bring to Mary all our sorrows, knowing that she understands what it is to suffer. This month is a good time to draw closer to Mary by meditating on the great hymn to the Mother of Sorrows, *Stabat mater*, or "At the Cross her Station Keeping." In this beautiful prayer, we ask for the grace to feel with Mary, to share her sorrow:

> Holy Mother! pierce me through,
> in my heart each wound renew
> of my Savior crucified:
> Let me share with thee His pain,
> who for all my sins was slain,
> who for me in torments died.

Catechetical Sunday

Each year in September, as faith formation programs get underway, the Church in the United States observes a Catechetical Sunday. In many parishes, the catechists who will help prepare children for the sacraments, and teach the faith to catechumens through the Rite of Christian Initiation of Adults, receive a special blessing.

Each year a different focus is chosen for Catechetical Sunday. In recent years, these themes have ranged from the dignity of Marriage to the celebration of the Eucharist, and the implementation of the third edition of *The Roman Missal*.

Labor (Labour) Day
First Monday in September

Today marks the time when working people around the country come to the end of summer vacation and students return to school. We set aside this day to reflect on the work we do. Over the course of our lives, most of us will spend more time working than we do at any other activity.

Until the last century or so, most people worked on farms. They worked long days, and the pace of life was slower. The Industrial Revolution changed that. New farm machines meant that fewer farming jobs were available. Farm workers moved to the cities, where they took low-paying jobs in factories. They worked as long as sixteen hours a day. Their jobs were dangerous because the machinery had few safeguards against accidents. Even children as young as six or seven years old were forced to work because wages were so low and families needed multiple incomes to survive.

The labor union movement was born in response to these conditions. Unions gave workers a way to stand together and fight for safe machinery, better salaries, and fair treatment. The first official Labor Day was celebrated in New York City in 1882. Peter J. McGuire, founder of the carpenters' union, suggested Labor Day at a union meeting. In its early years, it was a day when workers called attention to their grievances. Eventually this day became a national holiday. Now Labor Day is celebrated in Canada on the same day as in the United States. Many other countries observe a day to honor workers on May 1 (this day is also the optional Memorial of Saint Joseph the Worker).

Several popes of the last hundred years have written encyclicals, which are teaching letters, to speak for the dignity and rights of workers. The American bishops have also issued a letter about work. It's called *Economic Justice for All*.

Grandparents Day 🇺🇸 🍁

First Sunday after Labor Day

Marian McQuade of Fayette County, West Virginia, had a great idea. Reflecting on the many lonely elderly people in nursing homes, she decided to create a special day of the year when children could tap into the resource of wisdom and heritage that those elderly have to offer. In 1978, President Jimmy Carter signed National Grandparents Day into law. Mrs. McQuade died in 2008 at the age of 91, but some of her 15 children and 43 grandchildren still offer service to the National Grandparents Day Council. Now, variants of Grandparents Day exist in Australia, Canada, and several European nations. Many grammar schools offer Grandparents Day activities, encouraging children to create scrapbooks, essays, posters, poems, videotapes, or websites to tell their grandparents' stories.

2

OPTIONAL MEMORIAL OF Blessed André Grasset, PRIEST AND MARTYR 🍁

A Sulpician priest, born in Montreal, Quebec in 1758, Blessed André Grasset served in the Archdiocese of Sens, France. He was one of 191 Martyrs of September who were imprisoned by the Legislative Assembly druing the French Revolution because they refused to take an oath that supported the civil constitution of the clergy. This act, condemned by the Vatican, would give the state control over priests. Scholars are still debating whether they died for political reasons or for their refusal to submit to the civil authorities because it meant surrendering their religious independence. Grasset was killed on this date in 1792 in Paris. He and his companions were canonized by Pope Pius XI on October 17, 1926. Though he died in France, Grasset was the first Canadian-born saint. A college in Montreal is named for him.

3

MEMORIAL OF Saint Gregory the Great, POPE AND DOCTOR OF THE CHURCH

Saint Gregory the Great (540–604) was a mayor, a monk, a pope, and a writer. Unhappy with his life as mayor of Rome, Saint Gregory allocated half of his fortune to the poor and the other half to the foundation of seven monasteries. After joining a monastery in pursuit of a simple life, he was elected to the papacy. As pope, he cared for the poor, implemented the reforms to improve Church governance and clerical behavior, promoted the monastic vocation, and renewed the liturgy. His name is often associated with Gregorian chant (plainsong) and Eucharistic Prayer II (along with Saint Hippolytus). A prolific writer and Doctor of the Church, Saint Gregory composed numerous theological texts and is cited 374 times in Saint Thomas Aquinas' *Summa Theologia*.

4

OPTIONAL MEMORIAL OF Blessed Dina Bélanger, VIRGIN 🍁

A contemporary of Saint Thérèse of Lisieux (she's known as the "Little Flower of Canada"), Blessed Dina Bélanger was born in Quebec City, Canada in 1897. When Bélanger's brother died at three months old, her grieving mother starting visiting the poor and ill, bringing nourishment and compassion. Dina often went with her, which must have had a profound impact on the young girl. Discovering she didn't have a patron saint, she resolved to be the first Saint Dina.

Gifted in music, Dina studied piano at the Conservatory of Music in New York from 1916 to 1918. But instead of becoming a concert pianist, she entered the convent of Jesus and Mary in 1921 and taught music there. A great mystic, she revealed her intimacy with God in her diaries and autobiography. In prayer, she heard Jesus say, "You will do good by your writings." She died at age 32.

8

FEAST OF THE Nativity of the Blessed Virgin Mary

Exactly nine months after the Solemnity of the Immaculate Conception of the Blessed Virgin Mary (December 8), we come to an observance in honor of Mary's birth. This is one of only three birthdays in the Church's calendar, the other two being the birthdays of Jesus and of John the Baptist. This solemnity, like all Marian days "is less about Mary than it is about the wondrous work of God in Mary. As Saint Andrew of Crete said in a homily long ago, "The present festival, the birth of the Mother of God, is the prelude, while the final act is the foreordained union of the Word with flesh. . . . Justly then do we celebrate this mystery since it signifies for us a double grace . . . . Today this created world is raised to the dignity of a holy place for him who made all things. The creature is newly prepared to be a divine dwelling place for the Creator" (Office of Readings, Volume IV, p. 1371).

Our Lady of Charity (Cuba)

Today, as the Church celebrates the birthday of the Blessed Virgin Mary, the people of Cuba honor Mary under the title of *Nuestra Senora de la Caridad del Cobre*—Our Lady of Charity of Cobre—or, more simply, *Cachita*. The story is told that three young men, at least one of whom was a slave, went out to collect salt. A violent storm arose, and they were forced to take refuge on shore. Setting forth again when the sea was calm, they saw a strange object floating on the smooth water. They found that it was a small statue of the Virgin Mary holding the child Jesus, fastened to a board on which were written the words, *Yo Soy La Virgen de La Caridad*—I am the Virgin of Charity. In spite of the recent storm, the statue was completely dry. The sailors returned to land with the statue, and a chapel was built to house it. Our Lady of Charity of Cobre was proclaimed the Patroness of Cuba by Pope Benedict XV in 1916.

9

MEMORIAL OF Saint Peter Claver, PRIEST 🇺🇸

Saint Peter Claver (1580–1654), a Spanish Jesuit priest, spent his life tending to the needs of African slaves in Columbia, South America. While serving as a missionary, he ministered to the slaves by providing them with food and medicine, washing their wounds, preparing them for Baptism, and witnessing their Marriages. He actively recruited lawyers to plead the cases of imprisoned slaves and prepared criminals for death. Not only did he care for the slaves, but he also preached missions to plantation owners and sailors. The "saint of the slaves," as Saint Peter is often called, died after contracting the plague.

11

National Day of Remembrance and Mourning (Patriot Day) 🇺🇸

On this day, people in the United States of America recall the terrorist attacks of 2001, when hijacked commercial airliners flew into the Pentagon and the two World Trade Center towers in New York City, and crashed near Shanksville, Pennsylvania, killing 2,977 people. Firefighters and other first responders died and succumbed to lung contamination and trauma-related stress. In reaction to the event, the United States invaded Iraq and Afghanistan, resulting in the deaths of thousands of military personnel and uncounted numbers of civilians.

President George W. Bush proclaimed this day as Patriot Day on September 4, 2002. On this day, the flag is flown at half-staff at the White House, at government buildings, and at homes. At 8:46 AM Americans are to observe a moment of silence. This is the time in which the first plane struck the North Tower of the World Trade Center. Others who lost loved ones visit their graves or attend special memorial services. On the tenth anniversary of this tragic event, the 911 Memorial located at Ground Zero was opened to the public.

Our Lady of Coromoto (Venezuela)

On this day the people of Venezuela celebrate a feast in honor of Our Lady of Coromoto. The devotion goes back to 1652, when the Blessed Virgin Mary appeared to Coromoto, the native chief of the Cospes people. The Lady spoke to Coromoto in his own language, saying, "Go to the white house and ask them to pour water on your heads to go to heaven." Coromoto allowed his tribe to be catechized and baptized, but he resisted Baptism himself. The lady appeared to him again, and he struck out angrily at the apparition. She vanished, but in his hand he found a tiny picture of Mary holding the child Jesus on her lap. The image is barely an inch square. This tiny relic is venerated at the National Sanctuary of the Virgin of Coromoto, where countless pilgrims come to honor Mary each year and to recall the beginnings of the Catholic faith in Venezuela.

Saint Deiniol, Bishop (Wales)

Not much is known about the life of Saint Deiniol, save that he died around 584 and was the first bishop of Bangor in Wales, consecrated by Saint David himself. According to legend, he was the son of a noble family, and after studying for the priesthood, was given land to found a monastery on the site of present-day Bangor Cathedral. He is also said to have attended the Synod of Llanddewi Brefi in 545 with Saint David, where the rules for penance were discussed.

12

OPTIONAL MEMORIAL OF THE Most Holy Name of Mary

Three days after the Feast of the Nativity of the Blessed Virgin Mary, the Church observes an optional memorial honoring the Most Holy Name of Mary. In Hebrew, the name *Mary* is "Miryam," or "Miriam," which means "bitter sea." The name is an important one for the Jewish people: Miriam, the sister of Moses, sang in thanksgiving to God after the crossing of the Red Sea, and it was a common name for Jewish women (in the Gospel account of the Resurrection of Jesus, three women visit the tomb in the rock, and all of them are named Mary!). In the Middle Ages, the name *Mary* was often translated as "star of the sea," a title with which Mary continues to be honored today.

13

MEMORIAL OF Saint John Chrysostom, BISHOP AND DOCTOR OF THE CHURCH

After a short stint as a monk, Saint John *Chrysostom* (c. 350–407), whose surname means "golden mouth," returned to Antioch, where he was ordained a priest and became a noted preacher. During his free time he wrote commentaries on the Pauline letters as well as the Gospel according to Matthew and according to John. Due to his reputation for preaching and writing, he was appointed bishop of Constantinople. As bishop he initiated a program of reform that challenged clerical abuses and the extravagant lifestyle of the upper class. His reforms were not always received well, especially on the part of Empress Eudoxia; therefore, he was exiled from the city for a period of time. Saint John Chrysostom bears two distinctive titles in the Church: Father of the Church and Doctor of the Church.

14

FEAST OF THE
Exaltation of the Holy Cross

Today's Feast of the Exaltation of the Holy Cross began as a commemoration of a unique event: the miraculous finding of the True Cross by Saint Helena, the mother of the Emperor Constantine. Helena journeyed to the Holy Land to see the place of the Lord's Crucifixion. She found the spot and tore down a temple honoring the Greek goddess Aphrodite, which she found there, and began to build a new basilica in honor of Christ. As they began to lay the foundations, the remains of three crosses were discovered, but they did not know which was the true Cross. When a dying woman was healed after touching one of the crosses, they knew that the Cross of Christ had been revealed. The basilica was completed, and the Church in both East and West observes this feast in honor of the Cross on the anniversary of dedication.

"We are celebrating the feast of the cross that drove away darkness and brought in the light," said Saint Andrew of Crete in a sermon on this feast. "Had there been no cross, Christ could not have been crucified. Had there been no cross, life itself could not have been nailed to the tree. And if life had not been nailed to it, there would be no streams of immortality pouring from Christ's side, blood and water for the world's cleansing" (Office of Readings, Volume IV, p. 1390).

15

MEMORIAL OF
Our Lady of Sorrows

In the Gospel according to Luke, as Simeon holds the infant Christ in his arms, he tells Mary that her life will be full of suffering. Her son will be "opposed," and "a sword will pierce [Mary's] soul, too" (Luke 2:34, 35). That prophecy is fulfilled when Jesus is crucified and Mary stands at the foot of his Cross. The image of the *Mater Dolorosa*, the Sorrowful Mother, is the subject of one of the most famous works of art, Michelangelo's Pietà, which shows Mary with the dead Christ in her arms, her face revealing peace and acceptance, and yet profound grief. Today we ask the intercession of this sorrowful Mother for all mothers who suffer for their children, and especially those who have lost a child.

16

MEMORIAL OF
Saints Cornelius, POPE,
AND CYPRIAN, BISHOP, MARTYRS

Saint Cornelius (+ 253) and Saint Cyprian (+ 258) lived during a time of persecution at the hand of Emperor Decius. Saint Cornelius, the pope, faced the issue of whether or not Christians who renounced their faith during the persecutions should be welcomed back into the Church. With great compassion he publicly declared that these individuals could return to the Church after a period of penance. Saint Cyprian, bishop of Carthage, spent much of his life in hiding due to the persecutions, but this did not stop him from offering pastoral guidance and dispensing wisdom to the people of his diocese. Through letters he urged the people to remain faithful to their Christian call. Regarding those who apostatized, he maintained that they must be rebaptized before they can receive admittance back into the Church. Both Saints Cornelius and Cyprian shared the same fate—a martyr's death.

Independence Day (Mexico)

Until 1821, Mexico was a colony of Spain. The people keenly felt the burden and the injustice of foreign rule, but their efforts towards independence were scattered and ineffective until the morning of September 16, 1810, when the words of Miguel Hidalgo y Costilla, a Catholic priest, rallied them and launched the War of Independence. On that morning, shortly after dawn, Father Hidalgo rang the bells of his church in the small town of Dolores. The people gathered and Father Hidalgo spoke to them, urging them to be true to their faith and their land and to seize their independence. His impassioned speech came to be called the *Grito de Dolores*, "the cry of Dolores." It launched the Mexican War of Independence that ended in 1821 with the signing of the Treaty of Cordoba.

Each year, September 16 is observed as Mexican Independence Day. In addition to parades, the singing of the national anthem, and other displays of patriotic pride, bells are rung all over Mexico, a reminder of the bell rung by Miguel Hidalgo y Costilla, priest, general, and "father of the nation."

19

OPTIONAL MEMORIAL OF Saint Januarius, BISHOP AND MARTYR

Saint Januarius (c. + 305) was bishop of Benevento in Italy during the Diocletian persecutions. After suffering the fate of a martyr—being thrown to wild beasts and then beheaded—his relics were transported to Naples where it is said that a vial of his blood liquefies on three feast days related to his life: today, the day he supposedly prevented an eruption of Mount Vesuvius in 1631 (December 16), and the Saturday before the first Sunday in May, commemorating the transfer of his relics. He is the patron saint of blood banks and Naples, where he is referred to as *San Gennaro*.

17

OPTIONAL MEMORIAL OF Saint Robert Bellarmine, BISHOP AND DOCTOR OF THE CHURCH

Saint Robert Bellarmine (1542–1621), bishop and Doctor of the Church, was an astute scholar with a knack for diplomatically responding to the controversies of his day. As a Jesuit priest embroiled in the Protestant Reformation, he sensitively communicated through word and writing the Catholic perspective, especially regarding the relationship between Church and state. One of his most important contributions to the Church is a three-volume work, *Disputations on the Controversies of the Christian Faith*, which explained Catholic fundamentals in a non-defensive, systematic way. Saint Robert, a devotee of Saint Francis of Assisi, demonstrated heroic virtue by praying for his opponents, living simply, and embracing spiritual discipline.

20

MEMORIAL OF Saints Andrew Kim Tae-gŏn, Priest, Paul Chŏng Ha-sang, MARTYR, AND COMPANIONS, MARTYRS

During the eighteenth and nineteenth centuries, approximately 8,000 adherents to the Catholic faith in Korea were martyred (from 1839 to 1867); 103 of them of whom were canonized by Pope John Paul II in 1988. The canonized martyrs were victims of a particularly heinous series of persecutions happening between 1839 and 1867. During this time, Korea was ruled by an anti-Christian dynasty that did everything possible to eliminate Catholic ideology and influence, including the malicious mass murder of Christian missionaries and their followers. Two of the more notable martyrs are Saint Andrew Kim Tae-gŏn, priest and martyr; and Saint Paul Chŏng Ha-sang, a layman, both of whom were dedicated to the revitalization of the Church in Korea.

Venerable Mary Theresa Dudzik 🇺🇸

At an early age, Venerable Mary Theresa Dudzik (+ 1918) emigrated from Poland to the northwest side of Chicago where she encountered the poor, elderly, and abandoned. In a spirit of compassion, she ministered to the needs of these marginalized populations, sometimes even providing shelter in her own family home. In 1893, Chicago experienced a severe financial crisis that led to high unemployment rates. Amidst this depressed economy, Mary founded the Congregation of the Franciscan Sisters of Chicago to care for those in need, especially the disabled, poor, and elderly. She firmly believed that she could not love Christ or expect heavenly reward without tending to the needs of the afflicted and suffering. She died on this date in 1918. Dudzik's cause for beatification is still pending.

21

FEAST OF Saint Matthew, APOSTLE AND EVANGELIST

Saint Matthew (first century), referred to as the "tax collector," is one of the Twelve Apostles and the Evangelist who authored the first of the four accounts of the Gospel. His account has a two-fold purpose: one, to announce that Jesus is the eternal king of all creation; and two, to encourage faith in the face of doubt, especially regarding persecution. We have very little information about him, other than he invited Jesus to his home to dine with societal outcasts (see Matthew 9:9–13), and that he preached the Good News after the Resurrection. Tradition says he began preaching in Judea, then moved on to Ethiopia, Persia, Syria, Macedonia, and possibly Ireland. He is venerated as a martyr, even though history does not tell us how or where he died.

22/23

Autumnal Equinox

This celestial event marks the official change of seasons. After today, nights will be longer than days in the Northern Hemisphere. Autumn is beginning. (Of course, in the Southern Hemisphere the opposite is true and the season of spring begins.) The full moon closest to the autumnal equinox is known as "harvest moon." In the old days, the light of the full moon helped farmers harvest crops during the night. The next full moon, about a month later, is called "hunters' moon." It is a second harvest moon.

23

MEMORIAL OF Saint Pius of Pietrelcina, PRIEST

Early in life Saint "Padre" Pio of Pietrelcina (1887–1968), a Capuchin priest from Italy, demonstrated an unquenchable thirst for God. While praying one day before a crucifix, he received the visible wounds of Crucifixion that Christ bore in his Passion and Death, known as the stigmata. After an examination by a doctor, it was determined that there was no natural explanation for the wounds. Along with the stigmata, he experienced other mystical phenomena, including bi-location, the ability to be in two places at the same time, and "reading the hearts" of those who sought counsel and forgiveness in the sacrament of Reconciliation. These two miraculous gifts enabled him to lead both the sinner and the devout closer to God. Upon his death the stigmata were no longer visible.

24

Our Lady of Ransom (England / Peru)

Devotion to the Blessed Virgin Mary as Our Lady of Ransom dates to the time of the Crusades, when Saint Peter Nolasco established the Order of Our Lady of Mercy for the Ransom of Prisoners, or the Mercedarians, whose mission was to ransom Christian slaves held captive by Muslims. The Order survives today in seventeen countries. In England, devotion to Our Lady of Ransom was revived in the nineteenth century, with the aim of praying for the conversion of England and her return to the Catholic Church.

Today, as England honors Our Lady of Ransom, Peru celebrates Mary under the same title with great fanfare. Peru was evangelized by Mercerdarian religious, who brought the Gospel to Peru, and along with it their devotion to Our Lady of Mercy. Today, *Nuestra Senora de la Merced* is the Patroness of Peru, and September 24 is a national holiday.

OPTIONAL MEMORIAL OF
Blessed Émilie Tavernier-Gamelin, Religious 🍁

At the age of eighteen, Émilie Tavernier moved in to help her widowed brother: on one condition. They must set a table for the hungry, called "The Table of the King." In 1823, Émilie married Jean-Baptiste Gamelin, an apple grower, and they had three children. But her husband and children all died at about the same time.

Instead of being consumed by grief, she came to see the poor as, in a sense, her husband and children. They filled her home: the unemployed, indigent, elderly, orphaned, people with handicaps, prisoners, immigrants. They came to call it the House of Providence and for fifteen years, she opened more and more homes. Eventually, those who helped her formed a religious community, the Sisters of Providence, who now work internationally. She died in the cholera epidemic of 1851.

25

OPTIONAL MEMORIAL OF
Saints Cosmas and Damian, MARTYRS 🍁

Saints Cosmos and Damian (c. + 287) were brothers, possibly twins, who practiced medicine without accepting money for their services, which is why they are known in the East as the *anargyroi*, meaning "moneyless ones" or "moneyless healers." As vibrant witnesses to the Christian faith, they were arrested during the Diocletian persecutions. When they refused to renounce their faith and engage in idolatrous worship, they were beheaded and cast into the sea. They are patron saints of twins, confectioners, the sightless, and many medical professions (e.g., physicians, nurses, and dentists). Their names are included in Eucharistic Prayer I.

26

OPTIONAL MEMORIAL OF
Saints Cosmas and Damian, MARTYR 🇺🇸

Please see above for more information.

FEAST OF Saints John de Brébeuf, Isaac Jogues, PRIESTS, AND COMPANIONS, MARTYRS, SECONDARY PATRONS OF CANADA 🍁

On this day the Church honors the saints who gave their lives to spread the Catholic faith in North America: two Jesuit priests, Saint Isaac Jogues (1607–1646) and Saint John de Brébeuf (1593–1649), and their companions. Saint Isaac was captured and tortured for his preaching of the Gospel. He escaped and returned to Europe, but only to seek permission to offer Mass with his scarred and mutilated hands. The pope granted his wish, and Saint Isaac returned to the New World where he was put to death in 1646. Jean de Brébeuf dedicated himself to preaching the Gospel among the Huron peoples in what is now upstate New York and Canada. He translated the Catechism into the Huron language and wrote a series of "Instructions for Missionaries" that mingled divine and practical counsels: Love the Hurons as brothers, he urged, and bear with their shortcomings. Never keep them waiting, and learn to get into a canoe without carrying sand or water with you. Eat first thing in the morning, because that's what the Indians do. Work as they do, and serve them in whatever way you can. Jean de Brébeuf knew that only by understanding the Indians could missionaries hope to help them understand the Gospel. North American martyrs, pray for us.

27

MEMORIAL OF Saint Vincent de Paul, PRIEST

Saint Vincent de Paul (1581–1660), a French priest, gradually became aware of the growing disparity between the rich and poor; therefore, he laid the framework for a confraternity of caring, called the Servants of the Poor, which provided for the physical needs of the poor. Recognizing the call to care for not only their physical needs, but also their spiritual needs, he established a society of priests, the Congregation of the Mission (Vincentians), dedicated to preaching to peasants, catechesis of the marginalized, and other charitable works. In collaboration with Saint Louise Montfort de Marillac, he founded the Daughters of Charity, a new community of sisters not bound by traditional vows or enclosure, devoted to the sick, orphaned, and imprisoned. Saint Vincent is the patron saint of charitable societies. Many day care centers, hospitals, thrift stores, and soup kitchens are named in his honor.

28

OPTIONAL MEMORIAL OF Saint Wenceslaus, MARTYR

Most people are familiar with Saint Wenceslaus (c. 907–929), due to the popular Christmas carol *Good King Wenceslaus*. Although this ancient carol is not based on historical events, it illustrates the fame King Wenceslaus received because of his heroic life. As a Christian king in Bohemia, a primarily pagan country, he worked fervently to Christianize his people. His attempt to evangelize the Bohemians was not received well by some, including his brother who eventually murdered him. As he was dying, he prayed that God would forgive his brother. Shortly following his death, people proclaimed him a martyr.

OPTIONAL MEMORIAL OF
Saint Lawrence Ruiz and Companions, Martyrs

Saint Lawrence Ruiz (1600–1637), a married man with three children, fled to Japan from Manila to escape an unjust charge. Upon arrival, he was greeted with hostility, due to a recent edict that banned Christianity. When he and 15 other companions would not adhere to the state religion and trample on religious images associated with the Catholic faith, they were executed. Saint Lawrence and his companions join 231 other Catholics martyred in Japan between the sixteenth and seventeenth centuries.

29

FEAST OF Saints Michael, Gabriel and Raphael, ARCHANGELS

We celebrate the feast of three Archangels, Saints Michael, Gabriel, and Raphael, the great heralds of salvation and defenders against the power of evil. Saint Michael is guardian and protector of the Church, from its roots in Israel to the Church of today and beyond. In Hebrew, his name means "who is like God?" Saint Gabriel, whose name means "hero of God," announces that John the Baptist will be born to Elizabeth and Zechariah. He is entrusted with the most important task of revealing to Mary that she will bear the Son of God. Then, there is Saint Raphael, whose name is Hebrew for "God has healed." He is named in Tobit 12 as the one standing in the presence of God and in 1 Enoch (early Jewish writing) as the healer of the earth.

30

MEMORIAL OF
Saint Jerome, PRIEST AND DOCTOR OF THE CHURCH

Saint Jerome (c. 345–420) is the patron saint of scholars and librarians. With a great love of learning and books, as a monk and priest he developed a passion for the interpretation of Sacred Scripture. With a comprehensive knowledge of classical languages, Saint Jerome produced a Latin text of the entire Bible which came to be known as the Vulgate. He wrote numerous commentaries on several books of the Bible. Along with writing, he provided spiritual guidance to wealthy widows and mentored young monks in monastic discipline. Saint Jerome joins three other saints (Ambrose, Augustine, and Gregory the Great) as the four great Latin Doctors of the Church.

OCTOBER

Month of October

October means "eighth month" in Latin. Why is that? In the old Roman calendar, the year began in spring, not in winter. September was rich with feast days. November also will have several important days. But October was cut from rather plain cloth. There are valleys between mountains and ordinary days between extraordinary ones.

Month of the Most Holy Rosary

On October 7, we celebrate a well-loved memorial in honor of the Rosary, and according to a long-standing tradition, the entire month of October is dedicated to the Most Holy Rosary. In the Rosary, with its sequence of prayers and mysteries, we contemplate the Gospel in company with the Blessed Virgin Mary. As Blessed Pope John Paul II wrote in 2002, "the Rosary. . . . is a prayer loved by countless

Images of Saints in October (clockwise from left): Our Lady of the Rosary (October 7), St. Thérèse of the Child Jesus (October 1), Saint Francis (October 4).

Saints and encouraged by the Magisterium. Simple yet profound, it still remains, at the dawn of this third millennium, a prayer of great significance, destined to bring forth a harvest of holiness. . . . With the Rosary, the Christian people sits at the school of Mary and is led to contemplate the beauty on the face of Christ and to experience the depths of his love. Through the Rosary the faithful receive abundant grace, as though from the very hands of the Mother of the Redeemer" (*Rosarium Virginis Mariae*, 1).

Respect Life Sunday

First Sunday in October

The Church's teaching about life encompasses the whole spectrum of human life, "from womb to tomb." The Second Vatican Council proclaimed that "whatever is opposed to life itself, such as any type of murder, genocide, abortion, euthanasia or willful self-destruction, whatever violates the integrity of the human person, such as mutilation, torments inflicted on body or mind, attempts to coerce the will itself; whatever insults human dignity, such as subhuman living conditions, arbitrary imprisonment, deportation, slavery, prostitution, the selling of women and children; as well as disgraceful working conditions, where men are treated as mere tools for profit, rather than as free and responsible persons; all these things and others of their like are infamies indeed. They poison human society, but they do more harm to those who practice them than those who suffer from the injury. Moreover, they are supreme dishonor to the Creator" (*Gaudium et Spes,* 27). This Sunday, let us open our eyes to the many ways in which human life is at risk in our world and find constructive ways to preach the Gospel of Life.

Columbus Day 🇺🇸

Second Monday in October

October 12 marks the day in 1492 when three wooden ships landed at the tiny island of what is now San Salvador in the Bahamas. The ships had been provided by the king and queen of Spain. Their Italian captain, Christopher Columbus, was sure he had just reached "the Indies" (Japan and China) as he'd set out to do. His bold plan was to reach the Far East by sailing West. The "new world" Columbus found was filled with cultures older than those he had left behind in Europe. Many of these cultures were destroyed by diseases spread by the Europeans. Many more Native Americans died because of the cruelty of Columbus's sailors. When the Europeans realized they would not find gold mines, they turned to capturing and selling slaves as a source of income. The course of history would be changed by the blending of the "old" and "new" worlds. The native people of the Americas, their gifts, and their cultures have proven to be the new world's greatest treasure. In many Latin American countries October 12 is called "the Day of the Race." This refers to the new race of human beings formed by the marriages of Native American people and European people as a result of Columbus's voyages. In large cities of the United States, Columbus Day is a time for Italian Americans to celebrate their famous countryman with parades and church services. Parades are held in Chicago and New York City. San Francisco holds its *Festa Italiana* over the weekend before this day. Activities include a street fair, a waterfront cavalcade based on the life of Columbus, and ceremonies at Telegraph Hill, where a statue honors the explorer.

Thanksgiving Day 🍁

Second Monday in October

Few people know that the first formal Thanksgiving service in North America was celebrated in Newfoundland in 1578 by Sir John Frobisher and the European settlers after their safe landing. However, Thanksgiving Day didn't become an annual event in Canada until much later.

The tradition returned to the province of Nova Scotia with travelers who had celebrated Thanksgiving Day in New England. The tradition spread to the rest of the country, and in 1879 a day of thanksgiving for a good harvest and other blessings became an official holiday in Canada. Traditional Thanksgiving feasts include dinners of venison, waterfowl, and other wild game, as well as other North American foods, such as wild rice, corn, cranberries, and potatoes.

World Mission Sunday
Second-to-last Sunday in October

World Mission Sunday takes place on the second-to-last Sunday of October each year. Organized by the Vatican Congregation for the Propagation of the Faith, this is a time for Catholics worldwide to recommit themselves to the Church's missionary vocation. Each year, the need for support grows as new dioceses are formed and new seminaries are opened in mission territories, as areas devastated by war or natural disaster are rebuilt, and as countries where the faith was suppressed begin to open up to hear the message of Christ and his Church. More than a thousand dioceses around the world receive regular annual assistance from the funds collected on World Mission Sunday. Through our support of this important aspect of our Catholic life, we feel our connection with the global Church, and we respond to Christ's command: "Go . . . and make disciples of all nations, baptizing them in the name of the Father and of the Son and of the holy Spirit, teaching them to obey everything that I have commanded you" (Matthew 28:19–20).

Priesthood Sunday
Last Sunday in October

In the United States, the last Sunday of October is known as Priesthood Sunday and is set aside to honor the priesthood in the United States and to reflect on and affirm the ministerial priesthood in the life of the Church. It provides an opportunity for faith communities to express appreciation for the priests who serve them faithfully. This is also a day to pray for an increase in vocations to the priesthood. The lay faithful of each parish, school, or other ministry are invited to develop their own ways to mark the day and to honor the priesthood and their own priests. This nationwide event is coordinated by the United States Council of Serra International.

Pastoral Care Week 🏴
Last full week of October

Pastoral Care Week comes each year at the end of October. It was begun in 1985, an initiative of the National Association of Catholic Chaplains, and has since spread all over the world. The purpose of Pastoral Care Week is to honor and celebrate all who practice pastoral care, both clergy and lay, to raise awareness about the need for trained pastoral care ministers and to educate about the importance of providing pastoral care in hospitals, prisons, and other institutions.

1

MEMORIAL OF Saint Thérèse of the Child Jesus, VIRGIN AND DOCTOR OF THE CHURCH

Saint Thérèse of the Child Jesus (1873–1897), also known as the "Little Flower," was the youngest of Blessed Zélie and Blessed Louis Martin's five daughters. Zélie died of breast cancer when Thérèse was only four years old, a blow from which Thérèse took years to recover. The family moved to Lisieux, to be closer to Zélie's brother and his family. After their mother's death, Thérèse became very close to her sister, Pauline, but five years later, Pauline entered the Carmel of Lisieux. Eventually, all five sisters would become nuns, four of them at the Lisieux Carmel. When she was only fifteen, Thérèse, having received permission from the diocesan bishop because of her youth, joined the Carmel. As a Carmelite nun, she overcame the narrow, negative spirituality prevalent in nineteenth-century France, and focused on love—her love of God and God's love for her. She called her path of holiness the "Little Way," referring to her belief that every act, no matter how great or small, brings us as close to God as do heroic acts performed by spiritual giants such as Ignatius of Loyola or Teresa of Avila. She developed tuberculosis when she was only twenty-four and was unable to join a Carmel in the missionary territory of Vietnam. A year later, when only twenty-five, she died of the disease, after suffering through a period in which she doubted the existence of heaven. Thérèse left behind a memoir, *L'histoire d'une âme* (*The Story of a Soul*), which she wrote under obedience to her sister, Pauline, who had become prioress. It was published posthumously, after heavy editing by her sisters brought it into conformity with their idea of piety, but recent editions have restored the original material. Translated into over fifty languages, it has inspired faith in skeptics and strengthened the souls of believers. Because of her missionary spirit, Thérèse of Lisieux is the patron saint of the missions. Pope John Paul II declared her a Doctor of the Church in 1997, one of only three women so honored, along with Teresa of Avila and Catherine of Siena.

2

MEMORIAL OF
the Holy Guardian Angels

While not a defined teaching of the Church, the belief that each person has a guardian angel has roots deep in antiquity, among Christians and non-Christians. The ancient Babylonians and Assyrians believed in angels, and they are mentioned in the Old Testament as well, beginning in the Book of Genesis, where they deliver God's punishment on the cities of the plain and rescue Lot and his family from the

destruction (see Genesis 28—29). Perhaps one of the best and most touching examples of the activity of angels is found in the Book of Tobit, where the archangel Raphael leads and advises Tobiah on his journey (see Tobit 6—12). In the New Testament, Jesus himself seems to indicate that each of us is assigned a guardian angel, when he says, "Take care that you do not despise one of these little ones; for, I tell you, in heaven their angels continually see the face of my Father in heaven" (Matthew 18:10).

The memorial of the guardian angels developed as a local celebration in Spain, but in 1608, Pope Pius V added it to the general calendar, and Leo XIII made it obligatory in 1883.

4

MEMORIAL OF
Saint Francis of Assisi

The son of a wealthy merchant, Saint Francis of Assisi (1182–1226) seemed destined for grand castles, exquisite clothing, and fine food. After a conversion experience, he relinquished the trappings of this world to minister to the leper and preach to the spiritually hungry. His home became the earth; his clothing, humility; and his identity, an impoverished beggar seeking God. Many young men joined Saint Francis in this new way of life, leading to the foundation of the *frati minori* ("lesser brothers"), which eventually became known as the Friars Minor. He is perhaps one of the most popular saints in Church history due to his love of creation as exemplified in his famous "Canticle of the Sun." Pope Pius XI described Saint Francis as an *alter Christus*, meaning "another Christ." Given Francis's concern for creation, many parishes offer a blessing of animals on this day. The blessing is found in the *Book of Blessings*.

5

Blessed Francis Xavier Seelos

Blessed Francis Xavier Seelos (1819–1867), born in Bavaria, knew from an early age that he wanted to be a priest and model his life after Saint Francis Xavier. Due to his zealous and missionary spirit, he decided to enter the Redemptorist Order to train for their mission in the United States. After his profession of religious vows and priestly ordination, Blessed Francis was appointed to a parish in Pittsburgh where Saint John Neumann was pastor. Throughout his life, Blessed Francis served the Church and his religious order in several capacities, including pastor, novice-master, seminary director, and preacher of parish missions. Wherever he traveled, people came to him for Confession, spiritual advice, physical healing, and catechesis. His compassionate, yet challenging preaching style healed racial, ethnic, and socioeconomic divisions.

6

OPTIONAL MEMORIAL OF
Saint Bruno, PRIEST

Saint Bruno (c. 1035–1101) longed for a deeper relationship with God, nourished by solitude and austerity; thus, he and six companions built an oratory surrounded by several small hermitages, or cells, in a remote area in the French Alps known as La Chartreuse. This marks the beginning of the Carthusian order whose motto is *Stat crux dum volvitur orbis*, Latin for "The cross is steady while the world is turning." Following the *Rule of Saint Benedict* in a strict manner, Carthusian monks live an eremitical (reclusive) life solely seeking the will of God through prayer and manual labor.

OPTIONAL MEMORIAL OF
Blessed Marie Rose Durocher, Virgin

Blessed Marie-Rose Durocher (1811–1894) was raised in a large family just outside of Montreal, Quebec. From a young age, she expressed the desire to join a religious order, but her poor health stood in the way of this dream. With the approval of the bishop, she founded the Congregation of the Sisters of the Most Holy Names of Jesus and Mary dedicated to the education of the young and poor. Little did she know the ministry of the sisters would stem beyond Canada to the United States and some third world countries.

7

MEMORIAL OF
Our Lady of the Rosary

The Rosary, which is perhaps the most-loved devotion in the Catholic Church, dates to the Middle Ages, when a practice developed of praying 150 Hail Marys on a set of beads, echoing the monastic prayer that was based on the 150 Psalms. The Dominicans are credited with popularizing the Rosary across Europe. By the sixteenth century, the Rosary had taken its present form, with fifteen mysteries—joyful, sorrowful, and glorious. In 2002, Pope John Paul II added the "Mysteries of Light," or Luminous Mysteries: Christ's baptism in the Jordan, the wedding feast at Cana, the proclamation of the Kingdom, the Transfiguration, and the Institution of the Eucharist.

9

OPTIONAL MEMORIAL OF
Saint Denis, Bishop, and Companions, MARTYRS

Saint Denis of Paris (+ 258) was the bishop of Paris during the third century, martyred during the persecution by the emperor Decius. It's possible that Denis came from Italy to convert Gaul, settling in Paris on the Île de la Cité in the River Seine. According to Gregory of Tours, he was beheaded with a sword on Montmartre, the highest hill in Paris, which may have been a druidic holy place, and local tradition holds that the martyrdom of Saint Denis gave the hill its name. After his death, his body and those of his companions, Saints Eleutherius and Rusticus, were recovered by the Christian community and buried. Later, Saint Geneviève started the construction of a basilica on the spot. Saint Denis of Paris is often confused with Dionysus the Areopagite, who was converted by Saint Paul in Athens (Acts of the Apostles 17:34), and with Pseudo-Dionysius the Areopagite, a sixth-century theologian who's best known for describing the ranks of angels in the *Celestial Hierarchy*. Because he was martyred by beheading, Saint Denis is portrayed decapitated, dressed in bishop's vestments, and holding his own head. He is a patron saint of France, the city of Paris, and is one of the Fourteen Holy Helpers, invoked against headaches, rabies, and demonic possession.

OPTIONAL MEMORIAL OF
Saint John Leonardi

Saint John Leonardi (c. 1541–1609) was an Italian priest who founded the Confraternity of Christian Doctrine. Born in Diecimo, his father sent him to pharmacy school when he was seventeen, and John plied this trade for ten years before realizing that he had a vocation to the priesthood. He was ordained in 1572 and developed an apostolate among young people with the Confraternity of Christian Doctrine. In 1574, he founded a community of priests, the Order of Clerks Regular of the Mother of God. After Paul V approved his new order, John moved to Rome, where he cofounded the seminary of the Propagation of the Faith. He died during an influenza epidemic, after caring for his stricken brothers. Saint John is the patron saint of pharmacists.

12

Our Lady of Aparecida (Brazil)

Our Lady of Aparecida (*Nossa Senhora Aparecida*) is celebrated with a national holiday in Brazil. This dark-skinned image of Our Lady has a remarkable history. In 1717, three men were fishing in the Paraiba River but without success. Casting their net a third time, they were amazed to bring up a headless statue. They cast their net again, and brought up the statue's head. They soon realized they had discovered a black image of Our Lady of the Immaculate Conception. Casting the net again, they brought up a wondrous catch of fish. The statue was recognized as the work of a monk from Sao Paulo, Brother Agostino de Jesus, which had been made in 1650. It had been underwater for so long that all the bright colors with which it had originally been painted had faded away. The statue was placed in a chapel, and devotion to the image of Our Lady grew rapidly, especially among African Brazilians. In 1955, a mighty basilica rose to house the statue of Our Lady of Aparecida. It is one of the largest churches in the world and can accommodate up to 45,000 pilgrims. The parking lot has room for 4,000 buses and 6,000 cars! Even so, the basilica can be very crowded at times, with about 8 million visitors each year.

Our Lady of the Pillar (Spain)

Nuestra Senora del Pilar, Our Lady of the Pillar, is an image of the Blessed Virgin Mary and the Child Jesus venerated in Spain. The legend has it that the Apostle James the Greater was at prayer when Mary appeared to him and gave him a small wooden statue of herself and a column of jasper. She instructed him to build a church in her honor on that very spot, present-day Zaragoza, Spain.

The Blessed Virgin Mary has been venerated at Zaragoza for many centuries, and saints like John of the Cross, Teresa of Avila, and Ignatius Loyola have made pilgrimages to her shrine and venerated this well-loved image of Our Lady. The Patroness of Spain, Our Lady of the Pillar is also venerated in the Philippines and throughout Latin America. Pilar is a popular name for girls in many Spanish speaking countries, a tribute to Our Lady of the Pillar.

13

Saint Edward the Confessor, King (England)

Saint Edward the Confessor (1005–1066) was one of the last Anglo-Saxon Kings of England, the son of Emma of Normandy and King Æthelred the Unready. He survived the Viking raids that took place during his youth, and after being exiled during the reigns of Cnut and his sons, became king upon the death of his father and older brothers. Some accounts claim that he was pious and otherworldly, a weak king who made it easy for the Norman Conquest to occur after his death, but these may be from Norman sources. Others say he was a strong king. Edward had to deal with Scotland and Wales and received Malcolm of Canmore as an exile after Macbeth killed his father, Duncan I. In 1042, Edward began the construction of Westminster Abbey. Edward the Confessor was the first Anglo-Saxon and only king of England to be canonized. He is buried in Westminster Abbey and is a patron saint of those in difficult Marriages, separated spouses, kings, and the English royal family.

14

OPTIONAL MEMORIAL OF Saint Callistus I, POPE AND MARTYR

Following a life of slavery and hard labor, Saint Callistus I (+ 222) was appointed deacon in charge of the Christian cemetery on the Appian Way, now called the catacomb of San Callisto. Recognized for his abounding wisdom and natural bent for leadership, he was eventually elected pope. He had many critics, due to his liberal stance regarding the forgiveness of those who had apostatized during times of persecution. Saint Callistus, heeding the commands of Christ, believed the repentant should be forgiven and welcomed back into the Church. Tradition maintains that he began the ember days, periods of fast and abstinence, which were replaced by days prayer and penance determined by each diocese. He is commemorated as a martyr; he was probably killed during a public disturbance.

15

MEMORIAL OF Saint Teresa of Jesus, VIRGIN AND DOCTOR OF THE CHURCH

Saint Teresa of Jesus (1515–1582), more commonly known as Saint Teresa of Avila, joined the Carmelite Convent of the Incarnation at the age of 21. Disheartened by the laxness of its observance of the Carmelite Rule, in particular its opulent nature and overly social atmosphere, she began a reform movement laying the framework for the Discalced Carmelites. This new branch of Carmelites modeled themselves on the poor and crucified Christ, adopting a life of poverty and abstinence. In collaboration with Saint John of the Cross, she helped bring this new way of life to the male Carmelite communities. Although their reforms were met with great resistance, they moved forward with faith and persistence. Among her many writings, she is well known for two classics: *The Way of Perfection* and *The Interior Castle*. Saint Teresa is one of the first women to be named Doctor of the Church.

16

MEMORIAL OF Saint Marguerite d'Youville, RELIGIOUS 🍁

Saint Marguerite d'Youville (1701–1771) is the Canadian founder of the Grey Nuns of Montreal. She was born at Varennes, Quebec, a suburb of Montreal, and received two years of schooling at the Ursuline convent in Quebec City. At the age of twenty-one, she married François d'Youville, a bootlegger and fur trader, with whom she had six children before his death in 1730. Before she was thirty, Marguerite had experienced the loss of her father, husband, and four of her children, but her sufferings brought about a religious conversion. In 1737, her two surviving sons having entered the priesthood, Marguerite cofounded a group dedicated to helping the poor, which developed into the order known as the Grey Nuns. Saint Marguerite d'Youville died in 1771 in Montreal and was canonized by John Paul II, the first Canadian to be so honored. She is a patron saint of widows and those in difficult marriages.

OPTIONAL MEMORIAL OF Saint Hedwig, RELIGIOUS 🎏

Saint Hedwig of Silesia (c. 1174–1243) was Duchess of Silesia and of Poland and an aunt of Saint Elizabeth of Hungary. When only twelve, she was married to Henry I of Silesia. They lived a devout life, performed penitential practices, and together supported the founding of many religious communities in Silesia. When Henry died in 1238, Hedwig went to live in the Cistercian convent her husband had founded at her request. Hedwig was canonized in 1267 and is a patron saint of orphaned children.

OPTIONAL MEMORIAL OF Saint Margaret Mary Alacoque, VIRGIN 🎏

Saint Margaret Mary Alacoque (1647–1690) was a French Visitation nun and mystic, whose visions of Jesus led her to promote devotion to the Most Sacred Heart as we know it today. Margaret was a pious child and practiced prayer and penance. She entered the Visitation convent in Paray-le-Monial in 1671. Unfortunately, the nuns there were suspicious of her, and Margaret Mary found her vocation tried, especially by the delay of her profession. The following year, she began having the visions that revealed the devotion to the Sacred Heart and its practices such as communion on First Fridays, and the holy hour of Eucharistic adoration on Thursdays. She was discouraged from spreading this devotion until the convent's Jesuit confessor, Saint Claude la Colombière, declared that her visions were genuine. Saint Margaret Mary died in 1690, but after her death, the Jesuits spread the devotion to the Sacred Heart. She is a patron saint of polio sufferers, orphans, and those devoted to the Sacred Heart.

Saint Richard Gwyn, Martyr (Wales)

Saint Richard Gwyn (c. 1537–1584) is one of the Forty Martyrs of England and Wales who died during the Protestant Reformation. He studied at Oxford and Cambridge, but when Elizabeth I became queen, he was forced out of his academic career and moved to Douai in France, as did many British Catholics during this time. Eventually he returned to Wales, became a teacher, was married, and he and his wife had six children. He did not hide his devotion to his faith, even when pressured to become Anglican by the bishop of Chester. He and his family moved often to avoid the heavy fines levied on Catholics at this time. In 1579, a former Catholic who had become the vicar of Wrexham arrested him. He escaped but was recaptured after a year and a half. In 1581, Richard was shackled and forcibly taken to a church in Wrexham and laid in front of the pulpit, but he made such a commotion by rattling his chains that he drowned out the voice of the preacher. He and two other prisoners, John Hughes and Robert Morris, were forced to listen to a sermon by an Anglican clergyman, but they heckled him, one in Welsh, one in English, and one in Latin. In 1583, the three were indicted for high treason and brought to trial where they maintained their loyalty to the Catholic Church. Richard Gwyn was sentenced to die by being hung, drawn, and quartered. He was conscious during the disemboweling that was part of this gruesome means of execution, and his last words were "Jesus, have mercy on me." Some of his writings have been preserved, especially a number of poems.

17

MEMORIAL OF
Saint Ignatius of Antioch,
BISHOP AND MARTYR

Saint Ignatius of Antioch (c. 37–c. 107), an apostolic father and possible disciple of John the Evangelist, served the community of Antioch as bishop. Living during the anti-Christian reign of the Roman emperor Trajan, he was sentenced to be fed to animals in the Roman Colosseum because he would not engage in idol worship. His journey to Rome was marked by extensive writing in which he composed seven letters. These letters, directed to various churches, emphasized the humanity and divinity of Christ, the centrality of Eucharist, and the importance of Church unity.

18

FEAST OF
Saint Luke, EVANGELIST

Saint Luke the Evangelist (first century) is traditionally known as the author of the Gospel that bears his name as well as of the Acts of the Apostles. He is also identified with the "beloved physician" referred to by Saint Paul (Colossians 4:14). Luke was a Gentile from Antioch in Syria, and his roots show both in his writing style and in his sympathetic treatment of Gentiles in the Gospel that bears his name. According to Acts of the Apostles, he accompanied Saint Paul on some of his evangelizing journeys, and he stays with Paul when he is imprisoned in Rome. Some sources claim he was martyred, but it is thought that he died an old man of natural causes. A tradition states that he was the first icon painter, and the Black Madonna of Częstochowa is attributed to him. His symbol is an ox or bull because the Lucan Gospel begins with Zachary, the father of John the Baptist, offering a sacrifice in the Temple. Saint Luke is patron saint of artists and physicians.

19

MEMORIAL OF Saints
John de Brébeuf and Isaac Jogues, PRIESTS,
AND COMPANIONS, MARTYRS 🇺🇸

Please see page 120 for more information.

OPTIONAL MEMORIAL OF Saint Paul of the Cross, Priest 🍁

After having a vision of himself clothed in a black habit, Saint Paul of the Cross (1694–1775) established the Congregation of the Passion (the Passionists, or Congregation of the Discalced Clerks of the Most Holy Cross and Passion of Our Lord Jesus Christ). The Passionists, a community of priests, were to live a strict monastic life while fostering an intense devotion to the Passion of Christ through preaching and missions. Along with the traditional vows of other religious communities, they took a fourth vow to spread the memory of Christ's Passion. Unique to their habit is a large badge in the shape of a heart bearing a cross and the words *Jesu XPI Passio* (Passion of Jesus Christ). As they grew in numbers, they engaged in ministry to the sick and dying. Toward the end of his life, Saint Paul founded a community of Passionist nuns.

20

OPTIONAL MEMORIAL OF Saint Paul of the Cross, PRIEST 🇺🇸

Please see above for more information.

OPTIONAL MEMORIAL OF Saint Hedwig, RELIGIOUS 🍁

Please see page 129 for more information.

OPTIONAL MEMORIAL OF Saint Margaret Mary Alacoque, VIRIGIN 🍁

Please see page 129 for more information.

22

SOLEMNITY OF the Dedication of Consecrated Churches WHOSE DATE OF CONSECRATION IS UNKNOWN 🍁

Every parish, large and small, has a solemnity on its calendar, which is its very own: its anniversary of dedication. In the *Rite of Dedication of a Church*, a church building is consecrated to divine worship, its walls are anointed with sacred chrism, and Mass is offered on its altar for the first time. A church's dedication day is something like a birthday. It is a time to reflect on the history of the parish community and to give thanks for the great "cloud of witnesses" (Hebrews 12:1) who have worshipped there over the years and to pray that the Gospel may continue to be preached there for generations yet to come. When the date of dedication of the church is known, this solemnity is usually celebrated on the anniversary. But for parishes whose date of dedication is not known, it is customary to celebrate the solemnity sometime in October. In Canada, that day is today!

Blessed John Paul II, Pope 🇺🇸

To tell of Blessed John Paul II's 26 years of Petrine ministry is to provide a litany of encyclicals, travels, and historic events. Not only was John Paul II (1920–2005) the first pope to enter a synagogue since Saint Peter, but he appealed to both Jews and Christians to be "a blessing to one another," and offered repentance in the name of the Church for the Shoah.

From the moment Karol Wojtyla was elected pope in October 1978, the man who had entered a clandestine seminary while living under Nazi occupation mesmerized the world. In the early years, Catholics and non-Catholics alike were attracted to the athletic man who snuck out of his villa to ski and reached out to the young at World Youth Days.

People of many faiths prayed for him when he was shot in Saint Peter's Square and were awed with the mercy he granted his assailant. And none escaped the poignancy of a feeble John Paul II praying at the Western Wall in Israel, leaving a prayer inside the wall.

Even a scant follower of the pope knew that the man who forgave his assailant, traveled the world to evangelize, and sought healing in relations with the Jewish people looked to the Blessed Virgin as a model of faith. A week after taking on the Chair of Saint Peter, he brought reporters to the Marian Shrine of Mentorella outside of Rome. "I wanted to come here, among these mountains," he told them "to sing the Magnificat in Mary's footsteps." On that date, too, he told of his love for the Rosary, a remark that he recalled 24 years later in his apostolic letter *Rosarium Virginis Mariae* (RVM, 2): "The Rosary is my favorite prayer. A marvelous prayer! Marvelous in its simplicity and depth." In that letter, he explained the Christocentric nature of the prayer. "With the Rosary, the Christian people sit at the school of Mary and are led to contemplate the beauty on the face of Christ and to experience the depths of his love." In RVM, he notes Mary's conformity to Christ: "Mary lives only in Christ and for Christ!" It is such conformity that John Paul II sought. His motto was *Totus Tuus* (all thine).

To John Paul II, the woman who carried the Savior in her womb, who first gazed on him at birth, and stayed with him by the Cross, is the person who can bring followers closest to Christ. In the apostolic exhortation *Ecclesia in America*, he called Mary "the sure path to our meeting with Christ" (11). He also noted that Our Lady of Guadalupe's meeting with Juan Diego evangelized beyond Mexico and voiced hope that the Mother and Evangelizer of America would guide the Church in America, "so that the new evangelization may yield a splendid flowering of Christian life" (11).

The pope credited Our Lady of Fatima with saving his life when he was shot on May 13, 1981, the anniversary of the first apparition at Fatima. He believed that Mary guided the bullet away from his vital organs. A year after the shooting, he placed the bullet that was taken from him among the diamonds in the crown of the statue of Our Lady of Fatima. "I wish once more to thank Our Lady of Fatima for the gift of my life being spared," he said. With the Church, many surely are thanking the man who espoused the Rosary for modeling a life of faith.

At the time of this printing, the United States Conference of Catholic Bishops approved the addition of the deceased pope's feast day as an optional memorial on the *Proper Calendar for the Dioceses of the United States*. It is pending approval from the Holy See.

23

OPTIONAL MEMORIAL OF
Saint John of Capistrano,
PRIEST

Saint John of Capistrano (1386–1456) was an Italian Franciscan priest. He was born in the Kingdom of Naples and studied law at Perugia, got married, and became a magistrate. During a war, he was sent as a peace ambassador but was thrown in prison, and during this time realized that he was called to be a priest. He and his wife had never consummated their marriage, so they separated, and John entered the Franciscans. He applied himself to a life of extreme asceticism and developed a reputation as a powerful preacher, in Italy as well as in countries such as Germany and Poland. So great were the crowds who came to hear him that no church could hold them, and he had to preach outdoors. In addition to preaching, John fought heresy through his writing and led an army against an invasion of Turks. He survived the battle but died of bubonic plague in 1456. Saint John of Capistrano is a patron saint of those in the legal profession. The famous *Mission San Juan Capistrano* in southern California is named for him.

24

OPTIONAL MEMORIAL OF Saint Anthony Mary Claret, BISHOP

As a successful weaver and skilled printer in Spain, Saint Anthony Mary Claret (1807–1870) felt called to be ordained a priest and preach parish missions. He eventually gathered young men together in community to preach missions, which led to the foundation of a new religious congregation called the Claretians. Later in life he was appointed archbishop of Santiago, Cuba, a huge diocese with many problems, including racism, slavery, and anti-Christian persecution. His Christian response to the posing problems (i.e., credit unions to loan money to the poor) resulted in fifteen assassination attempts upon his life. Following his tenure as bishop, he served as confessor to Queen Isabella II and was able to exert his influence in the court to implement new projects, such as starting a natural history museum and schools of music and languages.

25

The Six Welsh Martyrs and Companions, Martyrs (Wales)

Today the people of Wales observe a special commemoration of their own martyrs within this group. The six are the John Jones, Philip Evans and John Lloyd, David Lewis, Richard Gwyn, and John Robert. After Henry VIII separated from Rome in 1534, those who did not acknowledge Henry as head of the Church were considered traitors. The punishment for treason at the time was a gruesome form of execution, to be hanged, drawn, and quartered. The condemned would be hanged until almost dead, disemboweled while still alive, and cut into four pieces. The head of the condemned would be cut off and displayed in a public place as a warning. Most of the Welsh martyrs died by this method, which became obsolete in England only in 1870.

28

FEAST OF Saints Simon and Saint Jude, APOSTLES

Today we honor two Apostles (first century) about whom we know very little. Tradition maintains that Saint Simon the Zealot preached missions throughout Persia and Egypt. Saint Jude, not to be confused with Judas Iscariot, is the patron saint of hopeless causes and is called Thaddeus in the Gospel according to Matthew and the Gospel according to Mark. It is believed that he engaged in missionary work in Mesopotamia and Persia. Both Saints Simon and Jude were supposedly martyred in Persia, and their relics were transferred to Saint Peter's Basilica in Rome sometime during the seventh and eighth centuries.

The Lord of Miracles (Peru)

The Lord of Miracles (in Spanish *Señor de los Milagros de Nazarenas*) is a mural venerated in Lima, Peru. The image shows the crucified Christ, with the Blessed Virgin Mary and Mary Magdalene at the foot of the Cross, while the Holy Spirit and God the Father are seen overhead. The painting received its name *Señor de los Milagros* following a massive earthquake that devastated Peru in the seventeenth century. Almost the entire city was destroyed, but the wall on which the mural was painted remained standing. Every year on this date a procession honors the Lord of Miracles. It is one of the largest religious processions in the world, gathering hundreds of thousands of faithful on the streets of Peru.

31

Halloween

By the end of October, in most of North America and Europe, days have become short and cold. The Church keeps two great festivals at this dark time of year—All Saints and All Souls, the first and second days of November. And, like every other Christian festival, the holiday begins at sunset on the day before. An old name for All Saints' Day was All Hallowmas. ("Hallow" is another word for *saint*.) The eve of All Saints was called All Hallows' Eve, which got shortened to Halloween (from Hallowe'en, i.e., Hallows' evening). This festival has an interesting history. Many of the peoples of northern Europe divided the year into four seasons based on the length of days, but these were a bit different from the seasons as we know them. "Winter" was the period of the shortest days. It began on November 1 and ended on February 1. On this night, huge bonfires were lighted on hilltops to welcome the dead who would return home for a bit of comfort by the warm hearthside. Food was set out. Any stranger was welcomed into the home. Who knew? Maybe the stranger was really a dead relative.

But the annual return of the dead brought trouble, too. Not all of them were friendly. So everyone stayed together all night for protection, and they told stories of the dead and of narrow escapes from cranky ghosts. People dressed up like the dead to make any ghostly visitors feel more welcome and also to confuse the angry ones. In the earliest days of Christianity, the remembrance of the dead and the celebration of the saints was kept at Easter Time, because we Christians look forward to the day of resurrection of all who have died. But in the tenth century in western Europe, the Church began to keep the remembrance of the dead in November, in autumn, when it seems as if the earth itself is dying.

In most of Europe, Halloween is strictly a religious event. Sometimes in North America the church's traditions are lost or confused. Still, All Hallows' Eve has been kept by the Church for over 1,000 years. Halloween night still can be a Christian celebration, kept as the holy eve of All Saints' Day. Halloween customs reflect the Gospel. Trick-or-treat is just good, old-fashioned hospitality. In the name of Christ, we welcome all who knock on our doors. Walking in the streets in masks and costumes reminds us of our journey to heaven. Once our journey is done, we will take our masks off and see ourselves as we truly are—the beloved children of God, the saints in glory.

November

Month of November

The name for the eleventh month really means "the ninth month." In the ancient Roman calendar November was the ninth month because the year began in March. In Church tradition, November is a month to remember the dead and to pray for them. The month begins with All Saints' Day and All Souls' Day. Either in the last days of November or the first days of December, Advent begins. In folklore, November had a strange name. It was called *Gossamer*, which means "goose summer." That meant something like "Indian Summer," which is a time of warm weather after the first frost.

Saint Martin's Day, the eleventh day of the eleventh month, was a time to feast on roast goose. Perhaps that's where "goose summer" comes from.

Images of Saints in November (L to R): Saint Andrew Dũng Lac (November 24), Saint Cecilia (November 22), Saint Frances Xavier Cabrini (November 13).

Month of the Holy Souls

"It is a holy and a wholesome thought to pray for the dead that they may be loosed from their sins," observes the writer of Maccabees in the Old Testament (2 Maccabees 12:45–46; quoted in *Catechism of the Catholic Church*, 958). Intercession on behalf of those who have died is a cherished tenet of our Catholic faith, springing from our belief in the resurrection of the body and the communion of saints. "Though separated from the living, the dead are still at one with the community of believers on earth and benefit from their prayer and intercession" (*Order of Christian Funerals*, 6). Trusting in God's mercy, we continue to pray for them, knowing that this spiritual bond with our brothers and sisters who have died can never be broken. In the month of November, when we celebrate All Souls, we pray in a special way for those who have died—those who are known to us, and those who are unknown.

National Bible Week

Week of Thanksgiving

National Bible Week is celebrated each year during the week of Thanksgiving, from Sunday to Sunday. This ecumenical and interfaith event has been celebrated every year since 1941. Its goal is to raise awareness of the importance of the Bible for us as individuals and for our nation. The Bible has profoundly influenced art, literature, language, and music; it has shaped our laws, government, and politics. This is a week to stop and give thanks for the enduring word of God and to come to appreciate it more deeply. Across the country, churches and ecclesial communities will be arranging public readings of the Bible, as well as small study groups, concerts, and other events celebrating the richness of sacred scripture.

Our Lady of the Thirty-Three

(Uruguay)

Second Sunday of November

Nuestra Senora de los Treinta y Tres (Our Lady of the Thirty-Three), Patroness of Uruguay, is celebrated each year on the second Sunday of November. In 1825, a group of revolutionaries known as the "Thirty-Three Orientals" or the "Thirty-Three Easterners" began an insurrection, seeking the independence of Uruguay from Brazil. These men entrusted their cause to a small baroque image of the Blessed Virgin Mary venerated in the small town of *La Florida*. After their successful insurrection, they immediately returned to the shrine and placed the new nation under her protection. In 1857, one of the "Thirty-Three," now president of the new republic, offered an extraordinary gold crown to honor the image of Our Lady. The disproportionately large crown has become one of the distinctive features of this image of Our Lady, who was named Patroness of Uruguay by Blessed Pope John XXIII in 1962.

Election Day

Tuesday after the First Monday in November

Every fourth year on this day in the United States, people choose their next president. Every second year, some United States senators and members of the House of Representatives are chosen. Many local elections are held today, too. In colonial times, only about 15 percent of the American people had the right to cast a ballot. At first, suffrage (the right to vote) was limited to free males age 21 and over who owned land. In some colonies, Catholics and Jews were not allowed to vote. Many years passed before women and African Americans were granted suffrage. In some states it was 1948 before Native Americans were given the right to vote, and in 1970 suffrage was granted to those between the ages of 18 and 21.

Thanksgiving Day

Fourth Thursday of November

Thanksgiving Day in the United States comes at the end of November, a bit late in the year for a typical harvest festival. The growing season is over. In some parts of the country snow has already fallen. The Pilgrims, the Calvinist settlers in New England, held the first Thanksgiving Day celebration in 1621. Many of the English settlers did not celebrate Easter or Christmas. They had abandoned Catholic feast days and seasons, but they were devoted to the Bible. They based their laws and customs on it.

After landing in Massachusetts the Pilgrims had a tragic winter. They found the New England winters far colder than in England, and half the settlers died. In the spring, help came from a Pawtuxet Indian named Squanto, who showed them how to plant corn and other native crops. Because of this, they had a bountiful harvest. Inviting their Native American saviors to join them, they prepared turkeys and other wild game, seafood, corn, dried berries, and vegetables. Their harvest festival lasted three days.

Thanksgiving Day didn't become an annual event until much later. In 1789, President George Washington proclaimed a day of thanksgiving for the new country. For many years after that, some states celebrated on one day, some on another. In 1863, in the midst of the Civil War, Abraham Lincoln proclaimed the fourth Thursday of November as the official Thanksgiving Day of the nation.

The Law of Moses calls the people to share their bounty with family, servants, strangers, widows, and orphans. Today in America many people have no way to share in Thanksgiving Day because they are hungry, homeless, or isolated from family and friends. On Thanksgiving Day we remember them and welcome them with our prayer and our service.

Native American Heritage Day

Day after Thanksgiving

2008 marked the very first observance of this event marked across the United States of America with ceremonies and celebrations honoring the contribution of Native Americans to every aspect of American life. Today is especially right for this remembrance, since the Wampanoag people hosted the very first Thanksgiving in 1621 in a spirit of peaceful welcome. They brought the Europeans new foods and farming methods that helped them survive the first harsh years in their new habitat. Later, important ideas such as the separation of powers and the right of freedom of speech would be based on what the colonists learned from Native American cultures such as the Iroquois Confederacy.

Today's festivals will often begin with a tipi raising, followed by varied kinds of native dance, music, and storytelling.

1

SOLEMNITY OF All Saints

On this day, the Church honors all the saints, those who have finished the race and now rejoice in God's presence. We honor the towering figures like Saints Peter, Paul, Augustine, Francis, and Thérèse of the Child Jesus, and we honor the humble saints as well, those whose names are known to few or to none: the grandparents and ancestors, the friends and teachers who lived their faith to the full and inspired faith in others. This is a day to celebrate them all.

An observance in honor of all the saints has been celebrated on November 1 since at least the seventh century, and it originated even earlier, with a feast in honor of all martyrs in the year 359. "Why should our praise and glorification, or even the celebration of this feastday mean anything to the saints?" asked Saint Bernard of Clairvaux in a homily on All Saints' Day. "Clearly, if we venerate their memory, it serves us, not them. But I tell you, when I think of them, I feel myself inflamed with a tremendous yearning. Calling the saints to mind inspires, or rather arouses in us, above all else, a longing to enjoy their company. . . . We long to share in the citizenship of heaven to dwell with the spirits of the blessed. . . . In short, we long to be united in happiness with all the saints" (Office of Readings, Volume IV, p. 1526). All holy men and women, saints of God, pray for us.

2

The Commemoration of All the Faithful Departed (All Souls' Day)

"Why would we doubt that our offerings for the dead bring them some consolation? Let us not hesitate to help those who have died and to offer our prayers for them," said Saint John Chrysostom (*Catechsim of the Catholic Church* [CCC], 1032). On the day after All Saints comes All Souls, the Commemoration of the Faithful Departed, in which the Church prays for all who have died. As Catholics, we believe in Purgatory, that cleansing fire through which must pass "all who die in God's grace and friendship, but still imperfectly purified" (CCC, 1030). Today, we pray for them, trusting that God will hear and answer our prayers that they know eternal light, happiness, and peace.

As we remember and pray for our loved ones who have died, the reality that we ourselves must one day die is also brought home to us as a gentle, insistent reminder. In Mexico, the *Dia de los Muertos* or The Day of the Dead is a way of praying for our ancestors, remembering and celebrating them, and making friends with death. As Saint Ambrose wrote, "Death is then no cause for mourning, for it is the cause of mankind's salvation. Death is not something to be avoided, for the Son of God did not think it beneath his dignity, nor did he seek to escape it" (Office of Readings, Volume IV, p. 1539). May the souls of all the faithful departed through the mercy of God rest in peace.

3

OPTIONAL MEMORIAL OF Saint Martin de Porres, RELIGIOUS

Saint Martin de Porres (15795–1639) had a special love for the marginalized in society; he knew what it was like to feel unaccepted. As the son of an unwed couple, a Spanish knight and a freed slave from Panama, he hardly fit the norm. His father essentially disowned him because he inherited his mother's features, primarily her skin color. Instead of wallowing in his own pain, he chose to become a Dominican brother, focusing on ministry to the "forgotten" in society. Saint Martin, called the "father of charity," cared for sick people in the monastery, fed the needy with food from the monastery, and began a home for abandoned children. He had a close friendship with Saint Rose of Lima and is considered patron saint of racial justice.

Saint Winefride, Virgin (Wales)

Saint Winefride was a seventh-century Welsh martyr. There is not much historical information about her. Tradition says that she was a noblewoman, engaged to a man named Caradog. When she decided to become a nun, he became so angry that he decapitated her, but she was miraculously healed by her uncle, Saint Bueno, and did succeed in becoming a nun. There are a number of healing springs associated with her, but the main one is at Shrewsbury, where a shrine was built. It was a popular pilgrimage site until Henry VIII had it destroyed in 1540. Saint Winefride is the patron saint of payroll clerks and is invoked against sexual harassment. She is shown in art dressed as an abbess holding a sword, sometimes holding her head under her arm.

4

MEMORIAL OF Saint Charles Borromeo, BISHOP

Saint Charles Borromeo (1538–1584), a doctor of civil and canon law, was a great champion of the Church redefining itself in light of the Protestant Reformation. As archbishop of Milan, he promulgated the reforms of the Council of Trent, giving special attention to liturgical and clerical renewal. Other significant contributions he made to the Church include the establishment of new seminaries for the education of the clergy, defining a code of moral conduct for clergy, and founding the Oblates of Saint Ambrose, a society of diocesan priests to enforce the reforms of Trent. Saint Charles adopted a simple life in which he responded to the needs of the poor and sick by providing monetary and spiritual support.

Saint Illtud, Abbot (Wales)

Saint Illtud was a Welshman who lived in the sixth-century. He founded and was abbot of Llanilltud Fawr in Glamorgan. A seventh-century account of his life claims that he was a disciple of Germanus of Auxerre and implies that he might have been married at one time and had some military experience. Devotion to Saint Illtud did not become popular until the eleventh-century, when a life full of implausible stories of miraculously tamed wild animals, islands merging with the mainland, and apparitions of angels was circulated. Regardless, Saint Illtud is thought to have introduced better farming methods to the Welsh.

9

FEAST OF THE Dedication of the Lateran Basilica

Today the Church throughout the world celebrates a feast in honor of a church in Rome: the Basilica of Saint John Lateran. Saint John Lateran is not just any church: it is the cathedral of the Bishop of Rome, who is, of course, the pope.

"Lateran" was the name of a Roman family whose lands were seized by the Emperor Constantine in the fourth century. He proceeded to build a great basilica dedicated in honor of Saint John the Baptist, but the name of the family that had once owned the land remained associated with it, and the church is called San Giovanni in Laterano, or "Saint John in the Lateran." For centuries, the old Lateran palace was the residence of the popes. It was only when the popes returned to Rome following the Avignon exile in the fourteenth century that they moved their residence to the Vatican Hill, which they considered to be a healthier part of the city.

Saint John Lateran continues to serve as the pope's cathedral and is as a sign of our unity as a Church under the leadership of the Holy Father. As we recall the dedication of this important church, the Mother Church of all the churches of the world, we should look inward as well. "My fellow Christians, do we wish to celebrate joyfully the birth of this temple?" asked Saint Caesarius of Arles in a homily on this feast. "Whenever we come to church, we must prepare our hearts to be as beautiful as we expect this church to be. Do you wish to find this basilica immaculately clean? Then do not soil your soul with the filth of sins. . . . Just as you enter this church building, so God wishes to enter into your soul" (Office of Readings, Volume IV, pp. 1547–48).

10

MEMORIAL OF Saint Leo the Great, POPE AND DOCTOR OF THE CHURCH

As pope and Doctor of the Church, Saint Leo the Great (+ 461) strongly supported the teachings of the Council of Chalcedon, especially on the humanity and divinity of Christ. He advocated papal authority by moving from the traditional approach that the pope is a successor to Saint Peter's chair to the pope as Saint Peter's heir. Under his leadership, uniformity of pastoral practice was encouraged, liturgical and clerical abuses were corrected, and priests were sent on a mission to extinguish Priscillianism, a heresy that claimed the human body was evil. Saint Leo is recognized as a "protector of the people" because he persuaded Atilla the Hun to not invade the city of Rome and later prevented the Vandals (East German invaders) from torching the city of Rome and massacring its people.

11

MEMORIAL OF **Saint Martin of Tours**, BISHOP

Saint Martin of Tours (c. 316–397) was forced by his father, a pagan officer in the Roman army, to join the military. While serving in the military he encountered a beggar freezing in the cold. Martin cut his own cloak in half and shared it with the beggar. Following this encounter he had a vision of Christ wrapped in the cloak. As a result of this experience, Saint Martin chose to be baptized and declared himself a soldier of peace for Christ, refusing to participate in any act of violence. He took up the life of a hermit, thus beginning monasticism in Gaul. When he was elected bishop of Tours he continued living as a monk, but made numerous trips to visit his people and found new monasteries. The people of Gaul became Christian due to his example.

Veterans Day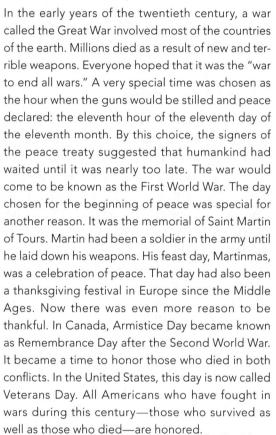

On November 11, 1918, World War I—called "the great war" or "the war to end all wars"—ended with the signing of an armistice between the Allies and Germany at Compiègne, France. It was eleven o'clock in the morning—the eleventh hour of the eleventh day of the eleventh month of the year. The day came to be known as Armistice Day, a day to commemorate the end of the war and to honor those who fell.

By 1954, the United States had been involved in two other major wars, and President Eisenhower officially changed the name of the holiday from "Armistice Day" to "Veterans Day." It is a day of solemn remembrance, a day to honor the veterans of all wars, both the living and the dead. It is also a day for looking to the future, a day when we "reconsecrate ourselves to the task of promoting an enduring peace so that their efforts shall not have been in vain" (Proclamation of President Eisenhower, October 8, 1954).

Remembrance Day

In the early years of the twentieth century, a war called the Great War involved most of the countries of the earth. Millions died as a result of new and terrible weapons. Everyone hoped that it was the "war to end all wars." A very special time was chosen as the hour when the guns would be stilled and peace declared: the eleventh hour of the eleventh day of the eleventh month. By this choice, the signers of the peace treaty suggested that humankind had waited until it was nearly too late. The war would come to be known as the First World War. The day chosen for the beginning of peace was special for another reason. It was the memorial of Saint Martin of Tours. Martin had been a soldier in the army until he laid down his weapons. His feast day, Martinmas, was a celebration of peace. That day had also been a thanksgiving festival in Europe since the Middle Ages. Now there was even more reason to be thankful. In Canada, Armistice Day became known as Remembrance Day after the Second World War. It became a time to honor those who died in both conflicts. In the United States, this day is now called Veterans Day. All Americans who have fought in wars during this century—those who survived as well as those who died—are honored.

12

MEMORIAL OF **Saint Josaphat**, BISHOP AND MARTYR

As a young man Saint Josaphat (c. 1580–1623) was excited about the possibility of the Orthodox metropolitan city of Kiev, comprising Belarussians and Ukrainians, reuniting with the Church of Rome. When he was elected archbishop of Polotsk, Lithuania, he worked tirelessly to continue the efforts to bring the Orthodox communities of Kiev in full communion with the Catholic Church. Many people were strongly opposed to this reunion; therefore, they established a rival hierarchy and set up groups to defame his name. While preaching in a particularly hostile city, he was murdered. His commitment to ecumenical relations was eventually realized in the Byzantine Rite of Catholicism. Saint Josaphat, the martyr, is the first Eastern saint to be formally canonized.

13

MEMORIAL OF Saint Francis Xavier Cabrini, VIRGIN 🇺🇸

Saint Frances Xavier Cabrini (1850–1917), also known as Mother Cabrini, was an Italian immigrant to the United States. She was the first American citizen to be canonized. As a girl, Frances dreamed of sailing to China as a missionary. In 1880, she founded the Missionary Sisters of the Sacred Heart of Jesus, and her community's work drew the attention of Pope Leo XIII. She hoped that he would send her to China, but he instead sent her to New York City in 1889 to minister to Italian immigrants, saying "Not to the East, but to the West." She founded sixty-seven institutions throughout the United States, Europe, and South America. After her death, her sisters fulfilled her dream of working in China. Saint Frances Cabrini is the patron saint of immigrants.

14

Saint Dyfrig, Bishop (Wales)

Saint Dyfrig (c. + 550) was the evangelist of southeast Wales. His mother, Efrddyl, was the daughter of the King of Ergyng and conceived him out of wedlock. He founded monasteries and taught many Welsh saints such as Teilo (see February 9) and

Samson. He was made bishop of Ergyng, attended the Synod of Llanddewi Brefi in 545, and retired to a hermitage on the Isle of Bardsey after handing over his diocese to Saint David. According to legend, it was he who crowned King Arthur.

15

OPTIONAL MEMORIAL OF Saint Albert the Great, BISHOP AND DOCTOR OF THE CHURCH

To the great disappointment of his father, Saint Albert the Great (1206–1280), known as "the universal doctor," entered the Dominican order, where he was recognized for his acumen. Ahead of his time, he believed that learning did not take place in a vacuum; one must be an interdisciplinary learner. He loved the world of academia, anywhere from studying the natural sciences to unearthing the connection between reason and experience to learning the geography of the earth. As a prestigious teacher, he had the privilege of instructing and mentoring Saint Thomas Aquinas, author of the *Summa Theologia*. Toward the end of his life he began to experience memory loss and dementia, which led to his gradual demise. He was declared a Doctor of the Church by Pope Pius XI.

16

OPTIONAL MEMORIAL OF Saint Margaret of Scotland

Saint Margaret of Scotland (c. 1045–1093), the wife of King Malcolm III of Scotland, managed to raise eight children while promoting Church reform, especially in the area of liturgical practice. As a woman of great faith, she founded and restored monasteries, provided hospitality to pilgrims, spoke out on behalf of the falsely accused, and fed the poor from her own dining table. All of her charitable activity was grounded in a strong prayer life.

OPTIONAL MEMORIAL OF
Saint Gertrude, Virgin

Saint Gertrude the Great (1256–1302) was a nun at the Benedictine monastery of Helfta, the abbey where two other great female spiritual writers lived: Mechtilde of Magdeburg and Saint Mechtilde (Matilda von Hackeborn-Wippra). Through prayer she was graced with many mystical and ecstatic experiences, which are recorded in a five volume work entitled *Legatus divinae pietatis*, commonly called *The Life and Revelations of Saint Gertrude the Great*. Her spirituality focused on the humanity of Christ and was characterized by a strong devotion to the Sacred Heart of Jesus. According to many scholars, Saint Gertrude's writings should be on the same shelf with other influential mystics, such as Saint Teresa of Avila.

17

MEMORIAL OF Saint Elizabeth of Hungary, RELIGIOUS

Saint Elizabeth of Hungary (1207–1231), the Queen of Hungary and mother of four children, had a special love for the downtrodden. She built a hospital in the basement of her castle, nursed the sick, fed the hungry, and provided life-giving work for the poor. After the death of her husband, she took the habit of a Franciscan tertiary (Third Order Franciscan), devoting herself to a life of simplicity and almsgiving. Along with her selfless service to those in need, she actively pursued God through prayer and spiritual discipline. Saint Elizabeth is the patron saint of Franciscan tertiaries, bakers, beggars, brides, the homeless, and charities (among others).

Venerable Henriette DeLille

During the time of legalized slavery and rampant prejudice in the United States, Venerable Henriette DeLille (1813–1862) was born to an interracial couple, a white man and "free woman of color," in New Orleans. Her affluent upbringing afforded her many educational opportunities. Her mother wanted her to marry a wealthy white man, but Venerable Henriette felt called to the religious life. After she was turned away from the Ursulines and Carmelites, she taught in a local Catholic school. Once she took over her family's assets, Henriette founded the Sisters of the Presentation, now known as the Sisters of the Holy Family, to provide nursing care for the elderly, safety for orphans, and education for the poor. Although her brother was outraged by her use of the family fortune, Henriette remained committed to the compassionate service of the marginalized. She died on this date in 1862. Her cause for beatification is still pending.

18

OPTIONAL MEMORIAL OF THE
Dedication of the Basilicas of Saints Peter and Paul, APOSTLES

"Basilica" has two meanings when it comes to church buildings. When it's written with a lower case "b," it describes a style of architecture. But when it has a capital "B," it refers to a church that is an especially important gathering place for Catholics, a church that has played an important role in the history of our faith. Today's memorial recalls two important centers for our faith: the Basilicas of Saints Peter and Paul in Rome. These two churches, built over the tombs of the Apostles, stand today as signs of our unity as a Church.

In the Basilica of Saint Paul, there are portraits of every pope, from Saint Peter all the way through to Pope Benedict XVI—with room for many more! It is a strong reminder of the continuity of the faith we profess, thanks to the power of God working through the authority given to Saint Peter and the preaching of Saint Paul.

A few miles away, on Vatican hill, rises the Basilica of Saint Peter, the church we associate more than any other with the Holy Father. In front of the great basilica is an enormous piazza or gathering place where people gather for Mass, audiences, and other events with the pope. The piazza is framed by two great colonnades, which the artist Bernini described as two great arms, reaching out to embrace the whole world and gather them in.

OPTIONAL MEMORIAL OF
Saint Rose Philippine Duchesne, VIRGIN 🇺🇸

Beginning her life as a nun in the Order of the Visitation in France, Saint Rose Philippine Duchesne (1769–1852) eventually joined the Society of the Sacred Heart, founded by Saint Madeleine Sophie Barat. Due to her missionary zeal, she was sent, along with five other sisters, to Saint Louis, Missouri, to care for the poor and educate Native Americans. Under her leadership, the sisters established numerous schools and orphanages. She is remembered for her remarkable work, including evangelization and catechesis with Native Americans, particularly the Potawatomi tribe. Recognizing her extraordinary ministry, amazing ability to navigate difficulties, and profound spirituality, a contemporary said, "She was the Saint Francis of Assisi of the Society."

19
Our Lady of Divine Providence
(Puerto Rico)

Today the people of Puerto Rico honor the Blessed Virgin Mary under the title of Our Lady of Divine Providence. Devotion to Mary under this title originated in thirteenth-century Italy and came to Puerto Rico in 1853. The image venerated in Puerto Rico is a statue that shows Our Lady seated with the infant Christ asleep in her lap, and as she holds his little hand in her own, she prays to the Father. The image speaks of peace and tenderness as well as trust and abandonment to God's will. Since 1969, her feast has been celebrated on November 19, coinciding with the date of the discovery of the island of Puerto Rico.

21
MEMORIAL OF THE Presentation of the Blessed Virgin Mary

The Gospel accounts tell of the Presentation of the Lord Jesus in the Temple but do not speak of the Presentation of Mary. Nevertheless, Christians in the East and the West have observed a day in honor of Mary's Presentation for centuries. Many artists have depicted the scene: a tiny girl (Mary is said to have been three or four years old when she was presented in the Temple), climbing the steps to go into the Temple to offer herself to God. This memorial speaks of Mary's total openness to God. God kept her free from sin from the moment of her conception, so that she, whose presentation in the Temple we commemorate today, would become a Temple of the Holy Spirit.

Our Lady of Peace (El Salvador)

In El Salvador today, Mary is venerated as Our Lady of Peace. The origin of the image is shrouded in mystery. According to the legend, some merchants found a box abandoned on the shore and decided to take it with them to San Miguel, a city in El Salvador. They reached their destination on this day in 1682, but as they rode past the church, the donkey carrying the box lay down and stubbornly refused to go any farther. Not knowing what to do, they opened the box and found a lovely image of Our Lady with the child Jesus. They placed the image in the parish church, and soon many miracles were attributed to her. Today, the little parish is a great cathedral, and the statue of Mary with her divine Son is known as Our Lady of Peace.

Our Lady of Quinche (Ecuador)

Our Lady of Quinche is a delicate wood carving of the Virgin and Child that has been venerated for more than four hundred years in the town of Quinche in Ecuador. The image, which stands about two feet high, shows Mary holding the child Jesus in her arms. Mary holds a scepter, and Jesus holds the globe crowned with a cross. The statue is covered in rich brocades, so that only the faces and hands are seen. The dark faces of the Virgin and the Child resemble the mestizo people of Ecuador, who refer to her affectionately as *La Pequenita*, the "little one."

22

MEMORIAL OF Saint Cecilia, VIRGIN AND MARTYR

According to legend, Saint Cecilia (c. third century) was beheaded because she would not forsake her vow of virginity and would not make sacrifices to the gods. She is the patron saint of musicians, singers, and poets. Her association with music is most likely related to a line from her *passio* (an account of her holy "passion," her martyrdom), where she is said to have sung "in her heart to Christ" as the musicians played at her wedding. Upon its foundation in 1584, the Academy of Music in Rome declared her the patron saint of musicians. Saint Cecilia's popularity grew so much that several hymns were written in her honor, and her life is referenced in Chaucer's *The Canterbury Tales*.

23

OPTIONAL MEMORIAL OF Saint Clement I, POPE AND MARTYR

Saint Clement I (c. + 100) was pope during a rather tumultuous time, when the early Christian communities were experiencing growing pains. He is most remembered for a letter referred to as 1 Clement, which was written to the Christian community at Corinth. His letter addressed division within the community, urging its members to live in charity and unity. An unverified tradition, but one accepted by the early Church historian Tertullian and Saint Jerome, claims that Saint Clement was consecrated by Saint Peter as his immediate successor. He is venerated as a martyr but the manner of his death is unknown.

OPTIONAL MEMORIAL OF Saint Columban, ABBOT

Saint Columban (Columbanus) (c. 543–615) was an Irish monk and missionary who established many religious houses in France and Italy. Through word and example, he urged the Church (and especially the clergy) to ever greater holiness.

OPTIONAL MEMORIAL OF
Blessed Miguel Agustín Pro,
PRIEST AND MARTYR

Blessed Miguel Agustín Pro (1891–1927), a Jesuit priest and martyr, lived under an anticlerical and anti-Christian political regime in Mexico. In the face of surmounting hostility and hatred, he chose to evangelize by performing Baptisms, witnessing Marriages, and conducting catechetical classes. Firmly grounded in both the corporal and spiritual works of mercy, he fed the poor, provided shelter for the homeless, and prayed with the dying. He was executed by a firing squad because he would not abandon his clerical call to care for the oppressed.

24

MEMORIAL OF
Saint Andrew Dũng-Lac,
PRIEST, AND COMPANIONS, MARTYRS 🏴

Saint Andrew Dũng-Lac (1795–1839), a Vietnamese priest, was one of 117 martyrs canonized in 1988 who died trying to establish and spread the Catholic religion in Vietnam. This effort, which began in 1533 and continued well into the nineteenth century, was fraught with periods of persecution. Although Saint Andrew was born into a Buddhist family, he was raised Catholic. His priestly ministry involved evangelization, parish catechesis, and service to the persecuted. Living under a particularly oppressive edict, Saint Andrew was killed because he would not renounce his Christian apostolate and succumb to idolatrous ritual.

25

OPTIONAL MEMORIAL OF Saint Catherine of Alexandria,
VIRGIN AND MARTYR

This fourth-century Christian woman lived in Alexandria, Egypt, during the reign of the Roman emperor Maxentius. Legend says that Saint Catherine of Alexandria bravely confronted the emperor about his pagan beliefs. Maxentius gathered fifty pagan philosophers and challenged her to a debate. Her arguments were so convincing that many of the philosophers converted to Christianity. He then threatened to kill her unless she married him and renounced her faith. She refused and was condemned to death by a spiked wheel, but the wheel fell apart when she touched it. She was then beheaded, and legend says that angels carried her to Mount Sinai. She has been venerated since the tenth century.

30

FEAST OF
Saint Andrew, APOSTLE

Saint Andrew (first century) was the first of the Twelve to meet Jesus. He was one of the two disciples of John the Baptist who saw John point out Jesus and say, "Here is the Lamb of God" (John 1:36). Andrew told his brother, Peter, "We have found the Messiah" (John 1:41) and brought him to Jesus. Saint Andrew is venerated as the *protoclete*, or first-called, by the Eastern Churches. Tradition says that he may have preached in parts of Asia Minor and Greece before being crucified on an x-shaped cross. The Scots claim Andrew as their patron saint, and his cross is on their flag.

DECEMBER

Month of December

The word for the last month of the year means, in Latin, "tenth month." The ancient calendar of the Romans began in March, which made December the tenth month. In ancient times, people of northern Europe stopped counting the days during winter. There wasn't any farm work to do, so there wasn't any reason to keep track of time. They called this free time *Yule*. This word comes from the same root word as the word *wheel*. The days of Yule connected the old year to the new.

Month of the Divine Infancy

During this month of December, as we look forward to Christmas, we recall the Divine Infancy of Christ. This month, let the paradox of Christ's birth and childhood strike us anew. Let us pray with Mary in the words of an ancient hymn by Saint Ephraem the Syrian: "I am your Mother but I will give honor to you. I have engendered you, but you are older than I am. I have carried you in my womb, but you sustain me on my feet. You have been born of me like a little

Images of Saints and Solemnities in December (L to R): Saint Lucy (December 13), Immaculate Conception of the Blessed Virgin Mary (December 8), Saint Nicholas (December 6).

one, but you are as strong as a giant. The height of the heavens are filled with your majesty, and yet my womb has not been too small for you."

1

World AIDS Day

Those simple loops of red ribbon that people wear on their lapels today are recognized around the world—because people everywhere have encountered AIDS (Acquired Immune Deficiency Syndrome) and the Human Immunodeficiency Virus (HIV) that leads to AIDS if left untreated. Unknown in 1980, HIV and AIDS have by now created a genuine pandemic. Those who suffer with these illnesses live mostly in middle- and low-income areas such as sub-Saharan Africa. Most of those who are ill have no access to the life-giving retroviral drugs that can stop HIV, ease the suffering of those with full-blown AIDS, and prevent the spread of the illness. World AIDS Day began in 1988 to call for greater awareness of their plight. Only universal access to prevention, treatment, and care can stop the disease.

3

MEMORIAL OF
Saint Francis Xavier, PRIEST

Saint Francis Xavier came from a noble family in the Basque region of Spain. He went to study at the University of Paris. There he met Ignatius Loyola, who invited him to become one of the first Jesuits. After Ordination, Francis became a missionary to Asia, first in India and then in Japan. He yearned to bring the Gospel to the Chinese and had made arrangements to enter the country, but worn out from his work, he died on the island of Sancian within sight of the coast of China. Pope Pius X named him patron saint of foreign missions.

4

OPTIONAL MEMORIAL OF Saint John Damascene, PRIEST AND DOCTOR OF THE CHURCH

Saint John of Damascus (or Damascene/c. 657–749), was a Syrian monk and priest, the "last of the Fathers of the Church." Islam had taken root in Syria, and John worked for the caliph for a time but left to enter the monastery of Saint Sabbas near Jerusalem. He is best known for his defense of the veneration of images and his summary of the teachings of the Greek Fathers, *The Fountain of Wisdom*. John also wrote hymns and prayers that are still used in the Orthodox and Eastern Catholic Churches and can be called "doctor of the Assumption" because of his writings on that teaching.

6

OPTIONAL MEMORIAL OF
Saint Nicholas, BISHOP

Little is known about this saint, the "wonder-worker," other than the fact that he lived sometime during the fourth century and was bishop of the city of Myra in Asia Minor. There is some evidence that he was imprisoned during the Diocletian persecutions and later condemned Arianism, a heresy that denied the Son was co-eternal with the Father. Many stories exist about Saint Nicholas, but one most frequently passed down speaks of a poor man who could not feed or clothe his three daughters. Upon hearing of this man's dire situation, Saint Nicholas tossed three bags of gold through his window one evening so the man could tend to his daughter's needs. Modern folklore about Santa Claus, Kris Kringle, and Father Christmas are based in the stories of Saint Nicholas and his great love for and generosity toward children. Whatever is known or not known about this great saint, it can be said, to quote an anonymous Greek from the tenth century, "All Christians, young and old, men and women, boys and girls, reverence his memory and call upon his protection" (as quoted in *Butler's Lives of the Saints: December, New Full Edition,* p. 60).

7

MEMORIAL OF Saint Ambrose, BISHOP AND DOCTOR OF THE CHURCH

Saint Ambrose (c. 340–397) was governor when he went to stop rioting that erupted during the selection of a new bishop of Milan. The crowd cried, "Ambrose for bishop," and he was chosen, although he was just a catechumen. The Arian heresy—which denied the full divinity of Christ—divided the Church of his time. When Empress Justina demanded that Ambrose give his basilica to the Arians, he and his congregation locked themselves in and sang antiphonally, the first recorded instance. He baptized Saint Augustine and was a great friend of Augustine's mother, Saint Monica. Ambrose is nicknamed the "honey-tongued doctor" for his eloquent preaching.

National Pearl Harbor Remembrance Day 🇺🇸

This day commemorates the 1941 attack by Japanese aircraft on the United States Pacific fleet, based at Pearl Harbor, Hawaii. The next day the United States of America officially entered World War II, which had already seen fierce fighting since 1937. Eventually 29 countries would be involved. No one really knows how many lives were lost in the epic struggle, perhaps as many as 60 million. A great percentage of those were civilians. They died by firebombing, germ warfare, slave labor, genocide, starvation, two nuclear bombs, and other forms of violence.

The December 7 attack damaged a sizable portion of the fleet, but since it did not destroy the base's shipyards and fuel storage tanks, the United States was able to mount a response. Even so, the war continued until August of 1945.

8

SOLEMNITY OF THE Immaculate Conception of the Blessed Virgin Mary, PATRONAL FEASTDAY OF THE UNITED STATES OF AMERICA

The dogma that Mary was kept free from original sin from the first moment of her conception was solemnly declared by Pope Pius IX in 1854, but it was by no means a new invention. The Eastern Church had celebrated this day from as early as the eighth century, and it soon spread to the West. It has been on the Church's universal calendar since 1708.

The Immaculate Conception is a singular grace, given to Mary to enable her to say "yes" to God. No stain of original sin touches her who is to become the Ark of the Covenant, the Temple in which God comes to dwell. This is a unique grace. And yet, Mary is our model for holiness. By our Baptism, we have been washed clean of the stain of original sin to become temples for the Holy Spirit. And we look to Mary for an example of the life of discipleship, open to God's word, obedient to God's will.

This Solemnity of the Immaculate Conception is celebrated with great festivity in many places around the world, particularly in Spain. In the Cathedral of Seville, there is a unique tradition called *Los Seises* or the "Dance of the Six." Six boys perform a solemn dance before the Blessed Sacrament as hymns are sung in honor of the Immaculate Conception. It is a tradition that survives to this day, a vivid image of the joy of the Church in this celebration of the grace of God at work in the Blessed Virgin Mary. Today's solemnity is the Patronal Feast Day of the United States of America.

Our Lady of Miracles (Paraguay)

On this Solemnity of the Immaculate Conception, the people of Paraguay celebrate Our Lady of the Miracles. Today, tens of thousands of pilgrims make their way to the shrine of the Virgin of the Miracles of Caacupé, also called the *Virgen Azul de Paraguay,* the "Blue Virgin of Paraguay." The image dates back to the early sixteenth century. A Christian native, threatened with death by a tribe that had declared itself the enemy of all Christians, hid behind a massive tree and vowed that if he escaped with his life, he would carve an image of the Virgin from the wood of the tree that saved his life. This he did, and the image of the Virgin and Child he carved has been venerated in Paraguay ever since.

OPTIONAL MEMORIAL OF Saint Juan Diego Cuauhtlatoatzin

Saint Juan Diego Cuauhtlatoatzin (1474–1548) was a native Mexican, a farmer, and a laborer. On December 9, 1531, on his way to attend Mass, he heard a woman call out from Tepeyac Hill. She was the Virgin Mary, and she asked Juan Diego to tell the bishop to build a chapel on the site. Juan Diego went to the bishop with the request, but the bishop scoffed at him. He returned with his cloak, or tilma, filled with roses, and when he unfurled it before the bishop, the woman's image was imprinted on the inside. The bishop believed, and the church was built. The image on Juan Diego's tilma is venerated as that of Our Lady of Guadalupe.

10

Saint John Roberts, Priest and Martyr (Wales)

Saint John Roberts (1575–1610) was born in Wales, studied at Oxford, and was a law student. During a trip to the continent, he converted to Catholicism and subsequently entered the Abbey of Saint Benedict at Valladolid. After Ordination, he was sent to England and arrived there in 1602. He was caught and banished to France but soon managed to re-enter England. Arrested and banished a second time, he returned and was caught in November 1605 and accused of conspiring to blow up Parliament as part of the Gunpowder Plot. Exiled a third time, Saint John went to Douai and founded a Benedictine abbey for English monks who had joined communities in Spain. This was the beginning of Downside Abbey. He returned to England in 1607, was captured, escaped, but was recaptured and banished. Once again, he returned to England and was caught celebrating Mass. He was hanged, drawn, and quartered at Tyburn, London in 1610.

International Human Rights Day

In 1945, when the Second World War ended, world leaders realized that new and better ways of solving disputes among nations must be found. They created the United Nations to provide a forum where countries can debate peacefully, rather than taking up arms to settle grievances. The United Nations works for peace. It works against hunger, disease, and poverty. In 1948, after much hard work, the United Nations produced a document called the Universal Declaration of Human Rights. Delegates from member nations all over the world hammered out their definition of 30 rights that all human beings need to live a decent life. The Declaration says that everyone on the planet, regardless of race, sex, language, or religion, has a right to certain basic freedoms. Among these freedoms are the right to life, health care, education, and privacy.

People also are entitled to freedom from imprisonment without trial. They have a right to leave and reenter their country. They have a right to seek protection in another country if they are persecuted in their own. Each of those freedoms is being denied to some of the world's citizens even as we celebrate the Declaration today. The United Nations will continue working for these basic human rights. They will also work to get the Declaration into the hands of people everywhere. People need to know that they deserve these rights and that the United Nations has pledged to uphold them.

11

OPTIONAL MEMORIAL OF
Saint Damasus I, POPE

As pope, Saint Damasus I (+ 384) commissioned his secretary, Saint Jerome, to revise the Latin Bible in use at that time by translating the Old Testament from the Hebrew rather than the Greek version. The Vulgate remained the standard Latin translation until 1979. Damasus presided over the Council of Rome, at which the canon of scripture, or recognized books in the Bible, was set. He fought to counteract Appolinarianism, an over-correction to Arianism (see December 7, Saint Ambrose) that de-emphasized Christ's humanity. He is also known for the verses he composed to adorn the tombs of the martyrs in Rome.

12

FEAST OF Our Lady of Guadalupe, Patroness of the Americas

Today the Church throughout America (North, Central, and South) celebrates Our Lady of Guadalupe, Patroness of America. Today is a feast in the United States of America, but in many Hispanic countries, such as Mexico, it is raised to a solemnity.

The story of the origins of the miraculous image of Our Lady of Guadalupe is well known. Juan Diego Cuauhtlatoatzin was a quiet, humble man, a poor peasant. When the Blessed Virgin Mary appeared to him and asked him to tell the local bishop to build a church in her honor, Juan Diego became a very reluctant messenger. The bishop would not believe him. So Mary filled Juan Diego's tilma, or cloak, with roses in December, and when he emptied out these beautiful flowers at the bishop's feet, there, imprinted on his tilma, was a wonderful image of the Virgin, dressed like a young Aztec woman.

Our Lady of Guadalupe, or *La Morenita*, as she is sometimes called—"the little dark one"—said to Juan Diego: "Know and understand that I am the ever virgin Mary, Mother of the true God through whom all things live. . . . Listen and understand, my humblest son. There is nothing to frighten and distress you. Do not let your heart be troubled, and let nothing upset you. Is it not I, your Mother, who is here? Are you not under my protection? Are you not, fortunately, in my care?" (*Benedictine Daily Prayer*, The Liturgical Press, p. 1698)

13

MEMORIAL OF Saint Lucy, VIRGIN AND MARTYR

Saint Lucy (c. + 304), even from a young age, had a burning desire to serve God and an infinite love for the poor. Living in Syracuse, a city in Sicily, she fell prey to the Diocletian persecutions, which eventually resulted in her martyrdom. She resisted a man, believed to be a Roman soldier, who tried to rape her. He, in turn, denounced her as a Christian and had her tortured and killed. Numerous legends revolve around her death, but one that has gained popularity is that she tore out her eyes in an act to resist her attacker. Her name comes from the Latin *lux* / Lucia, meaning light; therefore, many northern countries honor her at this time of year when darkness is pervasive. Sweden celebrates the virginity and martyrdom of Saint Lucy during a festival of light with a sacred procession of young girls clothed in white dresses with red sashes, and crowned with lit candles. She is the patron saint of those with eye troubles and those needing awareness.

14

MEMORIAL OF Saint John of the Cross, PRIEST AND DOCTOR OF THE CHURCH

John of the Cross (1542–1591) grew up near Avila in poverty. His father died when he was young, and his widowed mother struggled to support the family. Shortly after his ordination in 1567, he met Teresa of Avila and was drawn into her reform of the Carmelites. The reform set Carmelite brother against brother, and John was even imprisoned but used the time to write the *Spiritual Canticle*. For this, and for his other great work, *Dark Night of the Soul*, he is considered one of the greatest poets to write in Spanish.

16–24

Simbang Gabi

Please see page 9 for more information.

Las Posadas

Please see page 9 for more information.

16–26

Las Parrandas

Please see page 9 for more information.

17

The "O" Antiphons begin at Evening Prayer.

Please see page 4 for more information.

21

OPTIONAL MEMORIAL OF Saint Peter Canisius, PRIEST AND DOCTOR OF THE CHURCH

Saint Peter Canisius (1521–1597) was the first Dutchman to join the Jesuits. He is known as the second apostle of Germany for his work restoring Catholicism after the Reformation, writing a "German catechism," which defined basic Catholic beliefs in German. Peter felt that it was more effective to clarify the teachings of Catholicism rather than engage in polemics with the reformers. His last 20 years were spent in Switzerland, where he founded the Jesuit College that is the core of the University of Fribourg. He is credited with adding "Holy Mary, pray for us sinners" to the Hail Mary. This appeared for the first time in his catechism of 1555.

21/22

Winter Solstice

Today marks a turning point in the year. For people of the Northern Hemisphere, the winter solstice is the shortest day and longest night. From now on days will lengthen. For the ancient peoples of Europe, the winter solstice was one of the greatest feasts of the year. Once the harvest was in, there was little farm work to do, and so there was plenty of time to relax and celebrate. Sometimes the festivities lasted for two months! Many northern Europeans called these days "Yule," from the word *wheel*. They thought that the year was like a wheel. When the days started to get longer, it was as if someone had given the year a fresh turn.

23

OPTIONAL MEMORIAL OF Saint John of Kanty, PRIEST

Also known as John Cantius (+ 1473), Saint John of Kanty was a brilliant and multi-talented Polish theologian and professor of Sacred Scripture at Kraków. In addition to his theological work, he was also a physicist and anticipated the work of Galileo and Newton. He was known for his spirit of poverty and humility and gave most of his professor's salary to the poor, keeping just enough to live simply. Miracles were attributed to him in his lifetime, and he became a very popular saint in Poland. Many churches founded in North America for Polish immigrants are named in his honor.

25

SOLEMNITY OF THE Nativity of the Lord

Please see page 5 for more information.

26

FEAST OF Saint Stephen, THE FIRST MARTYR

Saint Stephen (c. + 34) is the protomartyr, the first martyr. When the Apostles chose deacons to help in their ministry, he was among the first seven. Stephen was arrested and tried by the Sanhedrin for blasphemy. His fate was sealed when he had a vision during his trial and cried out, "I see the heavens opened and the Son of Man standing at the right hand of God" (Acts of the Apostles 7:56). He was taken out to be stoned to death by a mob, which included Saul of Tarsus. Stephen is shown in art with three stones and a martyr's palm, sometimes wearing a dalmatic, a deacon's vestment.

Boxing Day
(Australia / New Zealand / Canada)

A public holiday in the British Isles, Australia, New Zealand, and Canada, Boxing Day began in the Middle Ages. Servants who worked on Christmas were granted the next day off, and perhaps given a new suit of clothing or some money. On this day, the poorboxes at churches were broken open so that the donations inside could be distributed to the needy. Nowadays people spend Boxing Day with family and friends feasting, watching major sports contests, playing board games—and sometimes, bargain-hunting. Many people also volunteer at food banks or otherwise serving the needy.

In Ireland, where this day is still known as Saint Stephen's Day, some places observe the ancient custom of "wrenning." Gaudily dressed carolers go door-to-door to raise money for charity or for a community party.

27

FEAST OF Saint John, APOSTLE AND EVANGELIST

Saint John (c. + 100) was one of the Twelve, the Beloved Disciple. He and his brother, the Apostle James, were the sons of Zebedee and Salome (the name tradition assigns to their mother). They were fishermen who worked in the Sea of Galilee. Jesus called the two brothers the "Sons of Thunder," and along with Saint Peter, they were present for the Transfiguration and the Agony in the Garden. John was the only Apostle who did not flee when Jesus was arrested, and Jesus puts his mother, Mary, into his care from the Cross. According to tradition, after the Assumption of Mary, he went to Ephesus, and from there was exiled to the island of Patmos, where he wrote the Book of Revelation. When he was an old man, he taught Saint Polycarp, who taught Saint Irenaeus. He was the only one of the Twelve to die a natural death, possibly near the beginning of the second century. Several New Testament books are attributed to him: a Gospel, letters, and the Book of Revelation. His symbol is the eagle because the Gospel attributed to him soars. He is the patron saint of authors, theologians, booksellers, editors, and friendship.

28

FEAST OF THE Holy Innocents, MARTYRS

Herod the Great, fearing for his throne after the Magi told him about the birth of Jesus, ordered the execution of all male children in Bethlehem, hoping that Jesus would be among those killed (see Matthew 2:16–18). According to Matthew, this fulfilled the prophecy of Jeremiah (31:15): "A voice is heard in Ramah, lamentation and bitter weeping. Rachel is weeping for her children." The haunting *Coventry Carol* refers to this episode as it asks, "O sisters too, how may we do, / For to preserve this day / This poor youngling for whom we do sing / By, by, lully, lullay."

29

OPTIONAL MEMORIAL OF Saint Thomas Becket, BISHOP AND MARTYR

Saint Thomas Becket (1118–1170) was born in London as the son of Norman parents (he was not a Saxon, as in the play, *Becket*). He received a good education at Merton Abbey, and later in Paris. When he left school, he became a secretary, a position of some prestige in a society with limited literacy. Eventually, he became assistant to Theobald, archbishop of Canterbury. Recognizing his talent, Theobald sent him to the court of King Henry II, and eventually Thomas was named Lord Chancellor of England. In 1162, hoping to gain control over the Church, Henry had him installed as archbishop of Canterbury, but Thomas had a conversion, resigned as Chancellor, and thus began a conflict between King and archbishop. When Thomas returned from exile in France and excommunicated Henry's followers, Henry said in a rage, "Will no one rid me of this meddlesome priest?" Four knights took this as a command and killed Thomas as he went to join the monks for vespers in the abbey church. The story is retold in T. S. Eliot's play *Murder in the Cathedral* and Jean Anouilh's play, *Becket*.

31

OPTIONAL MEMORIAL OF
Saint Sylvester I, POPE

Very little is known about Saint Sylvester I (c. + 335), in spite of his being pope during an eventful era in history, from 314 to 335. The only sources for his life are the *Liber pontificalis* and the *Vita beati Sylvestri*, both of which are filled with sketchy information or outright legends. According to these, his father was a Roman named Rufinus; his mother, Justa. We do know that shortly before the beginning of his papacy in 314, Constantine I issued the Edict of Milan (313), extending religious tolerance throughout the Roman Empire and enabling the Church to come out of hiding after years of persecution. During Sylvester's pontificate, some of the great churches in

Rome were built: the Basilica of Saint John Lateran, Santa Croce, the first Saint Peter's Basilica, and several others. The First Council of Nicea in 325, at which the Nicene Creed was adopted, occurred during his papacy. Sylvester himself did not attend, but he sent his legates, Vitus and Vincentius, who approved the council's decisions on his behalf. After his death, several fictional accounts of his relationship to Constantine appear, such as the Donation of Constantine (late eighth century), in which Sylvester cures the emperor of leprosy and baptizes him. Constantine is so grateful that he confirms the role of the Bishop of Rome over all other bishops and resigns as emperor. Sylvester then restores Constantine as emperor. This story implies that the pope is over all rulers, even the emperor, who can be deposed by papal decree. Saint Sylvester's memorial is celebrated on December 31, New Year's Eve, the day on which he was buried in the Catacomb of Priscilla. In some countries, New Year's Eve is called Silvester, in honor of the memorial. He is sometimes depicted in art with a dragon because of a myth that he slew one.

New Year's Eve

Please see page 30 for more information.

Orthodox Days

The year 1054 marked a tragic split in the Church, as Catholic Christians in the West became decisively separated from Orthodox Christians in the East. The schism arose over a variety of issues, including theological concerns (the *filioque* dispute was about whether the Holy Spirit proceeded both from the Father and the Son, or just from the Father — Catholics adhere to the former belief, Orthodox to the latter), but politics and geography also played into the separation, which endures to this day.

Nevertheless, Orthodox and Catholics share many of the same great feasts and holy days and honor many of the same saints. We all recall Christ's nativity on December 25 and Mary's nativity on September 8. We celebrate the Ascension of the Lord forty days after Easter and Pentecost ten days after that. We all observe feasts of the Transfiguration on August 6, the Assumption (or "Dormition") of Mary on August 15, and the Exaltation of the Holy Cross on September 14.

Images of Icons and Symbols of the Orthodox Church (L to R): Christ Pantocrator, Orthodox cross, the Theotokos.

But there are differences in our calendars as well—perhaps the most noticeable of these is the date of Easter or Pascha. In 1582, the Catholic Church began to use the Gregorian calendar, named for Pope Gregory XIII who initiated it. But the Orthodox Church never did; instead, they continued to use the ancient Julian calendar, which is 13 days behind the Gregorian calendar. When it is April 15 by the Gregorian calendar, it is April 2 by the Julian!

In addition, Orthodox Christians take into account the Jewish observance of Passover in calculating the date of Easter. Accordingly, they celebrate Easter on the second Sunday after the first full moon after the vernal equinox according to the Julian calendar. Thus, the Eastern Pascha can fall as much as five weeks later than the Western observance of Easter. But sometimes, amazingly enough, Easter can fall on the same day in both calendars (this will happen in 2014 and 2017).

Many wonderful customs surround the Eastern observance of the Pascha. On Good Friday, there is a procession of the faithful through the church and sometimes through the streets as well, with a cloth image of Christ, representing the linen shroud in which the faithful disciples wrapped his body. The shroud is placed in a tomb where the people keep watch through the night. At midnight or at dawn on Easter Sunday, the people gather before the church and knock on the doors with the cross. The doors swing open and everyone floods inside, singing in honor of the Resurrection. The cross opens the gates of Paradise! On Easter morning, it is customary for Orthodox Christians in many lands to greet each other with the words, "Christ is risen!" to which the other person responds, "He is truly risen. Alleluia!"

Catholics are often struck by the awe and mystery of Orthodox liturgy (and by its length—services can last for hours!). The wonderful singing of the entire congregation, the beauty of the icons, and the splendor of the churches, draw us towards the mystery of Christ and remind us of how much we share—and how much we have to learn from each other.

JEWISH DAYS

Jewish Days

All Jewish holidays begin at sunset since that's when the Jewish "day" begins. Hence, the holidays actually begin at sundown on the evening before the date shown and extends from sunset on that date until dusk on the last day.

Tu B'Shvat

Tu B'Shvat takes place on the fifteenth day of Shvat, which falls between mid-January and mid-February. Though not a widely observed holiday and one that existed long before the actual State of Israel, its purpose might be seen as similar to Earth Day and Arbor Day. However, to say that defies the significance of the holiday because its meaning is much more than

Images and Symbols of Judaism (clockwise from left):
Moses, the Star of David, Elijah, the Menorah.

planting a tree to add life and energy to our planet. The original significance of Tu B'Shvat was meant to honor the actual land beneath the State of Israel, for the region one lives in defines the culinary cuisine. Scripture teaches us to be stewards of the earth and that we are to be sustained by the earth's ability to nourish us. Thus, the land must be honored for the fruits that flourish to sustain its people. For the Jewish community, this is biblically based in Deuteronomy 8:7–9 (as well as other passages about vegetation): "For the LORD your God is bringing you into a good land, a land with flowing streams, with springs and underground waters welling up in valleys and hills, a land of wheat and barley, of vines and fig trees and pomegranates, a land of olive trees and honey, land where you may eat bread without scarcity, where you will lack nothing, a land whose stones are iron and from whose hills you may mine copper." Aside from planting a tree to honor and sustain the land, if Tu B'Shvat is traditionally observed, the foods listed in the Bible are prepared and eaten along with special blessings for the food and the chanting of the Psalms of Ascent. The ancient purpose of this feast was to calculate the age of the trees for tithing purposes. It's known as the New Year for Trees. Today, Tu B'Shvat has also become a tree planting festival when trees are planted in honor or in memory of a loved one or friend.

Purim

Purim is celebrated on the fourteenth and / or the fifteenth day of Adar (February–March.) It commemorates the salvation of the Jewish people in Ancient Persia from Haman's plot "to destroy, kill and annihilate all the Jews, young and old, infants and women, in a single day." Jewish people added this holiday to honor the deeds and leadership of Queen Esther and her relative Mordecai. The climax of the story comes when, during the diaspora, the Jewish people were threatened to extinction at the hands of man named Haman. Esther hid her Jewish heritage from her Persian King / husband for years until it was necessary to make a move to save her people. Each year on Purim, the entire scroll of

Esther must be read, word for word, and each time the name of Haman is read (over 50 times), the people are to make noise (booing, shouting, stomping) and then the reading continues.

Finally, likely due to the generosity of life given by the King to his Queen and her people, another commandment of Purim is to be charitable to everyone, those in true need, and those who simply ask to get something just because they want it.

Pesach (Passover)

Passover is a seven-day-long feast that begins on the fifteenth day of Nisan (March–April) and is most known for the Seder Meal. As is shared in the ritual of the Seder Meal, to understand the depth of Passover, the Exodus story must be known in its entirety, for this is essential history. The ritual of the Seder Meal is on the eve of the fifteenth day of Nisan.

The characters of the story are God, Moses, Pharaoh, and the Hebrew people. The themes of the story include murder, deception, slavery, conversion, the Ten Plagues, and faith in God. Exodus begins as the first-born son of each Hebrew family was under threat to be murdered, yet Moses is saved by the Pharaoh's daughter. Growing up under the Pharaoh's roof, not knowing his Hebrew roots, Moses is outraged at how the Egyptian leaders treated the Hebrew slaves, and he kills one of the leaders. Thus, Moses is sent into exile, and many years later God charges him to go back to save the Hebrews from slavery. Moses, full of God's strength and wisdom, has to overpower Pharaoh's stubborn and prideful nature in order to barter back the Hebrew's freedom.

In the climax of the Exodus story, the night before the tenth Plague was to take place (the killing of each Egyptian's first-born son), Moses instructed the Hebrews to kill a lamb and spread its blood on their doorposts so that the angel of death would literally pass over their homes. On the night of the tenth plague, Pharaoh finally gave the Hebrew people their freedom. Each family fled their homes so quickly, uncertain if Pharaoh would change his mind, that their bread did not have a chance to rise!

Thus, we reach the elements that make up the Passover Feast and Seder Meal. The first day of Passover begins, as a holy day, honoring when the Hebrew people were freed and left Egypt. The final day of Passover is when Moses led the people safely through the Red Sea.

The rabbis created the Haggadah, a separate book, to celebrate the Exodus story. In this text, the youngest child of each household asks four questions, beginning with: "Why is this night different from all other nights?" The full Exodus story unfolds as the child continues to ask questions to understand the significance of eating unleavened bread, (the bread did not have time to rise,) and dipping herbs in water or salt water before eating them.

Yom HaShoah

Yom HaShoah, Holocaust memorial day, is observed on the twenty-seventh of Nisan. The chosen date of this somber memorial was difficult to finalize, for the only date that actually made sense was April 19, 1943. Yet that date happened to be the fifteenth day of Nissan, the Passover—the same day Nazis wanted to destroy the Warsaw ghetto. On this Passover in 1943, the Jews in Warsaw revolted in an act of courage. In order to have a date that fell close to the actual event the Jewish people wanted to commemorate, a date was chosen in the same month, but that would not fall within the Passover celebration. However, this simple explanation still does not take into account much heartache, many divisions, and unique needs to observe such a horrific event in history. How is it possible to choose a day and create a ritual to honor millions of people who were annihilated at the hands of Adolph Hitler and his men? This was the task of many rabbis and Jewish leaders. Even in recent years, while the date has finally been set, a common way to commemorate all the souls who were lost has not been set. This day is not a celebration, and the usual thanks given to God in all other feasts is not readily seen on this day. The prayers are those of silent remembering. In spite of the lack of a unifying ritual, this feast day is needed. When all the survivors of the Holocaust have passed away, and the first-person accounts unable to be spoken, the Jewish people will still remember.

Yom HaAtzm'ut and Yom Ha-Zikaron

Yom HaAtzm'ut, Israel Independence Day, and Yom Ha-Zikaron, a day to remember Israeli soldiers who have fallen in battle, are two strongly intertwined days. Yom HaAtzm'ut is observed on the fifth day of Iyyar (April–May) and correlates directly to May 14, 1948, the day Israel became an independent state. Any group that has fought for independence can understand the significance of commemorating the day the dream is realized. For the Israelites, the dream took an eternity and began at the early onset of their group identity as they endured the Exodus to seek the Promised Land. Receiving the land was a quintessential part of their journey and hope in God's promise. The Jewish people were promised a home, fought for their space, had their land taken away again and again, and eventually were split into factions, both politically and religiously. The realization of the State of Israel is both political and religious in nature, for the land itself (as celebrated on Tu B'Svat) is also holy.

Yet, as part of the ritual and celebration to achieve independence, those who lost their lives along the way must also be remembered. Unlike the American tradition that celebrates Memorial Day more than a month before American Independence Day on July 4th, Yom Ha-Zikaron is celebrated the day before Yom HaAtzm'ut. The separate holiday came into place after the third celebration of Yom HaAtzma'ut. The Jewish people seek the joy of resurrection to happen for their own lives and those who are gone; remembering the fallen is an emotional burden. Jewish leaders, sensitive to this fact, felt that a day to ritualize the fallen and then celebrate the actualized dream (of independence achieved), honored all aspects.

Lag B'Omer

As translated literally from Hebrew, *Lag* is the combination of two Hebrew letters that numerically means thirty-three, thus stating that the feast day is the thirty-third day of Omer. Omer is not a Hebrew month but a reference to a specific seven-week period of time that begins on the second day of Passover and ends on Shavuot (see the following entry). In terms of the Gregorian calendar, it would fall in the months of April and May. Biblically this time period was very joyous as the land prepared to offer the people the feast of fruits and grain, yet during the rabbinic era, this changed. The Hebrew date is the eighteenth of Iyar.

While history is uncertain, all the stories refer to a group of Rabbi Akiva's students who endured some kind of plague, and on this thirty-third day of Omer, the plague was lifted. The plague referred to was probably an attack on the students who were supporting (fighting for) a revolutionary leader, Bar Kochba, who fought against the Romans. The Romans attacked and killed many of the students under Bar Kochba's military leadership. While the plague was lifted on this day, the whole period of Omer was remembered for the casualties and destruction. The joyous time this once celebrated took a drastic turn so that no joyous event or marriage could take place during the counting of Omer. The exception of this seven-week period of mourning was Lag B'Omer. Traditionally people have observed this day by taking their children to the park to play games that have some military origin (bows and arrows). And, since marriage ceremonies were banned during Omer, on this day of celebration, marriages could take place. A reference has also been made that Lag B'Omer is like a Valentine's Day for Jewish adults.

Shavuot

Simply explained, Shavuot commemorates God's giving of the Torah to the Jewish people and usually falls in the months of May or June. The Hebrew date is the sixth of Sivan. As in every other Jewish feast or holiday, the simple is not devoid of meaning of complex ideas, values, history, and the connection of the Divine to the created, both as person and thing—the earth. If one had to equate the massive significance of this feast, it would be equal to September 17, 1787, a day historians know and most Americans would need to research. On that day, the United States government agreed upon the *Constitution*, the set of laws that would govern, guide, and protect the American people, set them apart, and mark the country as a unique democracy. The Torah did this for the Jewish people.

The giving of laws to govern and guide the heart and soul is something to be celebrated. God chose to be the loving "parent" and give rules for the chosen people. This was personal. For a God who did not love would not call people into the covenant relationship that exists in the giving of Divine Law. God gave the law; the people then had to choose to accept.

Richly embedded within the Book of Genesis, some of the first rules of God are given to humankind, the root of why agriculture and foods are interconnected in Jewish feasts. In Genesis, God tells humankind "to cultivate and care for" the earth. Thus, the giving of the Law is also connected to the harvest of the earth. Shavuot has three names, one of which is the feast of weeks that began on Passover. As previously referenced, Lag B'Omer takes place during this time. Omer is actually a measure of barley, the first crop to ripen. Each day during the seven weeks of Shavuot, this Omer was waved in the temple until the crops of wheat were ripe and the first loaf of bread could be made and offered as gift back to God. Connecting the Passover to Shavuot equates God's blessings of saving the chosen people and a ritual of unleavened bread, to a true celebration enjoying all the grains and fruits of the earth. God gives and God protects. The covenant remains and should be richly celebrated.

Tisha B'Av

Tisha B'Av takes place on the ninth day of Av (July–August). As I read about this major fast day complete with nine days of deep mourning before the actual commemoration, my mind went immediately to September 11th. While absent of religious ties, the destruction of these steel towers was laden with symbolism. The lives lost, the attacks on the government, and the towers fallen were meant to hurt and possibly destroy the American people; it did not. Tisha B'Av commemorates the greatest symbolic loss for the Jewish faith community, the Temple in Jerusalem, the greatest religious home for an entire community of believers.

The Twin Towers fell in one day. The Jewish Temple fell twice, though centuries apart. In reading of the history and pain, the tradition of nine complete days of mourning before the actual day of reliving the loss of the great treasure, one can only imagine the pain the first Jewish community felt in 586 BCE at losing their beloved home. To have this happen again in 70 CE had to diminish hope in the Jewish leaders and force decisions to be made. And it did. The second destruction caused fringe Jewish followers to make a choice to remain a Jew or go with the Hellenistic tide. Christian Jews chose to lean more towards Christianity and less towards Judaism. The destruction of the Temple was symbolic, and a great change also took place, the beginning of synagogues for specific communities.

Thus, to honor Tisha B'Av, the mourning is meant to be great—hair should not be cut, clothes (unless necessary) should not be washed, wine and meat should be avoided except on the Sabbath, and anything that gives pleasure should be avoided. During the evening at synagogue, the faithful gather to hear and remember using words from the Book of Lamentations, which was written after the first fall of the Temple. The walls may have been crushed, but the faithful still gather and remember.

Rosh Hashanah

Rosh Hashanah takes place on the first and second days of Tishrei, the seventh month of the Jewish year. This feast is the Jewish New Year. Do not let the words "new year" in the name fool you into thinking of grand celebrations. The lightness of New Year's Eve, which celebrates a new year of life and resolutions to become a better person are the only vague similarities. This feast day is heavy with meaning and repentance, focusing upon death and life with great importance even to non-practicing Jews. Like "Chriseasters" who publicly celebrate their Christian faith only twice a year on Christmas and Easter, those Jews who do not celebrate their Jewish faith during the year will honor the observance of this first of two high holy days. (The second is Yom Kippur.)

Called to fully examine their life and all choices, Jews are reminded to focus upon God, to wake up from the deep sleep pulling them away from their Creator and to repent for all wrongs. The greatest symbols of the feast are the notes blown through the shofar, a ram's horn, with each note intending a deeper emotion to be called forth from the listener. Sounds to bring forth the wrong intentions that should be grieved and given to God; sounds to call forth protection from those "spirits" that would call one away for God's presence; sounds to provoke awe for God, as King; and sounds to remind the listener of wars and the destruction of the Temple.

Rosh Hashanah requires a person with a strong voice to read the special prayers specific to this holy day. Those present are there, in essence, to plead their case with God who is both Creator and Judge. This is a time to take stock everything and seek assurance that one's life is in accord with God's will. Due to the intensity of the feast day, a common observance was added to bring sweetness into the repentance; apples are dipped into honey and eaten to symbolize the blessing given to wish all a "sweet" new year. Another custom is to cast off sins into the river.

Yom Kippur

This well known high holy day of atonement is prescribed in the Torah in three places stating: "On the tenth day of the seventh month, you shall afflict your souls." This specific day, the tenth of Tishrei, is meant to be a complete cleansing for the body and soul to live now as if one's sins were not forgiven, to feel that awful effect, and thus to make the necessary reparations to alleviate that pain before death.

It is a known psychological fact that the act of reconciliation—atoning for ones sins, asking for forgiveness, and then receiving those words—offers great gifts for the psyche. How much more so then for the soul and in terms of a heavenly relationship! Thus, any sins committed against God are forgiven on Yom Kippur, but first the penitent must truly be in a state of penance and prepare for it in their body, mind, and soul. As for the sins against another person, these sins are not forgiven unless the appropriate measures are taken to ask for and receive forgiveness in person.

The best way to achieve this state is through the act of denial in pleasure-inducing goods. On Yom Kippur, there is no eating for twenty-five hours, nor are Jews allowed to bathe, engage in sexual relations, or wear leather shoes (though in current times this ban has changed in nature). However, those under nine, women who are pregnant, and those who are severely ill do not have to follow these rules.

On this day, synagogue services are longest of the entire year, lasting from morning until night, during which those present constantly repeat the Al Khet, "for sins that we have committed." All sins are confessed in the plural; even if you didn't personally commit that sin, you speak it as if you did. There is a communal sense of responsibility, akin to that of an unspoken but known vow to support those around you to live up to the common covenant accepted by all. The final prayer of the evening, unique to this service, strongly brings forth the imagery of God as final judge. Those present know their fate lies in God's hands alone. In truly seeking atonement, the catharsis received in forgiveness can then allow a new verdict from God for their coming days.

Sukkot

In Genesis, God spoke and God's words become reality. The Feast of Booths or the Feast of the Tabernacle is strongly biblical in nature, stemming from more than one passage in the Torah. The first day of these seven days of celebration starts on the fifteenth day of Tishrei (September / October), God's words found in Leviticus 23:33–44 are fully honored. The chosen people are to live in booths for seven days to remember their history and their freedom at God's hands from their prior slavery. Thus, a tradition of this holiday is the making of a symbolic sukkah (booth) to be part of each home and mealtime celebration and is decorated according to the gifts of the harvest season (best described in American feasts as Thanksgiving decorations.) This feast is the second time the liberating freedom of the Exodus experience is celebrated, and these days of celebration come five days after the severity of fasting during Yom Kippur, making the joy even more palpable.

There are many religious traditions, special prayers, blessings, and rituals that are observed during this week. One such tradition is known as the Four Species. Four plants, spoken of in Leviticus, are bound together, held in one's hand, and used (moved in different directions) while a specific blessing is recited. Another tradition is that of honoring special guests into one's sukkah and offering acts of lovingkindness that are usually overlooked. The tradition is to invite a biblical ancestor each night as an exalted guest; each night another one is added, so on the seventh night you have seven exalted guests. Today, people sometimes add the names of any guests visiting the sukkot along with the ancestors. During this time, the material gifts are also meant to be honored in gratitude and shared with those in need. It is, after all, a time of joy!

Shmini Atzeret

The Eighth Day of Assembly, while connected to Sukkot as the actual last eighth day (the twenty-second day of Tishrei), in all actuality does not have to do with the traditions of Sukkot. The only connection is that the joy and celebration of Sukkot is maintained, but the rituals, blessings, and Four Species are not used. Known more accurately as the "prayer for rain," this is one more feast celebrating the agriculture of the Israeli homeland as the Jewish people pray for rain during Israel's rainy season, not for where they currently reside. It is a reminder that they are called to live and honor their ties to Jerusalem. Another beautiful way to understand this day is read in Rabbinic literature: "Our Creator is like a host, who invites us as visitors for a limited time, but when the time comes for us to leave, He has enjoyed himself so much that He asks us to stay another day. . . . for a more intimate celebration" (see the website, Judaism 101).

Simchat Torah

Literally *Simchat Torah* means: "Rejoicing in the Torah." In the State of Israel this special feast happens concurrently with Shmini Atzeret, while in all other places this is the second day after Sukkot ends. Honoring the covenantal promise, the Jewish people allow the law given in the Torah to fully guide all their actions and rituals. Thus, the reading of the Torah is to be honored at all times. Simchat Torah is the most joyous holiday as it marks the completion of reading the Torah cycle. The Torah is read from Genesis 1 all the way through Deuteronomy in one year, and the cycle continues to repeat, eternally.

The feast is celebrated in traditional synagogues through individuals and groups offering a special blessing the Torah called an aliyah. This is one time boys who are not yet of age and even women and girls can give a blessing.

The atmosphere of the synagogue is very informal. As a true celebration, the Torah is marched around the synagogue, and when those holding the twenty-some pound Torah make it to the front, more dancing ensues, and the process is repeated seven times with a new person marching the Torah each time.

Chanukah

As in other feasts, Chanukah is centered on the importance of the centrality of the Temple in Jewish life. In the second century BCE (167) the Jewish Temple was seized by Syrian-Greek soldiers and dedicated to the worship of the Greek gods. The emperor Antiochus made the observance of Judaism an offense punishable by death and demanded that all Jews worship Greek gods. Bold mothers who chose to observe the Jewish custom of circumcising their sons were killed, as were their infant sons. After three years of brutal fighting, the outnumbered Jews reclaimed the temple. However, the Greeks had defiled the temple because they worshipped foreign gods, and the Jewish people wanted to reclaim the temple according to custom.

It usually took eight days to purify the temple, using oil to light the candles. Only one small container of pure olive oil was found, enough to burn a candle for one day. Miraculously the container burned for eight full days. This trampling of the Jewish religion, the boldness of mothers, the solidarity of community members, and the ensuing battle to claim the Temple led to this feast where Jews are called to celebrate for eight days.

The most common things associated with this feast are the Menorah, the Dreidl, and latke pancakes. The Menorah was created so that one candle would be lit at the end of the first day, two on the second day, and so forth. The light is meant to be placed near a window so as to boldly proclaim one's Jewish faith and belief in this miracle. The spinning of the Dreidl, a children's toy, is a game with a purpose to remember the feast. (Each side of the toy contains a Hebrew letter that turns into an acronym about the feast: A great Miracle Happened there.) Finally in America and other places, it is popular to fry potato and onion pancakes, as all holiday foods are usually fried in honor of the oil that miraculously burned.

ISLAMIC DAYS

Ramadan

The ninth month of the Islamic year

Ramadan is a special time for physical restraint and spiritual growth in the midst of daily routines. The word *Ramadan* comes from the Arabic meaning "parched thirst" and "sun-baked ground." It is evocative of the desert experience, when people feel thirst and hunger, uniting them with thirsty, hungry people around the world. Its purpose is to draw people closer to God and each other.

This yearly fast is considered one of the five "pillars" of Islam (bearing witness to the oneness of God, prayer, charity, fasting, and pilgrimage). During the day, devout Muslims don't eat or drink, they try to eliminate bad habits, and center themselves on God. Central to this period is taking time daily for quiet reflection, reading from the Qur'an,

Images and Symbols of Islam (L to R): The *Shahada* is the Muslim declaration of belief in the oneness of God and acceptance of Muhammad as God's prophet. During the Festival of Sacrifice, *Eid ul-Adha*, Muslims remember Ibrahim's obedience. The star and crescent is symbolic of Islam or the Muslim community.

showing gratitude, and having a family meal in the evening. The Arabic word for fasting (*sawm*) literally means "to refrain," a restraint practiced by all parts of the body. The tongue "fasts" from negative speech and gossip. The eyes don't look at unlawful things. The hand does not touch or take anything not belonging to it. The ears resist listening to empty chatter or obscenities. The feet do not go anywhere sinful. It is hoped that the generosity, self-discipline, and charity practiced during Ramadan will continue throughout the year.

Eid al-Fitr
The end of Ramadan / The first day of Shawwal, the tenth month

Eid al-Fitr means the "festival of fast-breaking" and ends Ramadan, although its good practices should be incorporated all the time. This three-day period expresses gratitude that the long fast is ended. It is a time for charitable giving and joyful celebrations with family and friends. It's a time to thank Allah for his abundant mercy. Appropriate greetings are: "*Kul 'am wa enta bi-khair!*" ("May every year find you in good health!") "*Eid Mubarak!*" ("Blessed Eid!") and "*Eid Saeed!*" ("Happy Eid!")

Before the feast, during the last few days of Ramadan, each Muslim family donates food to the poor for their holiday meal. The day begins with a special Eid prayer, early in the morning outdoors or in mosques. Afterwards, families visit friends and other relatives, phone their holiday wishes, and give gifts to children. Usually the three days are an official holiday for the government and schools. A thousand years after the death of Muhammad, founder of Islam, the religion has spread throughout the globe. Approximately 1.5 billion people are celebrating its holidays now.

Leyla al-Qadr
Last ten days of Ramadan

Leyla al-Qadr, the Night of Power, occurs during the last ten days of Ramadan and concludes the month of fasting. It commemorates the first gift of the Qur'an to the Prophet Muhammad, when he was called to be God's messenger. He experienced a significant vision of an angelic being, summoning him to an uncorrupted, monotheistic revelation. During this time, Muslims around the world study the Qur'an in the mosque, pray, and meditate on the meaning of Allah's message to humanity. At this time of intense spirituality, the believers are surrounded by angels, heaven's gates open, and God's blessings are especially lavish. Chapter 97 of the Qur'an describes this sacred night as "better than a thousand months": "We have indeed revealed this message in the Night of Power. And what will explain what the Night of Power is? The Night of Power is better than a thousand months. Therein come down the angels and the spirit, by Allah's permission, on every errand. Peace! Until the rising of the morn!" Furthermore, the prophet Muhammad is reported to have said: "Whoever stays up (in prayer and remembrance of Allah) on the Night of Qadr, fully believing (in Allah's promise of reward) and hoping to seek reward, he shall be forgiven for his past sins."

Al Hijra
The first day of Muharram, the first month

The Muslim calendar is used in Iran, Turkey, Arabia, Egypt, Pakistan, and certain parts of India and Malaysia. In the Muslim calendar, months last from one new moon to another. There are 12 months in the year.

The length of time from one new moon to the next is 29 1/2 days, so the 12 months of the Muslim year add up to 354 days. That's 11 1/4 days short of the 365 1/4-day solar calendar. This means that the Muslim New Year (like every Muslim holiday) comes 11 or 12 days earlier each year on the Western calendar. In about 30 years, it's back to where it started.

The beginning of the Muslim New Year or *Al Hijra* also marks the anniversary of Muhammad's move from Mecca to Medina. In Arabic, "Mecca" means "the place of the drinking cup," a center people want to visit. (In English, we use the word similarly, for instance: "Taos is a mecca for the arts.") It refers to the story of Abraham and Hagar. Because he had a child, Ishmael, with Hagar, God ordered him to abandon mother and child in the desert. When God created a spring of water for them, it meant they would not die of thirst. Mecca is believed to be the site of the spring. Abraham and Ishmael later built the Kaaba ("House of God") there.

Muhammad's tribe controlled the holy city Mecca in the seventh century, but many gods were worshipped and even the Kaaba was filled with idols. His migration is an important event theologically, because once he left Mecca for Medina, Muhammad's community in exile—now no longer persecuted—became the foundation for Islam's growth throughout the Middle East. While it is not traditionally a day of celebration, some Muslims at this time remember the early community's migration. Others simply reflect on the passing of time and on their own mortality.

Eid ul-Adha

The tenth day of Dhul-Hijjah, the twelfth month *Eid ul-Adha*, (the Festival of Sacrifice), follows the annual Islamic pilgrimage (Hajj) to Mecca, one of the greatest religious observances in Islam. During this celebration, Muslims honor the prophet Abraham. The Qur'an says of him "Surely Abraham was an example, obedient to Allah, by nature upright, and he was not of the polytheists" (chapter 16). Muslims kill a sheep, camel, or goat, saying the name of Allah as a reminder that life is sacred. (Muslims eat meat only if God's name is said during the act of taking life.) This action remembers how Abraham almost sacrificed his son Ishmael. (Read the story in Genesis 22:1–2, 9–13, 15–18, where the son is Isaac.) The immediate family eats one-third of the meat, and shares one-third with the poor, and one-third with other families.

The sacrifice of the animal isn't a matter of atonement. Instead, it symbolizes the many small sacrifices people must make to remain on the Straight Path. One gladly follows Allah's commands with total obedience.

Day of 'Ashura

'Ashura, for Sunni Islam, resembles the Jewish Day of Atonement. When he was alive, Muhammad learned of this observance, directed Muslims to fast, and fasted for two days himself. While the fast now is not required, it is recommended around the tenth day of Muharram, the first month of the Islamic year. It also remembers Moses' freeing his people from the slavery of Egypt.

After Muhammad's death, a division over leadership occurred between Sunni and Shi'a Muslims. Sunnis (now 85 percent of Muslims around the world) believed his successor should be elected, and chose his close friend Abu Bakr as the first Caliph. Shi'a Muslims believed that leadership should remain within the family. They thought Muhammad's cousin and son-in-law, Ali should succeed him. Therefore, they don't recognize elected officials, and follow Imams appointed by God or the Prophet. Both groups hold in common the central elements of Islamic faith, but they observe 'Ashura differently.

Shi'a Muslims see this as the anniversary of the death of Muhammad's grandson, Husain in 680 A.D., murdered during a battle against the ruling Caliph. Because this happened in Karbala (now Iraq), it has become the site of pilgrimage. Their mournful observance consists of grieving the tragic murder and presenting dramas to keep Husain's memory alive.

Mawlid an-Nabi

Mawlid an-Nabi (meaning "birthday of the prophet") celebrates Muhammad's birth in 570, reportedly on the twelfth day of the month of Rabia Awal. During his lifetime, the prophet did not celebrate his birthday. It was first celebrated in the thirteenth century with a month-long festival. Today in some Muslim countries, it's an official holiday, but it is not universally kept. Many Muslims observe the day by reading biographies, telling stories of Muhammad's life, studying the Qur'an, following the prophet's example and giving money to the poor.

Why is this day so important to Muslims? Muhammad is revered as the last messenger from God, after the twenty-five named in the Qur'an: for example, Adam, Noah, Abraham, Moses, and Jesus. He preached forgiveness and lived in simplicity. He believed that the wonders of the world were open books in which to learn about God.

The facts about his early life are scant. Orphaned at age six, he grew up in poverty. He married a rich widow, Khadījah, with whom he had six children, including Fātimah, a daughter who would be influential in the spread of Islam. He began reciting his revelations at age forty. At first, he incurred opposition from the wealthy clans because he advocated the redistribution of wealth. His move to Medina was perilous, a way to escape their animosity. His call was grounded in unity to God and accountability to God in the hereafter. Afterward, his message spread widely; today he is honored throughout the world.

Laylat al-Baraat

Laylat al-Baraat means "the Night of Salvation" and is celebrated the fifteenth night of Shabaan, the eighth month of the Islamic calendar. It is a time of repentance for sin and seeking forgiveness from God. On this night all Sunni Muslims try to honestly settle their debts to each other, and sincerely ask pardon from each other. Because Allah's mercy is so great on this night, he forgives millions of people. In a touching way, Allah asks graciously, "Is there any seeker of salvation, so that I may give it to him; is there any one in need of food, so that I may feed him; is there any one suffering, so that I may cure him?" A metaphor for this is that God forgives more than the amount of wool found on the sheep of the Bani Kalb, who owned more sheep than any other tribe.

On this night, certain prayers are recited a specific number of times after sunset. The departed souls of Muslims visit their relatives and friends, reminding them that they enjoy the fruits of their labors. Devout Muslims also visit the cemetery and pray for their dead. They also remember in prayer those undergoing tragedies throughout the world and those in need of strength. Following Muhammad's example, many people fast at this time.

Laylat al-Miraj

Laylat al-Miraj commemorates Muhammad's ascension to Heaven in 620, described in chapter 17 of the Qur'an. He traveled from Mecca to Jerusalem, where he ascended and received the directions from God for Muslims to pray five times a day.

The story consists of two parts. First, in the *Isra*, two archangels (or in some versions, Gabriel) visited Muhammad at the Kabaa in Mecca. They gave him a winged horse named Buraq, who carried him to the "Farthest Mosque," usually considered the Temple Mount or Noble Sanctuary in Jerusalem.

The journey's second part is called the *Miraj*, meaning "Ladder." After praying with past prophets, Muhammad ascended into heaven. When he returned to relate his experience, some followers thought it bizarre. But Abu Bakr, his good friend, defended the truth of the story. Today, there are different interpretations: the first that it was a physical journey. Others think that it was a dream, or a metaphor for Muslim growth into a world power. Indeed, Muslim forces overtook Jerusalem less than thirty years later. It is one of the most important events in Islam's history, observed by special prayer services at the mosque, followed by treats to eat, or private storytelling at home with special prayers at night.

Index